Insecure Majorities

Insecure Majorities

Congress and the Perpetual Campaign

FRANCES E. LEE

THE UNIVERSITY OF CHICAGO PRESS   CHICAGO AND LONDON

FRANCES E. LEE is professor in the Department of Government and Politics at the University of Maryland.

The University of Chicago Press, Chicago 60637
The University of Chicago Press, Ltd., London
© 2016 by The University of Chicago
All rights reserved. Published 2016.
Printed in the United States of America
25 24 23 22 21 20 19 18 17 16   1 2 3 4 5

ISBN-13: 978-0-226-40899-6 (cloth)
ISBN-13: 978-0-226-40904-7 (paper)
ISBN-13: 978-0-226-40918-4 (e-book)
DOI: 10.7208/chicago/9780226409184.001.0001

Library of Congress Cataloging-in-Publication Data
Names: Lee, Frances E., author.
Title: Insecure majorities : Congress and the perpetual campaign / Frances E. Lee.
Description: Chicago ; London : The University of Chicago Press, 2016. | Includes
    bibliographical references and index.
Identifiers: LCCN 2016001723 | ISBN 9780226408996 (cloth : alk. paper) |
    ISBN 9780226409047 (pbk. : alk. paper) | ISBN 9780226409184 (e-book)
Subjects: LCSH: Political parties—United States. | United States. Congress. |
    Representative government and representation. | Elections—United States.
Classification: LCC JK2265 .L38 2016 | DDC 328.73/0769—dc23 LC record available
    at http://lccn.loc.gov/2016001723

TO EMERY AND BEVERLY

Contents

Acknowledgments

In writing this book, I have incurred numerous debts. Most importantly, this book would not have been possible without the generosity of the former and current congressional staffers and members who sat down with me for interviews. They gave freely of their time to answer my questions, even though they had many more important things to do. Several also put me in touch with other interview subjects who had backgrounds or experiences relevant to my project. Their perspectives and insights tremendously enriched my understanding of congressional politics and shaped the book in innumerable ways.

I am grateful to the University of Maryland and the Government and Politics Department for supporting my research. A sabbatical and a Research and Scholarship Award from the graduate school together gave me a year off from teaching responsibilities in order to research and write. I had fantastic research support from Kelsey Hinchliffe (coauthor of chapter 8). The Center for American Politics and Citizenship also provided me with excellent research assistance, including from Cory Maks and Tim Cordova (coauthor of chapter 7). I had great help tracking down sources from Judy Markowitz and other staff at McKeldin Library. I benefited repeatedly from feedback at the department's American Politics Workshop and from many graduate students in the program, especially Mike Parrott. Mike Hanmer offered key methodological assistance. Jim Gimpel, Irwin Morris, Stella Rouse, Kris Miler, and Lily Mason provided valuable comments. I particularly thank my colleagues David Karol and Ric Uslaner, who read the entire manuscript and helped improve it in many ways large and small.

I have also had much help from beyond my home institution. Walter Oleszek gave me access to his amazing archives at the Congressional

Research Service, along with much great advice. Bruce Oppenheimer pressed me to get outside the comfort of my office to interview Capitol Hill insiders. Matt Green offered good counsel on conducting interviews. Richard Forgette shared his data on the frequency of party meetings in the House of Representatives.

This book took shape in response to the comments and criticisms I received at workshops and presentations over the past five years, including at UC Berkeley, the University of Chicago, Northwestern, the University of Minnesota, Stanford, the University of North Carolina, Oxford, Yale, the University of Texas, UC San Diego, UC Davis, the University of Illinois, Cornell, and the annual meetings of the Midwest Political Science Association. I especially benefited from the Congress and History Conferences at Columbia and Vanderbilt. I cannot adequately thank the many people whose remarks and questions in these settings helped me improve this project, but I'd like to single out Mo Fiorina, Rick Valelly, Tony Madonna, Adam Myers, and Collin Paschall, who each provided thoughtful discussant comments. I also thank Brian Gaines for suggesting the idea for chapter 8.

For feedback on key parts of this project, I thank Eric Schickler, Jenny Mansbridge, David Broockman, and Daniel Stid. I owe very special thanks to the scholars outside my home institution who read complete drafts of the book: David Mayhew, Sam Kernell, and Jim Curry. Their comments sharpened the analysis and saved me from numerous errors. The reports from the anonymous readers secured by University of Chicago Press were also tremendously helpful.

I am grateful to my longtime editor John Tryneski, whose guidance made this a better book and whose enthusiasm for the project continually encouraged me to get it done. I also thank others at the press, especially Rodney Powell and Jillian Tsui. For expert and careful copyediting, I thank Daniel King.

This book would never have come together without the love and support of my family. My husband, Emery, read and commented on everything, as he has ever since the first paper I wrote in graduate school. My daughter, Beverly, inspires me daily with her humor, cheerfulness, and curiosity. Both Emery and Beverly have tolerated me putting in too much time at the office working on this book. It is dedicated to them.

CHAPTER ONE

The Ins versus the Outs

The central variable in a party system is the level of competitiveness. — Joseph Schlesinger (1985, 1154)

Today, in 2016, the Democratic and Republican Parties face each other at roughly equal strength. Almost every election offers the prospect of a change of party control over one national institution or another. Since 1980, Democrats and Republicans have each held the presidency about half the time. The Senate majority changed hands seven times between 1980 and 2016, with Democrats and Republicans each in the majority for nine Congresses. The House majority shifted three times during the same period, also with Democrats and Republicans each holding the majority for nine Congresses. Nearly three decades have elapsed since the last presidential landslide. Divided government is the norm. Margins of control in Congress are persistently narrow. Both parties can generally count on receiving between 47 and 53 percent of all the votes cast in congressional elections any given year. In 2002, *The Economist* magazine dubbed the United States the "50–50 nation," and subsequent elections have altered the picture little. The two parties remain locked in a ferocious power struggle for control of US national government.

Yet it has not always been so. For decades after 1932, Democrats were, by all appearances, the nation's majority party. Democrats maintained majority control of both the House and the Senate for nearly a half century between 1933 and 1981, interrupted only by two brief Republican interludes (1947–48 and 1953–54). The Democrats controlled the presidency two-thirds of the time during this period. Divided government was atypical. The Democrats' margins usually seemed insurmountable.

On average, Democrats held 60 percent of the seats and, with some frequency, majorities of 2:1. Even after Richard Nixon won one of the presidency's largest popular-vote shares ever in 1972, Democrats still held 57 Senate seats and 291 House seats, and their margins swelled further in the 1974 midterms. In the Congress of this era, Democrats were "something of a 'party of state'" (Mayhew 1974, 104).

The central argument of this book is that these changed competitive circumstances have had far-reaching effects on political incentives in Washington. Intense party competition for institutional control focuses members of Congress on the quest for partisan political advantage. When party control seemingly hangs in the balance, members and leaders of both parties invest more effort in enterprises to promote their own party's image and undercut that of the opposition. These efforts at party image making often stand in the way of cross-party cooperation on legislation.

The primary way that parties make an electoral case for themselves vis-à-vis their opposition is by magnifying their differences. Parties continually contrive to give voters an answer to the question, "Why should you support us and not the other party?" In some form or another, the answer has to claim, "Because we're *different!*" Differences can be defined along ideological lines, and ideological differences are often useful for appealing to party base voters, activists, and donors. However, nonideological appeals accusing the other party of corruption, failure, or incompetence are at least equally valuable and can potentially attract swing voters, as well as fire up the base. Difference drawing by no means entails only a focus on cultivating the image of one's own party. In a two-party system, one party's loss is another party's gain. As such, a party benefits from harming the opposing party's image. A party looks for ways to make its opposition appear weak and incompetent, as well as ideologically extreme and out of touch with mainstream public opinion. As parties angle for competitive advantage using such tactics, the upshot is a more confrontational style of partisanship in Congress.

Party image making impels an active quest to define and broadcast party messages. Fellow partisans seek issues and talking points around which they can coalesce that will also favorably distinguish their party from the opposition. At the same time, party image making also involves a continual hunt for issues that allow a party to score political points by putting its opposition on the wrong side of public opinion. Parties in Congress routinely try to force recorded votes on issues that will cast their opposition in an unattractive light. When these votes work as intended, they elicit party conflict and foreground party differences. Party image making extends beyond floor votes to the whole arena of communications. Parties' pursuit of advantage in public relations has fueled the creation and institutionalization of extensive partisan communications operations inside the legislative branch. These increasingly large and professionalized staffs of party communicators produce a steady stream of tough criticism of the opposing party, along with advertising, issue positioning, and credit claiming aimed at burnishing the party brand.

The quest for party differences cuts against bipartisan collaboration on legislative issues. An out party does not win a competitive edge by participating in, voting for, and thereby legitimating the in party's initiatives. Instead, an out party angling for partisan advantage will look for reasons to withhold support and oppose. If a particular initiative championed by an in party is sufficiently popular, an out party may prefer to dodge a fight on that issue. But an out party nevertheless must stake out some ground on which it can define differences in order to make a case for retaking power.

Partisan calculations such as these will weigh more heavily on political decision making under more party-competitive conditions. When majority status is not at stake, there are fewer incentives to concentrate so intently on winning partisan advantage. Members of Congress have less reason to systematically pursue strategies of partisan differentiation or to establish party institutions designed to drive favorable news coverage. But when majority status is in play, members of out parties tend to think in terms of winning the long game of institutional control rather than the short game of wielding influence by cooperating in policy making in the present moment. When competing for majority status, parties focus more intently on public relations, messaging, and related strategies designed to win the high stakes in contention.

During the long years of the so-called permanent Democratic majority after 1932, Republicans did not see much prospect of winning majority status and Democrats did not perceive much chance of losing their majorities. Under such uncompetitive conditions, one would expect to find scant effort expended on party organization. Party collective action during much of this era was, in fact, quite meager. Parties rarely met in caucus. Legislative party organizations were bare bones. There was little to no partisan communications apparatus in either chamber. Reflecting on his party's long minority status, Rep. William A. Steiger (R-WI) said in 1976, "The seemingly permanent minority status debilitates party members" (Freed 1976). Jones (1970, 170–74) described the Republicans of the era as struggling with a "minority party mentality," in which members had given up on efforts to build toward majority status.

"The critical characteristic of a competitive party system is insecurity," argued Schlesinger (1985, 1167). Insecurity, in turn, motivates partisan exertions. Under competitive conditions, "both parties will put forth a high level of effort" to win; meanwhile, when a single party is dominant, "the effort of the controlling party will be minimal [and] that of the hopeless party will at best be token" (1154). These generalizations apply to parties at many levels. Presidential campaigns ignore states that are not in play (Gimpel et al. 2007; Shaw 2008). Incumbents in districts and states perceived as "safe" often fail to draw quality challengers or any challengers at all (Carson 2005; Jacobson 2013; Squire 1989a, 1989b). Donors give and candidates spend far more money in competitive elections than in uncompetitive ones (Gimpel et al. 2008; Herrnson 1992).

These same incentives apply inside Congress, as members decide whether or not to organize and participate in collective efforts to win or hold majority status. Members and leaders have little reason to invest in partisan enterprises when they perceive no chance for majority control to shift. Competition for majority control, however, incentivizes them to put forth more partisan effort. The prospect of collective reward or punishment gives members stronger motivation to cooperate as a party team. A secure majority party behaves differently from a party that fears losing power. A minority party optimistic about winning a majority behaves differently from a hopeless minority. Members of insecure parties worry more about partisan advantage and work harder to win it.

When neither party sees itself as a permanent minority or a permanent majority, leaders and members invest more heavily in party organization and partisan collective action. As one Senate Republican leader's communication director put it in 2001, "There's nothing more important than getting back our majority. It's an issue that unites all of us on communicating our message, on legislative tactics, and on outreach" (Straub and Fonder 2001). With both parties similarly motivated, the result is a better organized, harder-edged, more forceful style of partisanship in US national politics.

In the simplest terms, then, the thesis of the book is that party com-

petition strengthens partisan incentives and motivates partisan strategic action. In other words, the level of party competition serves as the
key independent variable in the analysis. Party competition is measured
both objectively, via the outcomes of national elections and the distribution of partisan identification in the electorate, and subjectively, via the
perceptions of members and journalists about the likelihood of shifts in
party control.

In treating party competition as an independent variable, my goal
is *not* to explain why American politics became more two-party competitive. I view the intensification of party competition as the result of
broader forces in American politics external to Congress, primarily
the breakup of the New Deal coalition and the partisan realignment
of the South. My argument is that this transformed electoral landscape
changed the political calculations of members of Congress in a fundamental way. For decades, members of Congress inhabited a political
landscape where one party seemed to have a lock on majority control.
Since 1980 and 1994, when Republicans finally ousted the long-standing
Democratic majorities in the Senate and House respectively, members
have served under conditions where the two parties compete for control of Congress at relative parity. Neither party perceives itself as a permanent majority or permanent minority. The argument is that this shift
altered members' partisan incentives and strategic choices in ways that
help drive the sharp and contentious partisanship that is characteristic of
contemporary American politics.

By itself, no single part of this book offers "smoking gun" evidence
in support of the thesis. The central difficulty is that the dependent variables—incentives and strategies—cannot be observed directly. One cannot ascertain intentions and motivations simply from behavioral indicators, such as votes, amendments, staff allocations, or other such data.
Instead, the book employs a methodology of triangulation (Denzin 1970;
Rothbauer 2008; Tarrow 1995, 473–74), in which an unobserved quantity
is ascertained via cross-verification from different data sources. Seeking insight into partisan incentives and strategies during different eras,
I turn to historical narratives as well as to data on leadership contests,
caucus meetings, the content and frequency of partisan communications, staff organization, floor amending activity, and roll-call votes. Together, these data tell a rich and compelling story about the important
changes wrought by increases in party competition.

Specifically, this book turns to five sources of evidence for the key claims:

1. *First-person testimony.* Members of Congress and their staff frankly admit to strategically pursuing partisan confrontation as a means of making an electoral case for their own party vis-à-vis the opposition. They discuss how the imperatives of party messaging trade off against bipartisan participation in legislating. How a party weighs these trade-offs is affected by its institutional position. Parties with more institutional power place more emphasis on legislating; parties with less power focus more on messaging. Across the board, messaging takes a higher priority when majority control is insecure.

2. *Internal party debates after 1980.* The surprise Republican capture of a Senate majority in 1980 set off internal debates about strategy and organization within minority parties in both chambers. Senate Democrats and House Republicans began to meet more frequently than they had throughout the 1960s and 1970s to plot strategy, messages, and tactics. These internal party debates and, in key cases, leadership contests largely centered on the choice between partisan confrontation aimed at winning majorities and constructive negotiation to influence policy making. After 1980, forces favoring more confrontation steadily gained advantage, and the minority parties in both chambers became more aggressive in using floor votes and floor debate to define party differences.

3. *The creation and institutionalization of partisan public-relations operations.* Since 1980, both parties have built an extensive apparatus for generating and disseminating partisan messages in both chambers of Congress. Analysis of the content of these messages reveals a strong emphasis on partisan blaming and finger-pointing. Professional communicators have become increasingly influential players in the Hill's power hierarchy, at some cost to staff with substantive policy expertise.

4. *The rise of the partisan message vote.* I examine the increased use of the partisan message vote, meaning votes staged for the purpose of highlighting differences between the parties with no expectation of influencing policy outcomes. Members and staff of both parties candidly acknowledge use of this tactic. Patterns in floor amending activity in the Senate point to wider use of amendments for party message purposes after 1980 than between 1959 and 1980. As a case study in message votes, the book also offers an analysis of congressional behavior on increases in the debt limit since the 1950s. Debt-limit votes were used for partisan position taking throughout the period, but parties have exploited these messaging opportunities more aggressively since 1980.

5. *Comparative state legislatures.* Given that this book's argument ought to apply to other contexts beyond Congress, variation across states is examined for evidence of a relationship between party competition and legislative party conflict. Analyses drawing upon an array of different measures show that more two-party-competitive states systematically have more party-polarized legislatures.

Scholarly Perspectives on Washington Partisanship

In the new political order, nothing is more important than either winning or holding a majority. — Veteran Hill-watcher Charlie Cook (2014)

Scholars have not sufficiently considered how the broader competitive environment affects the incentives for members of Congress to engage in partisan conflict. This book argues that when majority status is perceived to be "in play," members will be more willing to participate in partisan collective action in pursuit of partisan collective gains. As such, the book posits that the struggle for institutional power drives much partisan conflict. This argument stands in tension with political scientists' standard explanation for the scope and intensity of party conflict: ideological polarization. The ideological distance between the parties is generally viewed as the central challenge for lawmaking and governance (see, e.g., McCarty et al. 2006; Poole and Rosenthal 2011).

The ideological composition of the parties is unquestionably an important driver of congressional partisanship and the activities of party leaders (Cooper and Brady 1981; Rohde 1991). There is no denying that there have been significant ideological changes within and between the two parties. Regional realignment has contributed to the ideological homogenization of party constituencies (Black and Black 2002, 2007; Jacobson 2013; Rohde 1991; Theriault 2008). In particular, the major parties are much more cohesive now that civil-rights issues no longer divide them internally along regional lines (Noel 2013; Schickler 2013). Since the 1970s, the major parties have incorporated new constituencies, including gun-rights advocates, social conservatives, and LGBT-rights supporters, thereby bringing the "culture war" debates into the party system (Karol 2009, 2012). The preferences of contemporary Republican and Democratic Party activists are more distinct from one another than in the past (Layman et al. 2010), as are those of the attentive rank-

and-file partisans in the electorate (Abramowitz 2010; Ellis and Stimson 2012; Fiorina and Abrams 2009; Pew Research Center 2014).

The goal of this book is not to call into question the importance of changes in party coalitions and ideologies in American politics. Instead, my purpose is to draw attention to another significant factor: the intensification of party competition for institutional control. Scholars' nearly exclusive focus on policy preferences as a driver of partisan conflict underestimates the role of strategic behavior and the ways that party strategies are likely to change under different competitive conditions. In advancing this argument, the goal is not to rule out changes in policy preferences as a rival hypothesis. It is instead to insist upon an account that takes both factors into consideration. Ideally, I would like to be able to partition out the variance so as to nail down precisely how much party conflict can be attributable to ideology and how much to party competition. Unfortunately, the question is plagued by problems of observational equivalence. No existing method of measuring members' ideological preferences can offer traction, because these measures cannot ascertain the reasons the parties vote differently (Aldrich et al. 2014). Political science's standard measures of ideological preferences cannot differentiate partisan conflict rooted in competitive incentives from partisan conflict rooted in ideology (Lee 2009).

Both ideology and competition are likely to affect members' behavior for the simple reason that members of Congress have "power preferences" as well as policy preferences. They must also make strategic choices. These choices, in turn, depend in part upon whether members perceive any prospect for winning or losing majorities in Congress. Scholars generally recognize that holding majority status matters greatly to members. Over the past two decades, scholars have made members' motivations to win and hold party majorities a foundation for entire theories of congressional leadership and institutional organization (Cox and McCubbins 1993, 2005; Green 2010, 2015; Smith 2007). But this literature has not yet considered how members' concern with winning and holding majority status has differed depending upon the competitive context.

Party competition for institutional control has not been a constant fact of life throughout congressional history. It was not a prominent feature of the long-ago "textbook Congress" (Shepsle 1989). When Democrats seemingly held a permanent majority, members of neither party gave much thought to how they might better compete for majority status.

Accordingly, the scholarship on congressional parties and leaders published in the 1960s and 1970s had virtually no comment on any efforts being made to win or hold party majorities. For example, *Understanding Congressional Leadership*, a three-hundred-page volume with contributions from the field's leading scholars in 1981, devotes a mere five paragraphs to the subject (Mackaman 1981). None of the chapters on the House of Representatives mentions this facet of a party leader's job, and a chapter on the Senate (Peabody 1981, 89–90) just briefly references Sen. Howard Baker's (R-TN) hopes of winning a Republican majority. Similarly, Sinclair's (1983, 1995) early books on congressional leadership contain no sustained discussion of leaders' efforts to pursue or preserve majority status in Congress. This shift in the scholarly literature is probably not the result of scholarly misperception in either era. It is more likely that partisan messaging and image making were simply not very salient concerns for leaders and members during times when there seemed little prospect for changes in party control. The quest for majority status only became a priority for members when the return of competition threw control of Congress into doubt.

The renewal of competition for majority control stands at the root of much change in the behavior of parties and leaders in Congress. Heberlig and Larson (2012) detail how the ongoing contest for congressional majorities has transformed congressional parties into fundraising machines. Committee leaders and rank-and-file party members are assessed dues to be paid into the party's campaign committees. Ambitious members jockey for leadership positions by demonstrating their fundraising prowess (see also Cann 2008). Theriault (2013) documents the emergence of "partisan warriors" in the Senate, a group of hard-edged partisans primarily made up of Republican former House members first elected after 1978. In addition, a growing literature analyzes the enhanced media visibility of congressional leaders, the development of messaging campaigns, and individual members' willingness to participate in party messaging (Butler and Powell 2014; Evans and Oleszek 2002; Grimmer 2013; Groeling 2010; Harris 1998, 2005, 2013; Malecha and Reagan 2012; Sellers 2010).

Yet few scholars have seriously considered how party competition for majority control of the institution relates to the escalation and intensification of party conflict inside Congress itself. After all, party competition is not confined to the campaign trail. Members believe that what happens in Congress affects their party's electoral prospects. As

such, campaign strategizing intrudes upon the legislative process itself as members weigh how their behavior on issues might gain or cost
their party competitive advantage. Members actively enlist legislative resources, including staff time and floor votes, in the service of partisan
public relations.

For deeper consideration of how competition can structure party behavior on legislation, one might instead look to scholarship on legislatures in other democracies. A dominant cleavage in legislatures around
the world is "government-versus-opposition" or, put differently, the ins
versus the outs. Battles in many parliaments largely take place between
the parties in government and those in opposition, and not along left–
right lines (Dewan and Spirling 2011; Diermeier and Feddersen 1998;
Godbout and Høyland 2011; Hix and Noury forthcoming; Spirling and
McLean 2007). Members of parties not in government will typically oppose the government's bills, even when they prefer them to the policy
status quo (Dewan and Spirling 2011; Spirling and McLean 2007). As
such, parliamentarians do not vote according to their sincere ideological
preferences (Diermeier and Feddersen 1998).

Out parties in parliamentary systems methodically refuse to vote for
the government's bills in order to signal their opposition to the government overall and as the backdrop to their campaign for a change of majorities. By withholding their support, out parties increase the pressure
on the party or coalition in power by forcing it to marshal all the necessary votes from within the ranks of its own backbenchers (Dewan and
Spirling 2011). This obliges a majority coalition to bear the burdens of
governance on its own and allows the out parties to capitalize on public discontent with the in parties' performance. The prevalence of this
behavior has made parliamentary roll-call voting much less interesting
to scholars than the (historically) less predictable behavior in the US
Congress.

There is reason to think that this type of government-versus-
opposition partisanship also occurs in the US Congress, particularly
under conditions of increased competition for majority control. After
all, the United States has a rigidly two-party system, in which dissatisfaction with the party in power redounds to the political advantage of
the party not in power.

As in other democracies, the minority party in Congress stands to
gain political benefit from strategically resisting the majority. Strategic

opposition means voting no even when members would, in fact, prefer the proposed policy to the status quo (Green 2015; Jones 1970). First, voting no offers the minority party an opportunity to publicly criticize the deficiencies of the majority's efforts and to tout its alternatives (Egar 2015). The minority may still opt to oppose even after it has been granted significant legislative concessions (Schickler and Pearson 2009, 462). Second, the minority's opposition increases pressure on the majority, in that a majority deprived of assistance from the minority may struggle to maintain its unity and look less than competent in the process (Groeling 2010). Third, lack of help from the minority will force the majority party to attempt to whip its marginal members in order to carry the party's agenda. These controversial votes are likely to yield fodder for challengers' campaigns to take the majority's vulnerable seats in upcoming elections. One would expect all these kinds of political calculations to influence members' behavior more when majority control of Congress is perceived to be up for grabs.

In the United States, the government-versus-opposition dimension of partisan conflict is obscured by the lack of party responsibility in a complex political system in which confidence is not needed to sustain a government. Nevertheless, although party responsibility is much more diffuse in the US system, it is not entirely lacking, in that one party often has more institutional power and responsibility for outcomes than the other. As such, party politics in the United States to some extent still pits the ins against the outs, as in other democracies. The empirical challenge is teasing out this dimension of partisan conflict from the left–right disputes organized along ideological lines.[1]

Scholars have tended to overlook the possibility of this kind of partisan team play in Congress. Prevailing theories of congressional behavior postulate that members engage in sincere spatial voting on the basis of their individual policy preferences. In other words, members are thought to vote for a legislative proposal if they prefer it to the status quo and to vote against if they do not (Krehbiel 1998; McCarty et al. 2006; Poole and Rosenthal 2011).

Spatial theories do not incorporate the incentives minority parties have to strategically withdraw support, force the majority to bear the burdens of governing alone, and exploit dissatisfaction with the majority's performance as ways of regaining power. Even theories that emphasize majority party members' interest in retaining institutional control still assume that members of the minority party will cast sincere votes. In party cartel models, moderate members of the majority are thought to set aside their policy preferences in order to sustain the majority's agenda control in exchange for side payments and the perks of majority status (Cox and McCubbins 1993, 2005). But members of the minority party are not expected to engage in a parallel calculus in which they have political incentives to resist the majority's legislative initiatives, even when they might prefer them to the status quo, so as to publicly criticize the majority's performance and force its marginal members to take tough votes. If government-versus-opposition partisanship structures behavior in Congress, members of out parties will systematically withhold legislative cover from in parties for strategic, not simply ideological, reasons. Denying the opposition cross-party support permits a party to clarify differences with the opposition and to use those differences as part of its argument for retaking control.

Spatial theories also generally do not take into account the deliberate staging of roll-call votes for the purposes of partisan public relations. They do not consider how leaders and members may opt to demand recorded votes not to affect policy outcomes but to shape the parties' public images (for an exception, see Groseclose and McCarty 2001). Leaders and members regularly set up roll-call votes in full knowledge that these votes will have no effect on policy outcomes, but they nevertheless stage them for messaging purposes—that is, to define the differences between the parties in hopes of making their party look more attractive to voters or key constituencies than the opposition. To the extent that party competition for institutional control induces more pervasive use of the floor for party position taking, party conflict will become more frequent and party members more in lockstep.

For these reasons, intensified party competition for majority control of Congress may well foster a more parliamentary style of partisanship in Congress. If these types of strategic behavior are more prevalent under conditions of party competition, party conflict would be more frequent in the contemporary Congress than in the 1960s and 1970s, even if the underlying distribution of members' ideological preferences had remained unchanged. In other words, not all party conflict is "polarization" stemming from a widening gap between the two parties' policy preferences. Instead, much party conflict in the contemporary Congress is strategically engineered in the quest for political advantage as the two parties do battle for majority control.

Data and Methods

Because this book focuses on strategic behavior, the inquiry necessarily centers on perceptions. As such, much of the evidence relies upon first-person perspectives. To what extent do members believe their actions might affect their party's fortunes? How important is majority status to them? What is the perceived likelihood that majority control might shift? What strategies and tactics do they believe help build or sustain their party majorities? How do they implement them? What are the constraints they face? Given the centrality of such questions to the book, readers will encounter far more direct quotations than is typical for most works of political science. The book draws upon a wide and diverse array of published material for insight, including from congressional memoirs, historical texts, news coverage, and the *Congressional Record.*

In addition, I conducted interviews with a group of Washington insiders with long experience working in Congress. The subjects were thirty-one current and former high-level staffers for both the House and the Senate, as well as two former House members. The vast majority of the staff interviewed for the project served at the rank of chief of staff, staff director, or its equivalent (88 percent), and the remainder held senior roles, such as press secretary. On average, interviewees had sixteen years of experience working for Congress, with 79 percent having at least a decade of experience. In many cases, subjects had served multiple stints on Capitol Hill, interspersed with years of private-sector lobbying, and 61 percent worked or had worked directly for House or Senate party leaders.

Given the book's focus on competition for majority status, it was important to find interview subjects who had perspective on the institution before Democrats lost their long-standing Senate and House majorities in 1980 and 1994. Of the interview subjects, 24 percent had experience working on the Hill before 1980, and 73 percent had experience before 1994. The interviews were obtained using a snowball selection technique (Esterberg 2002, 93–94). Although some subjects were cold-called, in most cases I asked Hill insiders with whom I was already acquainted for introductions to appropriately experienced staff, and then I would ask interview subjects for additional referrals. In the end, the sample was reasonably representative: 57 percent were Republicans; 42 percent were Democrats; 45 percent had House experience; 55 percent had Senate experience. For additional information about the interview subjects and process, see appendix A.

These were in-depth, unstructured interviews. Nearly all were an hour in length, and some extended two hours or longer. The interviews were conducted with the understanding that sources would be kept anonymous. Each interview was different in that questions were tailored to the subject's experiences, though the same general themes were pursued. Subjects were queried on topics relating to party messaging and competition for majority control. I asked for explanations of how party messages were constructed and disseminated, how communications and policy staff interact, examples of effective and ineffective messaging campaigns, and how messaging related to legislating. I asked about the importance of majority status to members and how competition for congressional majorities affects interactions between members on legislation. For interview subjects with experience before 1980 and 1994, I sought to ascertain when they believed Democrats might lose control of Congress, what efforts (if any) had been made to either protect or undercut the long-standing Democratic majorities, and how members reacted to changes in majority status after they occurred. Evidence from the interviews is presented throughout the book. Each interviewee was assigned a number, and all quotations are identified by those numbers.

Beyond the first-person perspectives drawn from interviews and other sources, the book assembles a large amount of other data. For information on the scope and intensity of party competition for institutional control over time, there are data on election outcomes, seat divisions in Congress, and party identification in the electorate, as well as data on the incidence and content of news stories raising the possibility of a near-term shift in party control. Historical data on party activity before and after the 1980 elections is presented, including data on fundraising and the frequency of party caucus meetings. Leadership contests are examined for insight into members' preferences about overall party strategy. Congressional staff directories were culled for data on the number and percentage of aides working in party communications roles over time. A dataset of all amendments offered on the Senate floor between 1961 and 2013 was assembled to analyze whether floor amending activity is used more for party messaging purposes in the post-1980 period. A dataset of all House and Senate roll-call votes to raise the debt limit was compiled to shed light on how members handle the trade-offs between messaging and governing over time. Yet another dataset was amassed to examine the relationship between party competition and legislative party polarization across the states. Readers will encounter a large number of figures and tables in the book, in addition to many direct quotations.

Organization of the Book

Chapter 2 takes stock of variation over time in party competition for institutional control. This analysis has both objective and subjective components. The chapter presents objective data on election outcomes, margins of control in Congress, and partisan identification in the electorate. For insight into politicians' subjective perceptions, I also examine the incidence and content of news stories discussing the likelihood of a shift in party control, as well as what politicians and other close observers said about their party's prospects of winning or losing power during different periods. The chapter argues for the importance of 1980 as a key turning point in the intensification of party competition for control of US national government.

Chapter 3 lays out the argument that increased competition for majority control of Congress gives rise to a more confrontational style of partisanship. Drawing upon the interview subjects consulted for this book, as well as personal memoirs of former members of Congress and perspectives from news sources, the chapter elaborates a logic of partisan confrontation to unpack why members of Congress perceive political benefits from defining and dramatizing party differences. I examine how these party messaging efforts are implemented and how they disrupt bipartisan collaboration. Finally, the chapter analyzes how a party's incentives to engage in strategies of partisan differentiation are shaped by its institutional position in the constitutional system.

Chapter 4 presents a detailed history of how the minority parties in Congress reacted to the changed competitive circumstances after 1980. The seemingly permanent Democratic majorities before 1980 incentivized more "loyal opposition" behavior on the part of the minority party. Republicans and Democrats frequently collaborated on committees. Their apparently invulnerable majorities made Democrats complacent, and they rarely met in caucus and raised almost no party campaign funds. After 1980, a sharper style of partisanship began to emerge among both minority-party Democrats in the Senate and Republicans in the House. Senate Democrats and House Republicans began to meet more frequently. The minority parties in both the House and the Senate started looking for more ways to create partisan distinctions, publicize partisan controversies, raise campaign money, and make an argument for their party to retake control.

Chapter 5 examines how the parties in Congress have developed and professionalized their messaging capabilities after the reemergence of party competition for institutional control in 1980. The contemporary legislative branch now employs a large workforce of professional partisan communicators. This chapter sheds light on how party messages are constructed and disseminated. It provides a content analysis of the types of messages the parties broadcast. It also examines how the institutionalization of party messaging has affected power hierarchies inside the legislative branch and sparked rivalries between staff focused on policy and those focused on communications.

Chapter 6 examines how members and leaders set up recorded votes to drive party messages. The strategy and tactics involved are detailed, drawing upon perspectives from interviews and other sources. The chapter then presents an analysis of amendments that receive recorded votes on the Senate floor, one of the most frequent ways message votes are staged. Through an examination of floor amendments receiving roll-call votes in the Senate between 1959 and 2013, the chapter offers evidence that senators in the post-1980 period employ floor votes for purposes of partisan communications more often than did senators of the 1960s and 1970s.

Chapter 7 (coauthored with Timothy L. Cordova) uses votes to raise the debt limit to shed light on how parties weigh the trade-offs between messaging and legislating under conditions of competition for majority control. Even though raising the debt ceiling is something neither liberals nor conservatives ever want to be responsible for, the congressional politics of these measures is highly partisan, with members' willingness to support raising the debt limit heavily influenced by their party's institutional position. The more power members' parties have, the more willing they are to vote in favor of increasing the debt ceiling. Meanwhile, parties with less power exploit debt-ceiling votes for messaging purposes. The chapter presents evidence that government-versus-opposition conflict on the debt limit is sharper after 1980.

Chapter 8 (coauthored with Kelsey L. Hinchliffe) examines whether there is more legislative party conflict in more two-party-competitive states. Five different measures of party competition are employed.

Drawing upon new data on state legislative party polarization (Shor 2014; Shor and McCarty 2011), we show that all five measures of competition are associated with higher levels of party polarization in the lower chambers of state legislatures, and most are associated with party polarization in the upper chambers. No measure of party competition is associated with lower levels of polarization in either chamber.

Chapter 9 concludes with some reflections on the larger significance of the book's argument for both scholarship on Congress and the functioning of the US constitutional system.

A Protracted Era of Partisan Parity

"Our political solar system . . . has been characterized not by two equally competing suns, but by a sun and a moon," wrote Samuel Lubell (1965, 191–92). This widely quoted metaphor encapsulates what was once conventional wisdom: for one party to enjoy a significant electoral advantage over the other is the norm in American politics. Looking back from the vantage point of the 1960s and 1970s, students of American political history saw not two parties competing on equal terms for control of national institutions but long stretches with one dominant party and a second party only winning power when the majority coalition divided. This pattern explains, in part, pundits' and political scientists' long-standing fascination with "critical" or "realigning" elections marking the emergence of a new dominant party (Burnham 1970; Clubb et al. 1980; Key 1955; Nardulli 1995; Sundquist 1983).

For decades after 1932, no one doubted that the Democrats were the nation's majority party. "The Republican party is the minority party," wrote Rossiter (1960, 76). "All other things being equal . . . they should lose every nationwide election." Similarly, Jones (1970, 7) observed, "Presently, of course, we are in a period of Democratic Party dominance," dating the era to 1932.

For much of the twentieth century, there was little contest for majority party control of the House or Senate. "Alternation in party control has at least temporarily ceased," concluded Mayhew (1974, 103–4). Although Republicans successfully competed for the presidency, it was conventionally understood that Republicans stood at a competitive disadvantage in the contest for control of national governing institutions. Even Republican presidents persisted in the belief that Republicans were the nation's minority party (Galvin 2010).

How things have changed. The conventional wisdom that there is a dominant party in American politics is dead and has been for a long time. From time to time, journalists, pundits, and operatives declare a particular election a realignment, marking the rise of a new majority party. But no such claim has ever achieved widespread acceptance among adherents of both parties or among political scientists. Instead, the whole concept of the realigning election has fallen into disfavor (Mayhew 2002).

The purpose of this chapter is to take stock of these changed competitive circumstances. This analysis necessarily has both objective and subjective dimensions. Objectively, there are hard data on election outcomes, seat divisions in Congress, and partisan identification in the electorate over time. These data are obviously crucial for assessing the state of two-party competition. Yet more importantly, it is essential to understand how politicians' perceptions of political possibility have informed their strategic calculations. Does the out party see a path to reclaiming power, or is such an eventuality dismissed as highly improbable? Does the in party perceive its grasp on power as tenuous or instead as secure? How party leaders perceive the possibility of gaining—or losing—power will influence their behavior in myriad ways, both internally (within Congress) and externally (in campaigning). A secure party will behave differently than a fearful one. A hopeful party will behave differently than a hopeless one. So it is essential to consider party elites' subjective assessments of party competition as well. To that end, I examine the incidence and content of news stories discussing near-term possibilities of a shift in party control of Congress. I also draw upon what politicians and other close observers have said about their party's prospects of winning or losing power during different periods.

Measures of Party Competition

It is easy to see why American politics was once described in terms of a "sun" party and a "moon" party. Figure 2.1 displays a simple index of party competition at the national level between 1861 and 2016. It is an average of the Democratic Party's share of the two-party vote for president, its share of House seats, and its share of Senate seats. Then, for purposes of differentiating Republican and Democratic eras, fifty is subtracted from the average, so that years with Democratic majorities are shown with bars above the zero line and years with Republican majori-

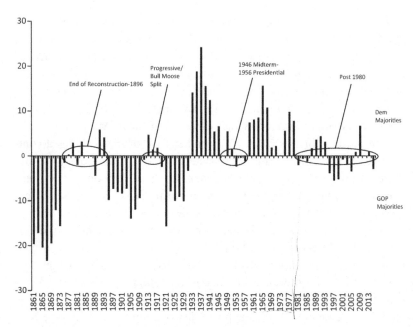

FIGURE 2.1. Index of two-party competition for control of US governing institutions, 1861–2016

The index is the average of the Democratic Party's share of the national two-party presidential vote, its share of House seats, and its share of Senate seats. Fifty is subtracted from the average to differentiate Democratic and Republican majorities.

ties are displayed with bars below the zero line. If one looks at the period before 1980, the patterns described by Lubell are immediately evident. There is no denying that Republicans were dominant in national politics for a decade after the Civil War and then again for most of the time between 1896 and 1932. Democrats were similarly dominant for decades after 1932.

These stretches of one-party ascendancy were punctuated by two relatively brief periods of strong party competition, each circled on the figure. Divisions within the Progressive Era Republican Party helped turn the House over to the Democrats in 1910, and then those divisions erupted with the Bull Moose insurgency in 1912. This competitive decade drew to a close in 1920 with the landslide victory of President Warren Harding, sweeping Republican gains in both the House and the Senate, and the so-called return to normalcy.

The other major burst of party competition during the twentieth century also lasted for a little over a decade during and just after the conclusion of World War II. The Democrats lost their long-standing majorities in Congress at Truman's first midterm in 1946, regained them with Truman's narrow reelection in 1948, and then lost them again with the 1952 election of Eisenhower, the first post–New Deal Republican president. At Eisenhower's 1954 midterm, Democrats recaptured their majorities in Congress, and then they held them through his landslide reelection in 1956 and for decades afterward. The narrow, seesawing majorities of this era fueled Republican exertions to improve their party's image, build its infrastructure, and break out of what they still perceived as its minority status (Allen 1992; Galvin 2010; Gellman 2015). However, this mid-century competitive period came to a decisive end with the crushing Republican defeat in the 1958 midterms, after which Democrats held nearly two-to-one majorities in both the House and the Senate.

Notwithstanding the years of party competition during the Progressive Era and the mid-twentieth century, the period since 1980 still stands out from the long time series (1861–2016) for its narrow and alternating party majorities. If the full sweep of US political history resembled the post-1980 period, no one would have ever described the American party system as being made up of a "sun" and a "moon."

The party competition of the last two decades of the nineteenth century stands as the most similar period to the post-1980 era. The late nineteenth-century partisan stalemate lasted just over twenty years, from 1874 to 1896. It began at the conclusion of Reconstruction as white Democratic "Redeemer" governments came to power across the former Confederacy. The Democrats first dramatically rebounded to national competitiveness in the 1874 midterms; then the contested 1876 Hayes–Tilden presidential election underscored the closeness of the new partisan balance. During these decades, national elections were fiercely contested, divided government was the norm, and there was regular alternation in congressional party majorities. Notably, this was also an era of pervasive and strong partisanship in Congress (Brady and Althoff 1974; Cherny 1997; Lee forthcoming; Poole and Rosenthal 1997). This period of intense party competition closed with the crushing Democratic reverses in the 1894 midterms, followed by the Populist take-over of the Democratic Party and its decisive defeat in the elections of 1896.

Although shorter than the late nineteenth century's competitive period, the stretch of party competition at the middle of the twentieth century also bears some underappreciated similarities to the post-1980 era. Looking back from the present, the Congress of the mid-twentieth century is often seen as one characterized by cozy bipartisanship and reduced party polarization. To be sure, the conservative coalition of Southern Democrats and Republicans decided the outcome of many important issues during this period. Congressional party leaders were weak, committee chairs were strong, and the parties were ideologically divided internally (Cooper and Brady 1981).

A closer look at the 1940s and 1950s, however, suggests at least some parallels to the post-1980 period. First, congressional politics at the middle of the twentieth century was more partisan than it would be during the 1960s and 1970s. Party strength in Congress, as gauged by a variety of measures, trended downward after the 1940s and 1950s (Brady et al. 1979) as the Democratic majority became more entrenched. Similarly, the conservative coalition emerged even more frequently in the 1960s and 1970s than it did during the 1940s and 1950s (Brady and Bullock 1980; Manley 1973). Second, there is no shortage of evidence that party competition nurtured some contentious national politics during that period. When Truman called Congress into a special session less than four months before the 1948 elections to ask the Republican majority to act on its own party platform, he was under no illusion that Congress would actually pass legislation. Truman's goal was party messaging, and the resulting deadlock yielded his campaign theme of the "do-nothing 80th Congress." As Sen. Arthur Vanderberg (R-MI) remarked at the time, "No good can come to the country from a special session of Congress which obviously stems from political motives" (Glass 2007). Similarly, the Republican leadership's long toleration and even encouragement of Sen. Joseph R. McCarthy's (R-WI) excesses also owed something to the potency of red-baiting for Republican electoral purposes. Sen. Robert A. Taft (R-OH) had specifically urged McCarthy to keep leveling accusations, saying, "If one case doesn't work out, then bring up another" (Latham 1966, 399; see also Gellman 2015, 92–93). Party competition, especially in the wake of the unexpected Republican defeat in the presidential election of 1948, at least partly underlay the era's ferocious Soviet espionage, communist subversion, and "Who lost China?" controversies.

Although a full investigation extends beyond the parameters of this study, it seems likely that the congressional politics of the 1940s and 1950s was more partisan than it would have been in the absence of com-

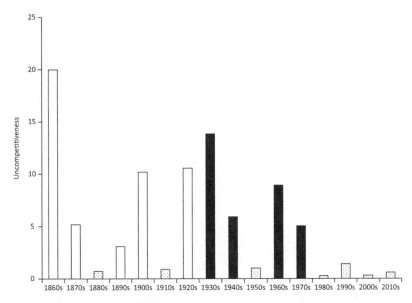

FIGURE 2.2. Divergence from partisan parity, 1861–2016
Higher bars indicate increasing dominance by one party, with Democratic-leaning eras
shown in black, Republican eras in white, and evenly balanced decades in dots.

petition for institutional control. Put differently, the insecurity of congressional majorities during that period probably fostered a higher level
of partisanship than one would have otherwise expected, given the underlying baseline of deep regional divisions within the parties on central
questions of public policy.

Figure 2.2 summarizes and simplifies the patterns in figure 2.1. The
figure tracks the size of the divergence from a 50–50 partisan balance
for each decade between 1861 and 2013. As can be seen here, the three-
and-a-half decades of narrow and alternating party majorities since
1980 stand out as the longest sustained period of partisan parity over
the whole period dating back to the Civil War. The post-Reconstruction
partisan stalemate lasted for only two decades. The other two similarly
competitive eras evident in figure 2.1 extended for just over a decade
each. Meanwhile, after more than thirty-five years, current party competition for control of US governing institutions shows no sign of abating.

More robust partisan competition in the post-1980 era is also apparent from public-opinion surveys. For decades after the development of
scientific public-opinion polling, far more Americans identified with the

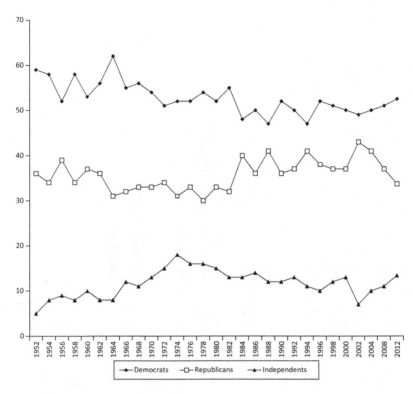

FIGURE 2.3. Party identification in the United States
Source: ANES Time Series Cumulative Data File.

Democratic Party than with the Republican Party. Figure 2.3 displays data on Americans' party identification between 1952 and 2012.

Between 1952 and 1982, there were always more than one-and-a-half times as many self-described Democrats as Republicans. On average, the ratio of Democrats to Republicans was 1.64. During this period, 55 percent of Americans self-identified as Democrats and only 33 percent as Republicans. In the 1980s, however, the two parties substantially converged in terms of their share of the electorate. Democratic identification had been slowly declining since the 1950s, and Republican identification surged in 1984 to 39 percent and then continued at that higher level. Although Republicans never pulled even with the Democrats in terms of party identification, by 1984 they had cut the Democrats' advantage roughly in half. Between 1984 and 2008, the ratio of Democratic to Republican identifiers was never higher than 1.44, and on average it was 1.3.

Republicans' worst showing in partisan identification post-1984 was in 2012, where the ratio of Democrats to Republicans once again stood at 1.55. However, it is worth noting that the share of the electorate identifying as Democrats in 2012 was no higher than it had been in 1996 or 1990; meanwhile, the percentage of Americans identifying as Republican stood at its lowest point since 1980. Some of the growth in the share of Americans identifying as "Independent" after 2002 appears to have come at the expense of Republicans. Starting in 2009, some proportion of these new Independents were Tea Party supporters, frustrated with the Republican Party but still strongly preferring Republicans to Democrats (Williamson et al. 2011). The bottom line is that, even with a larger Democratic advantage in voter identification after 2008, it is by no means clear that the party system was really any less two-party competitive.

The intensified party competition of the contemporary era is also reflected in the narrowness of the party divisions in Congress. Recent decades have seen slim congressional majorities by modern US standards. Figure 2.4 displays the party breakdown of the Senate starting in 1932. During the 1930s, Democrats had 2:1 margins over Republicans. The parties were closely competitive for roughly a decade under Truman

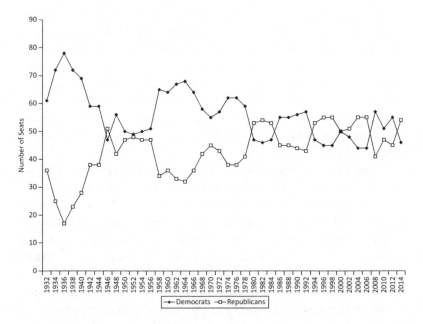

FIGURE 2.4. Party composition of the Senate, 1932–2015

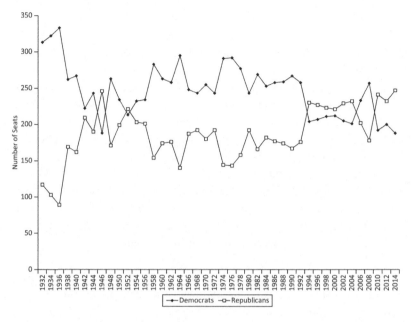

FIGURE 2.5. Party composition of the House of Representatives, 1932–2016

and Eisenhower. But after 1958, the Senate again stood with 2:1 Democratic margins of control. Democratic majorities held with only margin-
ally diminished strength throughout the 1970s. After 1980, by contrast,
no party possessed a majority the size of those typically held by Democrats during the preceding post–New Deal period. Between 1980 and
2015, party control of the Senate switched seven times, with Democrats
and Republicans each controlling Congress half of the time. To a considerable extent, majority control of the Senate has been an open question
ever since 1980.

Stronger party competition is additionally evident in the party breakdown of the House of Representatives, as displayed in figure 2.5. Democrats obviously held their majorities far longer in the House than in the
Senate, and the battle for majority control of that chamber was slower to
get under way in earnest. But since 1994, the party balance in the House
has been very close. Although the post-1994 House Republican majorities persisted until 2007, the GOP's margins of control were exceptionally narrow and could always have been reversed by a swing of merely
seventeen House seats at most. The Democrats' House majorities after
2006 were also narrow, as were the post-2010 Republican House majori-

ties. Between 1994 and 2014, the minority party in the House rarely fell below 200 seats; by contrast, between 1958 and 1994, the minority Republicans never held more than 192 seats, on average holding only 170. Republicans in the 114th Congress stand at their post–New Deal high-water mark, 247 seats, still a narrow margin in comparison to the Democratic majorities of most of the twentieth century.

Finally, it is important to note that even presidential elections have been markedly more competitive in recent decades. Figure 2.6 displays the winning presidential candidate's percentage of the Electoral College vote for each presidential election since 1932.

As is evident here, party competition for the presidency was stronger than for Congress throughout the period. The exceptionally close 1948 election brought to an end the lopsided Democratic victories of the immediate post–New Deal period. Republican Dwight D. Eisenhower then won two overwhelming victories in 1952 and 1956, though his war-hero status left the electoral appeal of the Republican Party more generally open to question. But the narrow 1960 election that returned the Democrats to power indicated that Republicans could field viable presidential contenders even without the unique magnetism of Eisenhower.

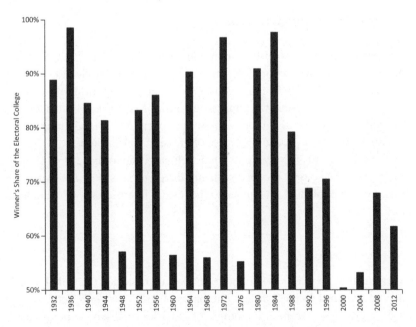

FIGURE 2.6. The winning presidential candidate's electoral vote share, 1932–2012

Despite a longer history of tough party competition for the presidency, the presidential contests of recent decades still stand out for their fierce intensity. It was once typical for presidential candidates to win all across the country and to amass large majorities in the Electoral College. Between 1932 and 1988, the winning presidential candidate received at least 80 percent of the Electoral College vote in ten out of fourteen elections. In contrast, since 1988 no presidential candidate has won more than 70 percent of the Electoral College vote. There has not been a presidential landslide since 1984—seven cycles (and counting). The 2000 presidential election was almost an Electoral College and popular-vote tie.

In short, the two parties in post-1980 US national politics are more evenly matched than was typical for most of the preceding modern era. By any of these objective measures, a party out of power in the post-1980 period has had much better prospects for near-term electoral success than the out party had throughout most of the twentieth century. By the same token, parties in power have also had much more reason to fear the loss of majority status. These changed prospects are likely to have pervasive effects on political incentives in national politics.

Perceptions of Competitiveness

The level of party competition in national politics is as much a question of perception as of election outcomes or other objective indicators. In an effort to reconstruct how understandings of party competition have varied over time, I pursue two approaches. First, I examine the incidence of news articles discussing the possibility of party control switching during the two months preceding every congressional election between 1958 and 2014. Second, I draw upon what Beltway insiders have said about their party's electoral prospects during different eras. For the latter, I turn to both published accounts and the insider interviews conducted for this project.

News Coverage

Turning first to predictions about change in majority control, I conducted searches in the full-text databases of the *New York Times*. Figure 2.7 displays a count of the number of articles discussing a possibility for a shift in majority control of either chamber of Congress, as well as

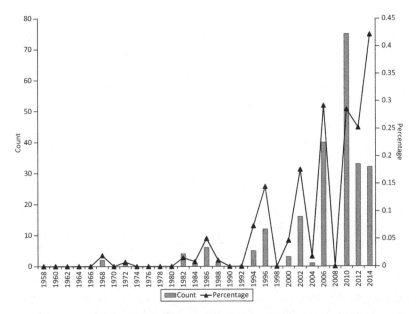

FIGURE 2.7. *New York Times* articles discussing prospects for a change in majority control in the two months preceding the November elections

Source: Online searches of the ProQuest Historical Newspapers (1851–2010) Database and ProQuest *New York Times* Database.

The bars track the number of articles discussing the possibility of a shift in majority control of either chamber of Congress. The lines track the percentage of the total number of articles about the congressional elections that discuss the possibility of a change in party control.

the percentage of all articles about the upcoming congressional elections that referenced a potential change in control.[1]

The most obvious and important conclusion to be drawn from these data is that there is far more speculation about prospects for changes in party control of Congress after 1980 than there was between 1958 and 1980. News articles much more frequently discuss prospects for changes of majority control in the post-1980 period, in terms of both a raw count as well as a percentage of all the articles about congressional elections identified in these searches.

Before 1982, in only two election years was there speculation in the *New York Times* about possible shifts in control of Congress. In 1968, there were two such stories (Apple 1968; Herbers 1968), each reporting on candidate Richard M. Nixon's and some Republican leaders' optimism that Republicans "might conceivably manage to win control" (Apple 1968, 31) of one or both chambers. Neither article, however, quotes Democrats or neutral analysts expressing similar sentiments or suggesting such a change was likely. A single *New York Times* story in 1972 referenced the outside possibility that a Nixon landslide would "carr[y] throughout the ticket" to Congress, though it went on to say that "political leaders do not foresee such a strong coattail effect" (Weaver 1972, 25).

A second noteworthy point is how limited the speculation was regarding the possibility of Republicans winning majorities before both the 1980 and the 1994 elections, the years when Republicans first overthrew the Democrats' long-standing control of the Senate and House, respectively. The outcome of the 1980 Senate elections seems to have been a complete surprise as far as the *New York Times* coverage is concerned. Looking more broadly to the ProQuest Historical Newspapers Database, there was occasional acknowledgement of the possibility of a Republican Senate take-over in 1980, though everywhere it was dismissed as unlikely. For example, the *Chicago Tribune* reported, "Republican strategists are talking about gaining control of the Senate and picking up 25 to 30 seats in the House. In reality, however, GOP gains are not likely to be that great" (Siddon 1980, 6). The relative dearth of articles discussing the Republicans' prospects for a take-over in 1994 is also glaring. The few articles that even broached the possibility tended to quickly discount it. In one article acknowledging that a Republican sweep could happen, the *New York Times* (Berke 1994, 1) reported, "Although no leading analysts have predicted that the Republicans will gain the 7 seats necessary to win back the Senate, or the 40 seats needed to take control of the House after four decades of Democratic control, they acknowledge that shifts of such magnitude are not inconceivable."

This relative lack of news reports examining the potential for Republican take-overs in the lead-up to the elections when Republicans first won control highlights that the conventional wisdom heavily discounted the possibility of a loss of Democratic control before it had actually occurred. Political observers markedly underpredicted the Republican victories of 1980 and 1994. But since the Republican take-overs, journalists seem to overpredict switches in majority control, although there are too few observations for any firm conclusions. Notably, a fair number of news stories discussed possible switches in both 1982 and 1996, when neither chamber of Congress changed hands. The small number of pre-election news articles that raised the prospect that Republicans would win control of Congress in 1994 ($n = 5$) markedly contrasts with the substantially larger number of articles that discussed whether Democrats might retake power in 1996 (n = 12). In other words, once the long-standing Democratic majority had been broken, changes in party control of Congress seem to have become easier to imagine and a greater subject for journalistic attention.

Finally, it is important to note that the data show that speculation about near-term shifts in majority control is not a constant fact about the contemporary, post-1980 era. Although most years feature some discussion along these lines, there are clearly elections when a change seems likely and others when the possibility seems remote. Reasonably enough, discussion of potential shifts in congressional majorities concentrates intensely on midterm years when the party not controlling the presidency might win control of Congress aided by the traditional off-year boost to the presidential out party, such as in 1982 (Senate only), 1986 (Senate only), 1994, 2002, 2006, 2010, and 2014 (Senate only). By comparison, there is far less speculation about party shifts in midterms under divided government, where the midterm penalty to the president's party stands it in very poor stead to win back unified party control of government (e.g., 1990 and 1998). There has also been little news speculation about changes in control of Congress during presidential election years. This may reflect, at least in part, the extent to which the battle for the presidency dominates news coverage, though it also tracks with the reality that no change in party control of Congress has coincided with a presidential election since 1980.[2] Despite this variation, the narrow congressional majorities across the whole contemporary period mean that every election can make a significant difference to a minority party's prospects of winning back control in subsequent cycles.

First-Person Perspectives

Drawing upon interviews with congressional insiders, as well as upon memoirs, reflections, and historical accounts, I turn now to reconstruct, in broad-brush terms, how party competition for control of Congress was perceived during three different periods: (1) during the 1960s and 1970s, (2) after 1980 but before 1994, and (3) after 1994.

1960s–70s   At no point after 1958 and before 1980 were Democratic majorities in Congress seen in serious jeopardy. During this era, Democratic control of Congress was largely taken for granted on both sides of the aisle. "When I entered Congress in 1969," said former Rep. David Obey (D-WI, 1969–2011) at a 2014 roundtable, "nobody thought there was much chance Democrats would lose control."[3] "When I served in Congress," recalled former Rep. Mickey Edwards (R-OK, 1977–93), "the Democrats had been in charge, with only a couple of exceptions, for forty years. It was just perceived as the normal state of affairs. . . . We were not chafing at it. It's perhaps what it's like to be a minority citizen who maybe feels that being in the minority is just 'my place.'"[4] When I asked one former House Republican leadership staffer who began his service in the late 1970s how Republicans saw their chances of winning control at that time, he laughed and said, "Nobody talked about it. Ever. This was a time when there was a joke postcard showing Bill Archer and Jim Collins in a phone booth, with the caption 'The Texas Republican Party.'"[5]

During much of the 1960s and 1970s, House Democrats were embroiled in internal party battles between liberals and conservatives over institutional reforms (Rohde 1991; Zelizer 2004). Some of these reforms—including open meetings, televising of hearings and floor proceedings, and the liberalization of floor procedure—would eventually afford significant new opportunities for the GOP minority to embarrass Democrats and to promote their own policy proposals (Farrell 2001, 626–38; Lawrence 2014; Roberts and Smith 2003; Zelizer 2004, 2007). But at the time these battles were being waged, the possibility that Republicans might gain partisan advantage from these reforms was simply not a pressing concern for Democrats, who felt secure in their majorities. "It was the furthest thing from Democrats' minds that [the reforms] would help Republicans," reflected one longtime former Democratic staffer. "At that point, the fighting in Congress was centered within the Democratic Party—that was the focus."[6] Republicans, for their part, were more alert to the possible advantages, and many strongly favored the sunshine reforms (Wolfensberger 2001, 86–128). "Open meetings, televised hearings—Republicans were for all these things," observed a former Republican staffer who served through the 1970s. "They understood that transparency would help them. . . . Many Democrats were out of step with their constituencies, and Republicans felt that anything they could do to raise the visibility would be helpful to the party."[7] One wonders whether Democrats would have been as interested in pursuing these institutional reforms had they anticipated how useful they would soon become to Republicans.

Between 1958 and 1980, the only two election years when Republicans perceived any notable possibility of winning majorities in Congress were 1968 and 1972. In those years, Republicans held out hope that presidential coattails might sweep in a sufficient number of Republicans to win a majority in Congress. Republican prospects, however, were not so great as to arouse serious alarm in Democratic ranks. In the lead-up to the 1968 elections, House Republicans hoping to win the 31 seats needed to take control of the House sported lapel buttons inscribed with the number 218 (Shepard 1968). More sober analysis suggested that such a number was out of reach. Given the number of seats in play, a net gain of 3 seats for Republicans seemed more likely, according to a *New York Times* estimate (Herbers 1968, E3). In the end, the 1968 Republicans won 5 seats each in the House and Senate, leaving Democrats in control of 243 House seats and 58 Senate seats.

There was also some optimism in Republican ranks in 1972, given the divisions evident in the Democratic Party and the weakness of its presidential nominee, George McGovern. A *Christian Science Monitor* state-by-state assessment showed the possibility that a strong Nixon landslide might edge the Senate into Republican hands, though the "scenario . . . [was] quite speculative and less than likely, in the assessment of the *Monitor* observers" (Sperling 1972). Nixon's assessment of the situation in 1972 was not optimistic, and he was criticized for remaining aloof from the congressional races and failing to campaign on behalf of Republicans. "His reasoning," reported the *New York Times*, "is that the Republican party remains a minority party" (Semple 1972). At the conclusion of the 1972 campaign, Republicans gained 12 House seats and 2 Senate seats, leaving Democrats in control with 242 House seats and 56 Senate seats.

Beyond these two elections, I failed to uncover any evidence that Republicans perceived significant prospects for winning control of Congress during this era, much less that conventional wisdom credited them with any serious chance or that Democrats worried about it. When *Congressional Quarterly* interviewed House Republicans about their prospects in 1976, none foresaw the party even "coming close to winning the House" (Freed 1976). Rep. Marvin L. Esch (R-MI), then age forty-eight, remarked that he had decided to run for the Senate because "at least there's a greater chance for Republicans to gain control of the Senate than the House within my lifetime" (Freed 1976, 1638).

1980–94   The Republican take-over of the Senate in 1980 was a surprise to nearly everyone. "For liberals, the shock of losing control of the Senate has been far more traumatic than even the loss of the White House," began one *New York Times* postelection analysis. "This is understandable. The Presidency has been won and lost many times, but a Democratic Senate was something you could count on" (Steinberger 1980, A35). In the lead-up to the election, *Congressional Quarterly* had projected that Republicans would gain less than 15 House seats and 2 or 3 Senate seats. "Not even the most daring prognosticators predicted that the GOP would pick up more than seven seats in the Senate and thirty in the House" (Busch 2005, 153). The Republicans gained 12 Senate seats for a new majority of 53. They also won 33 House seats, bringing them to 192 seats for the 97th Congress, the GOP's high-water mark in the chamber between 1958 and 1994. Senate Democrats "were just gobsmacked after 1980," recalled one former Senate staffer. "They were just as stunned as they could be. It seemed inconceivable that they could lose."[8]

The Republicans' Senate victory in 1980 heralded a new era of party competition for control of Congress. Although shocked by their losses, Democrats did not see themselves as out of striking distance of retaking control of the chamber. Reflecting back, a senior Senate leadership staffer at the time said, "We had no idea how long the Republican majority would last . . . but Democrats never thought they were a permanent minority. They thought they could get it back."[9] Some Senate Democrats expected to return to the majority right away. In February 1981, Sen. Russell B. Long (D-LA) dismissed the new Republican majority: "Bless their sweet hearts. They are in such a state of euphoria. . . . They're in control in the Senate for the third time in the 33 years I've been here. Now they're back in, in my opinion on a fluke, for another two years" (Sandoz 1981, 3). "Democrats had hope about 1982," remembered a Senate Democratic leadership staffer, "but not big hopes. Democratic incumbents were petrified after what had happened in 1980. So challengers in 1982 had no resources."[10] In the end, the Republican Senate majority would last six years, not two. Since 1980, no party's Senate majority has extended for longer than four Congresses; on average, Senate majorities have changed hands every three Congresses.

Although Republican House majorities remained far in the future, the 1980 elections also inspired new optimism among House Republicans. Reagan's sweeping national victory, combined with the surprise Republican majority in the Senate, gave House Republicans fresh rea-

son for hope. "This was a time of great optimism for Republicans generally," recalled one former Republican staffer serving at the time.[11] Right
away, some House Republicans began to talk about the possibility that
they might win a majority of that chamber in 1982 (Roberts 1981; Cohen
1982a; Smith 1988, 675). When I asked one former House staffer who
had served from the late 1960s through the late 1990s if there was any
particular year before 1994 when Republicans were especially hopeful,
he pointed specifically to 1982.[12] In the end, the 1982 midterms, in which
Republicans lost twenty-six House seats, were a dispiriting reversal for
the party.

Despite the disappointments of 1982 and several subsequent elections, an activist cadre of House Republicans persisted steadfastly all
through the 1980s in the belief that a Republican House majority was
in reach. Undeterred by the Democratic gains of 1982, Rep. Newt Gingrich (R-GA) organized the Conservative Opportunity Society (COS)
in early 1983. One former staffer for a member associated with the COS
recalled, "[After 1980] every two years we convinced ourselves that it
was our year. We didn't get too discouraged in 1982, despite the terrible
beating we took. . . . In 1984, with the Republican landslide on the horizon, we thought, 'This just *has* to be our year!' But then it didn't happen.
'If not then, *when*?' 1986 was a bad year. 1988, no coattails. By 1990, we
had nothing to show for all those efforts."[13]

Among these eternal optimists was Rep. Dick Armey (R-TX). In
October 1993, House Majority Leader Dick Gephardt (D-MO) asked
Armey why he was passing up the opportunity to run for whip, given the
vacancy opening up. Armey replied, "Well, that's because I'm running
for majority leader." Gephardt laughed and said, "That's a good story,
you ought to stick with it" (Garrett 2005, 66–67).

Most other House Republicans, however, questioned or rejected the
COS's perennial optimism. Gingrich himself reportedly warned Armey
to be more circumspect with his optimistic speculation: "Dick, you gotta
quit talking about being in the majority, people are laughing at you"
(Garrett 2005, 67). "Republicans had a serious inferiority complex," recalled another of those younger, more aggressive members, Rep. Tom
DeLay (R-TX). "I remember hearing [Republican Leader Bob] Michel
comment in his speeches that not one Republican who had served during his time had ever been part of a majority. He said this as though it
belonged in the *Guinness Book of World Records*" (DeLay and Mansfield 2007, 77). A former Republican House staffer of the era recollected,

"Going right up to the 1994 election, you could count on one hand the folks who thought we could win a majority."[14] "Reagan's election, along with the Senate sweep, provided the first glimmer of hope for [House] control," remembered another former House staffer from the era. "Even so, there wasn't much hope for taking control of the House. The Democrats were still so entrenched."[15]

AFTER 1994   The 1994 elections mark another turning point in the intensification of party competition for control of Congress. Like the 1980 elections, the Republican House take-over of 1994 was very much a surprise. The Democrats' losses that year massively exceeded forecasts and even included the first defeat of a sitting House Speaker since 1862. News reports had offered little inkling that the Democratic majority was at risk.

Despite the presence of a hard core of inveterate optimists, most Republican House members had remained doubtful of their 1994 prospects. "I don't think I thought myself that the Republicans were really going to win the majority until about two weeks out from the election," recalled one House Republican leadership staffer of the era. "I remember how in January 1994, Gingrich asked Dick Armey to be our transition chairman for taking over the majority. Lots of people, lots of *Republicans*, ridiculed the idea."[16] He went on, "I remember walking back with the House Republicans after the public event on the Capitol steps in support of the Contract with America [on September 27, 1994]. There was so much bitching and moaning, 'We're never going to win!'"

Most Democrats were taken by surprise as well. "Did we think Democrats could lose our majorities?" recollected a former House Democratic staffer. "Well, we worried about marginal members, loss of seats. We knew in 1993 and early 1994 that marginal members would have a difficult time. . . . But never in their wildest dreams did most Democrats really think [Republicans] would win control."[17] Former House Speaker Tom Foley (D-WA) recalled that "[Rep.] Vic Fazio [D-CA, chairman of the Democratic Congressional Campaign Committee] kept reporting in late spring and early summer 1994 on the tracking polls that were indicating that we had 60 or 70 seats that were in serious jeopardy. . . . But I think it was a shock to some when the curtain actually fell and the reality appeared that, after forty years, the majority had switched" (Biggs and Foley 1999, 244). "Democrats were really surprised by 1994," remembered an aide to one of the House Democratic leaders at the time.

"There was no sense of threat, particularly after having survived the bank scandal [in 1992] with so little loss of seats."[18]

Senate Republicans were more optimistic than House Republicans about their prospects in 1994. After all, they had only been in the minority since 1987. Some staffers whom I interviewed suggested that one reason Senate Republicans were unwilling to sign onto the Contract with America is that they believed they would win a majority without it. It was easier to get House Republicans to endorse the Contract, because the prospect of actually winning a House majority seemed remote. Members and prospective committee chairmen in the House would have been reluctant to precommit themselves to a policy agenda written by party leaders if they had expected that they would have to implement it. "One of the reasons why so many [House] members signed onto it was because they didn't actually think they'd have to do it," remarked one House Republican staffer from the period.[19] When I asked a Republican Senate staffer serving at the time whether he expected his party to win the majority in 1994, he replied, "Absolutely." He continued, immediately making the connection to the Contract, "The House Republican leadership approached the Senate leadership to ask if we wanted to be a part of the Contract with America, and Cochran and Dole said, 'No, thank you.'"[20] The Contract was less attractive to Republican senators because they did not want to make prior commitments about their agenda priorities once in control.

After 1994, House Democrats did not see themselves as destined for long-term minority status. "The margins were so narrow," remembered one House Democratic aide. "Democrats believed they would get back the majority. We thought we would get it back in 1996, with the next presidential election."[21] A House Democratic leadership staffer recalled, "We had a meeting, with sixty House members, in a DC ballroom over three days in late November or early December 1994 to talk about what we needed to do. At first, there was a lot of complaining about all the problems with leadership, a lot of airing of views about why we'd lost. Then we turned to focus on what we needed to do to get the majority back. This was the focus from day one."[22]

Republicans perceived threats to their new House majority immediately. House Speaker Gingrich recalled, "What people failed to understand is the hardest election was going to be in 1996. Republicans had not won a second consecutive election since 1928. . . . And I would argue the second election was much harder. . . . Democrats did a brilliant job of orchestrating resources, designing images, and really taking it to us" (2004, 102). Democrats persisted in seeing themselves as within reach of majority status, even though it took them until the 2006 midterms to retake the House majority. "The narrowness of the margins in the late 1990s is important," remembered one House Democratic staffer. "We were just a few seats short of what was needed."[23]

In both chambers, narrow majorities have been a stubborn reality since 1994. Not every election year has offered a good prospect for a minority to retake the majority, but the two parties remain fiercely competitive. The national electorate stands closely divided between the two parties. The Senate majority is persistently in play, with Democrats optimistic about yet another possible shift of party control of that chamber as soon as 2016. However, at this writing, House Democrats see themselves as facing a sharply uphill battle to retake control of that chamber. With Democratic voters less efficiently distributed across House districts than Republican voters, Democrats do not typically win a share of House seats commensurate with their performance in national or statewide elections (Chen and Rodden 2013; Jacobson 2013, 17–20; Schaller 2015). Particularly since the 2010 redistricting, Democrats recognize that a large electoral wave would be necessary to lift Democrats to a new House majority. In the meantime, Democratic lawsuits have been pressing the courts, with some success, to overturn Republican-gerrymandered House districts (Wilson 2015).[24] Despite House Democrats' more difficult path back to power, pundits have not ceased speculating about how Democrats might regain a House majority (Cillizza 2015; Gonzales 2015; Rothenberg 2015). No one is yet proclaiming Democrats a permanent House minority.

1980 as a Turning Point

I believe it is a mistake to see 1994 in isolation. . . . Reagan helped to bring us back from a distinct minority party status to being competitive. We, I think, helped get ourselves to parity, recognizing that much of the Contract was in fact standing on Ronald Reagan's shoulders. — Former House Speaker Newt Gingrich (R-GA; US House of Representatives 2004, 115)

The 1980 elections ushered in a protracted era of partisan parity in the contest for control of American national institutions. This is evident in the overall index of two-party competition (in figures 2.1 and 2.2). It is also apparent in the narrower margins of control of Congress that have prevailed since that time (figures 2.4 and 2.5), as well as the closer balance in partisan identification in the electorate (figure 2.3). The 1980 elections reintroduced competition for party control of the Senate, in that these were the first elections since 1954 in which the Republicans won a majority of seats in the Senate.

The 1980 election is also important in a qualitative sense. It was the first election since the New Deal in which Republicans captured the presidency with a candidate from the conservative wing of the party. Ronald Reagan—a conservative hero, unlike Nixon or Eisenhower—gave Republicans a sense that they could offer a full-fledged, politically viable national alternative to the Democrats. "With Reagan's election and the dramatic shifts in the Congress, you could feel the political ground shift," recalled former Sen. Trent Lott (2005, 77). "Standing on Ronald Reagan's shoulders," as Gingrich explained, gave House Republicans new hope for their party, even though it would be a long while before Republicans would succeed in winning a House majority.

While 1980 stands out as a turning point, party competition for control of US national government intensified further after 1994. Most importantly, the persistent Democratic majorities in the House finally came to an end. Switches in party control of Congress have occurred with greater frequency in the post-1994 era (figures 2.4 and 2.5). In addition, presidential elections have been more narrowly decided in the Electoral College relative to historical baselines (figure 2.6). News coverage of Congress also reveals a much more intense focus on the contest for congressional majorities, with most election years featuring some amount of speculation about the possibility for a shift in control (figure 2.7).

Neither party since 1980 has suffered from the defeatism that characterized Republicans for so much of the preceding post–New Deal era. By 1980, Democratic majorities extended back close to half a century—to the advent of the New Deal, with the sole exceptions of the 80th and 83rd Congresses. By the same token, neither party has been able to feel as complacent about holding its majorities as the congressional Democrats of the low-competition period. Of the pre-1994 Democrats of his era, former Rep. Bill Frenzel (R-MN) remembered, "After sixty-two years of ascendancy, with two small imperfections, most Democratic members believed they were born to rule and that their rule was ordained by the Almighty" (US House of Representatives 2004, 76). "We had always been in the majority, and thought we always would be," recalled a House Democrat. "[The loss in 1994] was a huge shock that everyone had to deal with" (Green 2015, 26).

The result is a Congress in which elections have become a more central preoccupation for members. To be sure, concern about one's own re-election is a constant fact of life for congressional incumbents. But elections take on greater significance in an era where majority control of Congress is in doubt. With congressional majorities at stake, members take much greater interest in how what happens in Congress might affect the prospects for their party to win or retain majority status. When I asked a senior House staffer how prospects of change in party control of Congress affect congressional politics, he said simply, "It is one of the most important factors. It affects everything about how Congress works."[25] A Senate leadership staffer of long experience said, "There has not been much time at any point when elections and concern about holding the majority hasn't been a consideration."[26] "Elections occur every two years without fail," observed a Senate leadership aide with three decades of service. "You can set your clock by it. Everyone is aware of this. Over time, elections have become more and more a focal point. Everything is seen through the prism of elections. It's never been more apparent than now."[27]

CHAPTER THREE

The Logic of Confrontation

Competition for majority status affects strategic decisions in Congress. When there is little competition for party control of Congress, members will, of course, weigh how the politics of various issues might affect their own individual electoral interests. But there will be less collective strategizing about how to influence the parties' overall image, reputation, and public standing. When control of Congress hangs in the balance, however, members will ponder how they might affect their party's common fate. As one former staffer put it, "When you think you have a chance [to win the majority], you're just going to go all out."[1] Members competing for majority-party status thus take a wider view of politics beyond their own reelection. They will be more likely to view issues and political decisions with an eye toward partisan (as well as personal) advantage.

This chapter argues that increased competition for control of Congress fuels a more confrontational style of partisanship, as parties in their quest for power seek to define the stakes for voters. I begin by laying out a logic of partisan confrontation: why members of Congress perceive political benefits from defining and dramatizing party differences and how they go about doing so. *Messaging* is the term that congressional insiders use to describe their efforts to highlight party differences. Next, I examine how party messaging disrupts bipartisanship. Finally, I analyze how a party's incentives to engage in strategies of partisan differentiation are affected by its institutional position in the constitutional system (e.g., majority vs. minority status, unified vs. divided party control, House vs. Senate). On each of these themes, I rely upon the interview subjects consulted for this book, as well as personal memoirs of former members of Congress and perspectives from news sources.

The Quest for Majority Control

What is the job of [a] Republican leader in the minority? It's to hold the job for as short a time as possible. — Rep. John A. Boehner (R-OH) in a 2006 letter to House Republican colleagues[2]

There is no question that members care about which party holds a majority. When I asked interview subjects whether majority status mattered to members, I would often get an incredulous look. "Without the majority, you have nothing," responded one senior Senate aide.[3] "Absolutely! It matters hugely," answered another. "Every senator in the majority party will get a gavel [of at least a subcommittee]."[4] When Republicans lost the majority in 2001, he continued, Republican senators' reactions "were as if someone had taken a beloved old dog out and shot him. These are all alpha males, Type A personalities. They want the ball." A staffer serving during the immediate aftermath of the 1994 elections recalled former House Energy and Commerce chairman John Dingell's (D-MI) reaction to his new minority status: "At first, he asked '*What do I do now?*' He couldn't set the agenda; he couldn't legislate. It was as if he had died, or as if they'd cut off both legs and both arms."[5] When I asked one senior Senate aide if his boss closely watched elections outside his own state, he said that "[his boss] would be chair if Republicans won a majority, which would mean a major change for him, a very big deal. There is a lot riding on the outcome."[6] Members are "acutely aware" of the stakes in the quest for majority control, said another Senate staffer.[7]

It is perhaps not surprising that majority status is very important to members during periods characterized by pervasive partisan conflict, where the minority party is routinely voted down. But even during the 97th Congress (1981–82), when House Republicans won many legislative victories in coalition with conservative Democrats, a former House Republican staffer remembered, "Republicans [at that time] cared about getting a majority very much, though there were conservative Democrats with whom they could work in the House."[8] Near the nadir of party conflict in Congress in the early 1970s, House Minority Leader John J. Rhodes (R-AZ) complained about the sense of "futility that comes from being locked into the minority" (1976, 4), and his book spins out an imaginary scene of him "mount[ing] the rostrum," "tak[ing] the gavel from my good friend Carl Albert," and basking in the "long and loud" applause (82). Although Rhodes labels his vision a "fantasy," the fact that he indulges it indicates that majority status is prized even when partisanship in Congress stands near historic lows.

Members value majority status even when the parties are not ideologically polarized, because members of the majority party chair all the committees in Congress.[9] Committee chairs generally decide what issues will move forward and which subjects will receive hearings. They also exercise significant gatekeeping power on the floor. Members desire and strive for this source of power, even under conditions where the parties share overlapping policy goals and there is prospect for bipartisanship on legislation. Put differently, the value of majority status is not conditional on the existence of ideologically polarized parties, though it stands to reason that ideological polarization would raise the stakes of party control further. "It's always better to be in the majority," summarized a veteran Senate Democratic staffer. "The Senate minority has more leverage than the House minority . . . but anybody who wants to be in the minority needs to have his head examined."[10] "Who controls the majority sets the agenda," said a Republican Senate aide. "It's always in the back and front of our minds."[11]

Individual members vary in how much they care about majority status, of course. "There's always a few, the 5 percent, who set up shop on their own and don't work with the party—[Senators Jim] DeMint (R-SC), [Mike] Lee (R-UT), and [Rand] Paul (R-KY) right now," said a Senate staffer.[12] "Some members don't care much about what the party is doing," reflected another Senate aide. "They are focused on their local media. They are focused on Twitter. They are going to the local Rotary or football games in their state."[13] But it is safe to say that the typical member of Congress prefers to be a member of a majority party. These preferences are undoubtedly even stronger for members who hold or expect to hold significant leadership positions.

Not only is majority status important to members; they also believe that their own actions can make a difference to that end. Members recognize that many factors beyond their control affect their party's political fortunes: the fixed timing of midterm and presidential elections, the state of the economy, critical events, war and peace, presidential success or scandal. But I did not speak with any congressional insider who believed that there was nothing that members themselves could do to affect their party's ability to win or hold a majority of seats. The general attitude is that "you have to try."[14]

What members can do to help their party's electoral prospects is universally known as "party messaging." Every interview subject approached for this project—in both chambers and both parties—was comfortable with using the term and discussing party efforts in this vein. To a person, they all saw it as an important enterprise and potentially consequential for electoral outcomes.

Messaging has become an institutionalized responsibility for congressional party leaders, as well as for many members and staffers in both chambers. It is a prominent part of the contemporary party leader's job (though it has not always been so). In particular, leaders experience continuous pressure from rank-and-file members whenever their party suffers electoral reversals, seems to be failing to "get its message out," or otherwise appears to have wound up on the wrong side of public opinion. News coverage of Congress—especially in Beltway outlets like *Roll Call*, *The Hill*, *National Journal*, and *Politico*—make it clear that party messaging is an ongoing preoccupation for members, leaders, and staff.[15] A representative news story begins, "Sen. Bill Frist (R-TN), seeking to rebound from several high-profile setbacks in his message battle with Minority Leader Harry Reid (D-NV), is beginning his last year as majority leader with a newly assembled rapid response and message development team" (Stanton 2006). Party messaging is the focus of constant strategizing, experimentation, institutional innovation, and creative effort.

Defining and Dramatizing Party Differences

[The 1992 election] is our shot. . . . We've just got to go all out. We've got every reason to define the differences between the parties. — House Minority Leader Bob Michel (R-IL), 1991[16]

Control of Congress will be the issue in 1982. We've got to give Democratic voters a sense that they have something at stake in 1982: their jobs, their homes, their children's future, their retirement. — Kirk O'Donnell, chief aide to House Speaker Tip O'Neill (D-MA), 1982[17]

In waging these party message battles, members and leaders have one primary goal: to give voters reasons to choose their own party over its opposition. Underneath this strategy is an implicit view of voters as rational actors. Put in Downsian (1957, 39) terms, party messaging aims to increase the "expected party differential": the difference voters perceive in utility between each party being in power. The underlying belief is that voters need to be convinced that the parties are different and that they should care about which party holds the reins of power. Politicians seeking to help their party win and hold majorities operate under the assumption that they must be able to offer clear reasons as to why voters should choose their party over the alternative. They want sharp contrasts so as to motivate supporters to make the effort to turn out to vote or to engage in more demanding forms of political activity, such as donating to campaigns.

Making the case for one's own party thus involves an active quest for issues to differentiate the two parties. "We committed to fashioning an alternative to every bill or amendment the Democrats proposed," explained former House Republican Whip Tom DeLay (R-TX) about his party's efforts in the lead-up to the 1994 elections. "This proved to be an effective strategy. . . . It illustrated to the American people that they had a choice" (DeLay and Mansfield 2007, 93). One former senior Senate leadership aide stated, "The key to effective party messaging is finding a way to illustrate the differences between the parties, finding a concrete example."[18] "To the extent that you're not drawing distinctions, you're making it harder to make your case," said a former House leadership staffer.[19]

To clarify the partisan choice, the issue must unify one's own party and create contrasts with the opposition. The Democrats' "Six for '06" agenda, for example, contained a set of modest, incremental policy proposals that were both uncontroversial among Democrats and designed to poll well.[20] But the agenda would only serve as a reason for voters to oust Republicans and install Democrats as the congressional majority if Republicans were seen as opposing the proposals. So each of these agenda items was also selected because it was known to provoke Republican resistance. One leadership aide explained the process: "In developing the 'Six for '06,' we only wanted issues that no one in the party could object to. . . . We needed to maximize unity and singularity of purpose. . . . And in constructing the agenda, we had one other consideration: the GOP had to be against it. That's the only way it works!"[21]

Put simply, party conflict is necessary for party messaging. If an issue is to serve as a reason for voters to prefer one party to the other, it cannot be a question on which there is bipartisan consensus. For an issue to work for message purposes, it must elicit some party differences. Another staffer pointed out that a unified response from the opposition party is not essential for effective party differentiation. As long as your party is cohesive on the issue, he said, "it can be good if the issue divides them. Roll a grenade into the midst of them."[22]

Wide consultation within the party is required to identify issues around which its members can coalesce. "The Hill is multiheaded. No one is in charge. It is hard to coordinate," said a former leadership aide. "Not everyone agrees with what the central message should be. You have to get general buy-in. . . . It is hard work."[23] Sen. Dick Durbin (D-IL) explained the message-development process as follows: "What we are trying to do here is get into the substance, and when all is said and done we will have three or four ideas that we think are really responsive to what the country needs and distinguishes what Democrats stand for and Republicans don't" (Preston 2002, 1). Many meetings and conversations are necessary to develop a congressional party's message and strategies for disseminating it.

A sense of shared threat or opportunity generates incentive for fellow partisans to work past disagreements and unite around a party message. Message discipline does not generally happen by accident. It occurs because members believe they have a common stake in the outcome of the effort. One longtime Senate staff director said, "Only years of getting our clock cleaned got us to our political consensus now that we work together on messaging. Unless there's an issue that is uniquely personal to your state, you work with the party. . . . There are some members who are complainers. But generally speaking, members don't take their criticisms of the leadership out on the talk circuit. They raise their issues in caucus, but then present a unified front to outsiders."[24] Asked how Minority Leader Nancy Pelosi (D-CA) was able to build agreement around a party message for the lead-up to the 2006 elections, another staffer echoed this point: "In the end, no one else, aside from Pelosi, had a road back [to the majority]. So Democrats were able to sublimate their own personal ideological and programmatic goals to the common agenda."[25] A Republican leadership staffer made the same observation: "If [Minority Leader] McConnell says, 'Let's avoid self-inflicted wounds,' [members] get the stakes. They get the importance. This is true for members generally, not just those in line to be chairmen."[26] In short, a competitive context in which the majority is perceived to be in contention strengthens members' incentives to accept some message discipline.

Importantly, the differences between the parties need not be defined along ideological lines. Downs (1957), of course, is famous for the proposition that competition will induce parties to converge to the ideological center rather than stake out divergent positions. However, ideological distinctions are often not the centerpiece of party messaging efforts. Partisans frequently just aim to paint their opponents as incompetent or untrustworthy. One senior Republican Senate aide explained, "If you're messaging, you're trying to create a difference between the parties. It's not just a matter of emphasizing the positives, your own alternative agenda. It's also a matter of focusing on weaknesses and failures of the other side. It can be a way of reducing the president's approval rating. You are trying to create an impression, to affect the sorts of things that you hear in focus groups when you ask, 'Do you think the president is doing a good job?'"[27] Another Senate leadership staffer explained his view of the public's priorities: "Most people are not very ideological. People just want to see some level of competency."[28] Democrats got a lot of "messaging mileage" out of the Farm Bill between 2012 and 2014 observed another, because "it's an issue that gives you a place to be that's not liberal, but that also allows you to hit the Republicans for not being helpful. You can be profarmer and probusiness."[29] In the lead-up to the 2006 elections, Democrats hammered on the theme of a Republican "culture of corruption"—a message all Democrats, whether they were liberal or conservative, could coalesce around.[30]

When messaging on the ideological disputes that separate liberals from conservatives, parties highlight issues on which they believe voters are on their side. Republicans, for example, do not build a messaging campaign around lower taxes for the wealthiest 1 percent of earners, even if they might favor such a policy if it is put to a vote. Democrats do not message on higher taxes for the middle class, even if they might vote for tax increases that would hit middle-class taxpayers. Party messaging is not about objectively and dispassionately cataloguing all the issue positions that differentiate the two parties. Parties message on issues where they believe themselves to be on the right side of public opinion and/or where they perceive the opposing party to be on the wrong side (Egan 2013; Petrocik 1996; Sigelman and Buell 2004). Pollsters are routinely brought into the strategy sessions where party messages are hammered out.[31] The goal of messaging is to foreground and dramatize those differences between the parties that will cast one's own party in a favorable light. "You're seeking to draw a contrast," said one longtime former press secretary. "And of course, it goes without saying, you want to put the other party on the wrong side of that contrast."[32] The differences parties want to highlight are those they believe are electorally useful.

Some messaging campaigns are aimed at swing voters, others at party-base voters. "Messaging involves both tasks: (1) motivating the base and (2) winning over the persuadables," said one veteran Senate staffer. "You make messages for commercials as well as to speak to your base."[33] "You try to have a balance of both" swing voter and base appeals, explained another Senate aide: "We see the polling about people's economic worries—anxiety about being able to afford a middle-class life, the future for their children. That agenda includes things like a minimum-wage increase, equal pay for equal work, the child tax credit. So these are not straight base excitement appeals."[34] On the other hand, sometimes the goal simply is just to "get the base fired up, really capture them and get them talking."[35] "Drawing clear lines definitely helps" with fundraising, remarked a senior Senate aide. "People who give money are more fringy—those giving low dollar amounts, those responsive to e-mail solicitations. The votes held to repeal Obamacare—they unquestionably help with fundraising."[36] But messaging aimed only at party-base groups can be a risky proposition: "Miscalculation seems to happen when a party forgets to focus on the broad set of issues that work for the party as a whole and starts narrow-casting to particular groups. . . . Other voters in the party may react by saying, 'What is going on here? That doesn't speak for me.'"[37]

Across the board, party messaging aims to magnify party differences for voters. Sometimes the message is directed toward stimulating and mobilizing base constituencies. At other times, the aim is to appeal to uncommitted voters and groups. Regardless, messaging "requires drawing clear lines between the parties."[38] Party messaging always says, as Rep. Bill Archer (R-TX) put it, that "there is a dramatic difference between Republicans and Democrats in this capital city, and this is the dividing line" (Mitchell 1999, E1).

Trade-Offs between Legislating and Messaging

Drawing clear lines between the parties stands at odds with the conciliatory efforts that are typically necessary to legislate, especially in a political system with so many veto points. Bicameralism, separation of powers, and other aspects of American national institutions almost always force congressional leaders to legislate by assembling large, bipartisan coalitions. Important legislation rarely passes on the strength of one party alone (Krehbiel 1998; Mayhew 2005).

Bipartisan participation in legislating, however, undercuts party messaging efforts. This is a theme that emerged repeatedly in interviews, and it often crops up in members' quoted comments in published media as well. How can members legislate across party lines on important issues and then proclaim to voters that it makes a big difference which party controls Congress? How will a party draw clear contrasts with the opposition while voting to pass major legislation on a bipartisan basis? How does a minority party vote in support of the bills the majority party leadership brings to the floor and then convincingly denounce the majority's performance in a campaign for change in party control? "You just apparently don't want to be caught being bipartisan," said Rep. Sander Levin (D-MI). "It's going to blur the political message" (Hulse 2010, A18).

There is no doubt that congressional action is multidimensional, such that messaging and legislating are often occurring simultaneously. Nevertheless, members engaged in a battle for majority control of Congress are likely to weigh the political costs of blurring party lines on any issue where they discern possible advantage from staking out partisan differences. There are, of course, circumstances when it is politically advantageous for a party to dodge a partisan fight. On issues where a party is perceived as being on the wrong side of public opinion, party leaders may want to arrive at a bipartisan deal or otherwise avoid party-line votes. (The other party, perceiving an advantage on the issue, may not be willing to cooperate.) Minimizing party conflict, however, is never a good way to increase the expected party differential. Members and leaders who want to amplify the differences that voters perceive between the parties need to provoke partisan fights, not tamp them down.

The tension between legislating and messaging is a key reason so many present and former members of Congress express anxiety about the trade-offs between governing and messaging. "We're all frustrated. We all wish there was more legislating and less messaging," said Sen. Max Baucus (D-MT; Kane 2013). "Today, Congress is constantly campaigning. Governing has fallen by the wayside," wrote retiring Rep. Elton Gallegly (R-CA) in a 2013 op-ed. "They keep saying, 'the election,'" said Sen. Olympia Snowe (R-ME). "And I say that's a year and a half from now. In the meantime, could we just sort of legislate?" (Mitchell 1999, E1). "What is disturbing about our current situation is that we seem to have forgotten the concept of legislative compromise," said Sen. Robert C. Byrd (D-WV). "There is no give and take. Instead, members seem more concerned with sowing the landscape with political seeds that can be cultivated and harvested during next year's election campaigns."[39] Each of these statements explicitly acknowledges perceived conflicts between the requirements of message politics and legislative deal making.

Legislation that draws support from both sides of the aisle does not simply blur the lines between the parties. It also constitutes an implicit "stamp of approval" for the status-quo allocation of party power. Passing bills with bipartisan assent communicates to external audiences that the minority party is still able to achieve legislative results it supports, even though it is in the minority. The minority's acquiescence thus constitutes a grant of legitimacy from the minority to the majority. Such an act is not generally helpful to the minority's argument for retaking control of Congress. It is tantamount to saying, "We agree with what the majority party is doing in these areas, but we are asking you to throw them out of power anyway."

Insiders perceive that bipartisanship redounds to the credit of the party in power and hinders the minority's argument for retaking control. "In the minority, you don't want to fuel the success of the majority," explained one veteran Senate leadership staffer. "Too much deal making can perpetuate them in the majority."[40] When waging the fight for party control of Congress, "it's self-defeating to work in a collaborative way," stated a longtime House leadership aide. "It's a constant fight. This is true on the floor, but it's also true in committees, as well. You look for opportunities to differ with the other party. You want to stigmatize the opposition. . . . The stakes are huge, so you do this all the time."[41]

Legislative compromise is also detrimental to party messaging because it often disappoints and demoralizes fellow partisans. If a bipartisan deal is to be struck, concessions usually have to be made, or at least maximalist ambitions curbed. This is not generally a good strategy for firing up one's supporters. "Bipartisan deals are dangerous, more often than not," reflected one veteran Senate leadership aide. "The pressures from the [party] bases get in the way."[42] After hard negotiations on a budget during conditions of divided government in 1987, conservative Democrat Rep. Marvin Leath (D-TX) lamented the tensions between governing and campaigning:

> Is this budget something that I like? No, it is not something I like. Is this budget we are talking about and debating what is best for the country? No, it is not what is best for the country.

> I do not like this budget . . . but I was sent here to make the hard decisions and ultimately to govern. My daddy told me a long time ago that 20 percent of something is better than 100 percent of nothing. So if that is all I can get in the legislative process, I am going to take it and accept the responsibility.
>
> Someday I hope I can live long enough that we can get together in this town and figure out that we ought to run for reelection three months out of every two years, and during the other 18 or 20 months we ought to govern.[43]

Leath perceived a conflict between members' electoral interests and supporting a policy that achieves "20 percent of something" desirable as opposed to nothing at all. The clear implication is that it would have been politically easier for him to simply vote no rather than bear responsibility for supporting the imperfect outcome of a negotiated agreement.

Reflecting on the problem of campaigning on the difficult deals one strikes during the course of the legislative process, former Rep. Barney Frank (D-MA) said he joked with his staff about a bumper sticker he wanted to use for his reelection campaign: "Barney Frank: 'Things would have sucked worse without me!'"[44] It hardly needs to be noted that no self-respecting political consultant would endorse such a campaign slogan. What is true for individual members' campaigns is true for party messages as well. It is not easy for a party to win praise by cutting disappointing deals and then telling its supporters, "Sorry, this is the best we could do under the circumstances, but it's better than nothing. And by the way, please give us more money and turn out to vote for us." Legislative compromises will often dishearten constituencies whose enthusiastic support a member or party needs. A glorious defeat is believed to work better for base mobilization than a successful deal where both parties get some share of the loaf.

Finally, party messaging undercuts the prospects for legislative success because it is aimed at defining "us versus them" rather than finding common ground. "Messaging escalates the conflict. It makes it harder to legislate," stated a longtime Senate leadership aide. "If we are trying to set up a message vote, we are not trying to find the common ground. Instead we often find something that's easy for the Republicans to vote against. . . . If you are trying to legislate, you wouldn't take such a hard line."[45]

The rhetoric deployed in party messaging is also characteristically blunt and harsh. It is not conciliatory, respectful of differences, or conducive to collaboration. Explaining why he was not "more confrontational" in his approach, Minority Leader Bob Michel (R-IL) once said,

"It's difficult at times to go out on the floor and just beat the hell out of your opposition and then expect them within a half hour to sit down and have a rational discussion" (Pianin 1991). Relatedly, one senior House aide observed,

> I look at the minority website for the Energy and Commerce Committee. They say this is the most antienvironmental Congress ever. They demonize Republicans. They say we are evil for even thinking the things we do. I think to myself that these are not the kind of things you say if you want to work with the majority on legislation. These are the kinds of things you say if you want to win back the majority. Statements like these do not facilitate negotiation or any effort to find common ground.[46]

In order to clearly define "us versus them," roll-call votes designed for messaging purposes will force members to select between simplistic "either/or" alternatives. As such, messaging does not entail an effort to wrestle with policy complexity or to identify inclusive "both/and" solutions. As a Senate leadership staffer put it, "With messaging, you're setting up simple choices: pay equity, motherhood, and apple pie. Are you for it, or are you against it? Of course, you and I know that these issues are not so simple. But they're designed for use in the thirty second ad."[47]

Even though messaging may undermine the prospects for successful lawmaking, legislative achievements are not necessary for parties to advance their political goals of creating favorable contrasts with the opposition. "In some ways, the failure to get things done makes these issues as clear and sharp a distinction between the two parties as if they get through," said Democratic pollster Guy Molyneux (Hollander 2014). In fact, for messaging purposes, failure often works better than success. A bill or amendment offered for message purposes makes the following implicit argument: "Here is a good idea we have. I'll bet you agree with us. But we cannot pass it, because we don't yet have enough power to do so." Failing to move the attractive bill thus becomes a way for a party to say to an outside audience, "If you like our ideas, we need your help to win more seats in Congress and/or take control of the presidency."

As such, legislative proposals put on the floor for the purpose of highlighting differences between the parties are generally not serious attempts to pass laws. Insiders can be quite frank about this fact. "Messaging bills aren't crafted in a way that they're intended to become law.

The level of detail is just not here," stated one veteran Senate leadership staffer.[48] Along the same lines, a former House Republican aide explained, "When you're serious about a bill and you intend to legislate, when you're preparing a bill to be marked up in committee, you do more legal research. You go through it with a fine-toothed comb. With a campaign bill, all you need is to make it look good."[49] Reacting to the Senate Democrats' "Fair Shot" agenda on the floor in the lead-up to the 2014 elections, Senate Minority Leader Mitch McConnell (R-KY) remarked, "These are bills designed intentionally to fail so that Democrats can make campaign ads about them failing" (Cox and Bolton 2014). This losing-to-win strategy becomes even more attractive as elections approach and the need to set up campaign issues takes precedence. "We used to basically shut down legislating after Labor Day in election years. But now it's earlier and earlier," observed one veteran staffer.[50]

Taken together, legislating and messaging frequently stand at cross-purposes, in terms of both outcomes and processes. Bipartisan legislative outcomes will obscure differences between the parties, thus directly contradicting the central purpose of partisan messaging, which is to draw partisan contrasts in hopes of winning greater or more enthusiastic support for one's side. Furthermore, the barbed rhetoric and polarizing choices entailed in party messaging contrast sharply with the skills of conciliation and accommodation usually necessary for successful legislating. A preoccupation with honing partisan messages in Congress undercuts the prospects for legislative deal making.

Power, Responsibility, and Weighing the Trade-Offs between Messaging and Legislating

Ain't opposition fun? We don't have to be responsible. All we have to do is watch them self-destruct. — Anonymous Democratic Congressman, 1995[51]

When faced with trade-offs between legislating and messaging, members have to make strategic choices about their priorities. They have to decide whether to make legislative deals or to withdraw from negotiations and instead focus on setting up issues for electoral purposes. "The classic legislative dilemma is how far you go in participating in a compromise," observed Rep. Henry Waxman (D-CA) during a 1985 Democratic intraparty debate over how to respond to President Reagan's budget (Cohen 1985, 2588). As Rep. Vic Fazio (D-CA) explained, "We were divided on the question of whether we wanted to win [a partial victory] or go down in glorious defeat" (ibid.).

To prioritize messaging over legislating means abjuring opportunities to influence policy in the present moment while looking with hope toward a future electoral victory. Rep. Barney Frank (D-MA) explained the dilemma: "Am I better off making a deal and making the policy better? Or am I better off just opposing?"[52] After Republicans won control of the House in the 2010 elections, they debated among themselves whether to try to strike an agreement with President Obama to reduce the budget deficit. Even though it might have been possible for Republicans in 2011 to advance some of their fiscal goals in exchange for concessions, a contingent of House Republicans pressed Speaker John A. Boehner (R-OH) to cease negotiations with the president altogether. "It's no longer policy season," said one Republican member in January 2011, nearly two years before the 2012 elections. "It's message season" (Stanton 2011).

Where parties stand in the constitutional division of power affects how they weigh the priority they give to legislating versus messaging. In democratic politics, power and responsibility go together. "If you have the majority and you have the ability to get something done, you have to realize that you have to come to the table to make it happen," said former House Speaker Dennis Hastert (R-IL). "If we're not doing anything, we're going to lose our majority" (Lawrence 2013). One Senate aide put it simply: "The priority you place on cutting deals depends on your responsibility for governing."[53]

By the same token, a lack of power is a freedom from this sense of governing responsibility. As the anonymous Democrat quoted above joked in 1995, "Ain't opposition fun?" Parties that have more power to govern are better able to enact policies they prefer, and they also expect to be held more accountable for governing failures. As a consequence, they are generally more eager to obtain the bipartisan cooperation necessary to successfully legislate, even if it comes at some cost to the clarity of their party's message. Parties less satisfied with their institutional power likely will be more focused on messaging, even if it entails some loss of influence over policy outcomes.

Insiders can be quite candid about how much easier it is to focus on messaging instead of legislating when one's party is not accountable for making the government function. "The minority is much more fun," recollected a former veteran Senate leadership staffer. "It's more fun because you don't necessarily need to achieve a result. It's much easier to throw a grenade than to catch it."[54] "In the minority it's easy, because you don't have to pass anything," said a current Senate leadership staffer. "It's easy to be a bomb thrower. . . . You just come up with ideas that will rile up somebody."[55] "You don't have the same demands on your time in the minority as you do in the majority," observed a former House leadership aide with experience in both the majority and the minority. "In the majority, you're trying to get things done. There's an awful lot of work involved in trying to pass things."[56] Being in the minority is also politically easier, said a longtime former House staffer, because "when the party all holds together in opposition to something, nobody has to compromise. You could all feel good about what you were doing."[57] "It's a lot easier to get people to vote no than to vote yes," said one former White House legislative affairs director. "But voting no is not governing."[58]

Freedom from having to produce results offers much wider scope for party messaging. A party unburdened by policy responsibility can simply oppose without specifying what, if any, policy alternative it might support. It can champion appealing but unrealistic initiatives that are "all gain and no pain," such as tax cuts or new program expenditures without regard for fiscal balance. It can outbid the party in power by promising more benefits with none (or fewer) of the pay-fors. An out party's economic stimulus package, for example, can purport to guarantee twice as many jobs created at half the cost.[59] An out party's prescription-drug plan can stipulate both more generous benefits and lower deductibles and premiums.[60] Championing attractive but impracticable policies has much upside and little downside for a party that does not expect to pass legislation.

By the same token, a party relieved of governing responsibility has much less cause to ask its base constituencies to either accept painful compromises or even understand the policy trade-offs involved. "You have more freedom when you don't have to be responsible," observed a longtime Republican Senate aide. "Just look at the Democrats after the next elections [when they go into the minority after 2014]. They'll be thinking: 'We don't have to be the party of domestic surveillance and the NSA. We don't have to raise the debt limit. We don't have to vote for free trade. We don't have to worry about the highway trust fund. We're the party of the $15 minimum wage. We're for equal pay for equal work.' Once they're in the minority, they can liberate themselves."[61] Regardless of his prescience on any specific prediction, this insider highlights policy areas where being in power and taking the lead on actual policy making forces members of Congress—in the case of these issues, especially Democrats—to contend with tough policy trade-offs: How high can the minimum wage reasonably go without harming job growth? How much can one spend on infrastructure without raising taxes or fees? How much regulation of private employers' personnel practices in the pursuit of equal opportunity is feasible and desirable? How much should civil liberties be protected at the expense of the president's powers to fight terrorism?

Leaders and members of a party that intends to pass legislation must figure out how to balance competing goods such as these. A party that does not expect to actually make policy does not need to identify workable solutions to such difficult questions. It can take politically easy, often simplistic positions that will go over well with external constituencies. It can promise to balance budgets by eliminating "waste, fraud, and abuse" and without specifying what taxes will be increased or what programs will be cut. On this theme, a former House leadership aide remarked, "There's a big difference between governing and campaigning. Governing is a hell of a lot harder."[62]

Being responsible for outcomes pressures a party to confront the choices among competing goods and the hard bargaining involved with actual policy making. Former Rep. Bob Walker (R-PA) acknowledged the challenges, reflecting on his experience transitioning from the House minority to the House majority after the 1994 elections:

> The main lesson that we learned very quickly was that governing is hard. When we had been in the minority, we never had any responsibility to do any governing. We had fought the good fights, we had charged up the hill every day, we had gotten bloody fighting with our flags flying, and so on. We would come down off the hill if we lost, but we felt really good about it because we had fought glorious battles. All of a sudden, we found ourselves in a position where we actually had to govern, where it did require compromise, where it did require a lot of work with individual members. And at the end of the day, you got part way to where you wanted to go. You won, but you didn't feel really good about it.[63]

When trade-offs have to be balanced against one another in policy making, some people or political interests will be unhappy with the outcome. Those in positions of political responsibility will become a lightning rod for disappointment. Meanwhile, in a two-party system, those not responsible for policy making can reap political dividends from discontent with those in power.

Operating within the constraints of the doable—especially in a political system of divided powers that puts a premium on compromise—actual policy making is much more politically dangerous than mere position taking. Former House Speaker Tom Foley (D-WA) recounts how, as a new member of Congress, he was advised by a senior Democrat on the House Agriculture Committee to dodge personal responsibility for policy outcomes (Biggs and Foley 1999, 215). "When it comes to the big agriculture bills," he told Foley, "always vote for the ones that fail and against the ones that pass." The then-freshman Foley asked, "Why should I do that, sir?"

> "Oh," he said, "it's so obvious. . . . Sooner or later the secretary of agriculture will do some damn fool thing, and his excuse will be that the law required him to do it. . . . But you can say, when the farmers complain to you about it, 'Well, you know, I voted against the bill because of that. I knew it was going to be trouble.' On the other hand, if the bill goes down and fails, run right down to the well and change your vote if you voted against it, and get a positive vote up there."

The Foley example focuses on how individual members might realize political benefits from shunning the burdens of policy responsibility. Members of parties that do not expect to be held accountable for making the government function can similarly benefit from a refusal to bear the burdens of policy choice. It is often more politically advantageous for an out party to sit on the sidelines and criticize rather than seek to play a junior role in the exercise of authority.

Even though it will bear the brunt of any dissatisfaction with its decisions, a party in power both stands to win more credit from any legislative achievements and feels a greater sense of responsibility to its constituents and stakeholders for delivering on policy promises. This sense of responsibility gives members of parties in power a stronger incentive to compromise as needed to win legislative enactments.

One former House Republican leadership staffer explained the transition from campaigning to governing after 1994 as one of moderating items in the Republicans' Contract with America as needed in order to garner House majorities. "I was part of the group that put the Contract together," he said. "One of the planks of the Contract was the Balanced Budget Amendment (BBA). . . . We had a question about which version of the BBA we'd include. . . . We decided to put the purest version in there, the one that would require a three-fifths majority to raise taxes. That's what you do when you're putting together campaign documents— you look for the clearest contrast ideologically and you put that version in."[64] After House Republicans took power, however, the ideologically pure version of the Contract was recognized to be politically unrealistic and impossible to move in the House. So, he continued,

> Once we won the majority, I had to go tell the members the bad news: you know that version we put in the Contract, that everyone signed, that everyone campaigned on? That's not going to pass! So we had to drop the three-fifths majority, had to go to a simple majority. This was actually Charlie Stenholm's (D-TX) Balanced Budget Amendment, which was somewhat embarrassing. But the Democrats' version is the one that could pass the House. All the items in the Contract needed to go through a similar process. But what choice did we have? We could remain pure, or we could do what would pass. We can't look incompetent in front of the American people, so we had to make the compromises necessary to show that we could govern.[65]

In short, the campaign imperative in the lead-up to the 1994 elections was to present partisan contrasts with maximum clarity. But to succeed legislatively after 1995 required more flexibility.

As a party struggles to get legislative results, partisan distinctions are likely to blur. Under such circumstances, obtaining legislative success in a decentralized political system trades off against constructing clear campaign contrasts. Members of a party in power are more willing to tolerate such trade-offs, because they want to produce results. Former Speaker Gingrich recalled a speech he gave to fellow Republicans trying to induce some realism about what was legislatively achievable in divided government. Gingrich said that he told his colleagues that President Clinton was "a liberal Democrat who legitimately represents the views of his party" and unless the budget was acceptable to both chambers of Congress as well as the president, "we do not have a bill worthy of being passed" (Lawrence 2013). Gingrich's stance on the need for compromise at that point was quite different from his view on the same strategic question during his long years in the minority, but from the vantage point of the speakership, he realized that flexibility was required to legislate. "The need to make compromises was already getting Gingrich a reputation for going soft," noted the former House staffer who had worked on the Contract with America. "It happens to all the leaders. You stand on principles, or you show you can govern."[66]

Along similar lines, one regularly encounters stories in the Beltway press about other former bomb throwers "maturing" after they assume positions of policy responsibility. For example, a news story (Cohodas 1987) shortly after Democrats had retaken control of the Senate began, "[Sen. Howard] Metzenbaum (D-OH) has a new look these days. He's become more of a pragmatist, less of an obstructionist. . . . But he's in the majority now, and as chairman of two key subcommittees, he wants to move his own agenda. And that nearly always means compromise." Of the transformation, Sen. Orrin G. Hatch (R-UT) remarked, "When you are in the majority, you cannot hold absolutely extreme positions. I think Howard has come to that conclusion faster than most" (ibid., 1582).

The political incentives are quite different for parties not in power. Members of parties not in power have greater incentive to stand on principle and refuse to support painful compromises that will disappoint party constituencies and stakeholders. Out parties do not expect to be held accountable for governance and thus do not feel the same pressure to achieve results. "Whoever is in the majority wants bipartisanship . . . because they get credit [for policy achievements]," said one Senate aide. "[But] it's in the minority party's interest to stop their members from peeling off" (Newmyer and Pierce 2010).

An out party's members may even conclude that any significant policy successes whatsoever could help perpetuate the in party's power. This logic can potentially devolve into a calculation of "the worse, the better." A minority party may reckon that the more unhappy voters are, the more likely it is that they will opt for a change. For example, Rep. Gingrich advised his minority Republican colleagues in 1987 to refuse to participate in budget negotiations and to just let the majority Democrats proceed without House Republican input. "Our No. 1 drive is to make sure the country understands who is running the House and Senate," Gingrich said, so he advocated that Republicans give voters a "taste of just how bad a Democratic presidency could be" (Hook 1987). Similarly, journalist Paul Kane (2014) observed how legislative successes could undercut the Senate minority's case for change in power in the upcoming elections: "If [Minority Leader] McConnell (R-KY) were to work with [Majority Leader] Reid (D-NV) to allow the Senate to function more

smoothly and effectively, he would undermine a key component of the
Republican campaign argument this fall: that the Democrats have mis-
managed the Senate and the GOP must take over." In a 2014b editorial, the *National Review* offered a frank explanation of how a party can
capitalize on governing failures for electoral benefit. The editors recommended that Republicans, newly in full control of Congress in 2015,
refuse to take up the challenge of "proving they can govern" by striking bipartisan agreements with President Obama: "Even if Republicans
passed this foolish test, it would do little for them. If voters come to believe that a Republican Congress and a Democratic president are doing
a fine job of governing together, why wouldn't they vote to continue the
arrangement?" The obvious implication is that the *National Review* editors judged that a continuation of difficulties in working across party
lines would help make a stronger case for a Republican as president in
the 2016 elections.

A party's political incentive to thwart its opposition's legislative success can even extend to minor, uncontentious policy proposals. "When
the parties are fighting for control, [the opposition] will withhold legislative success even on very small, uncontroversial matters," reflected a veteran Senate staffer. "Let's not let [Sen. Jon] Tester (D-MT) get his bill;
don't let [Sen. Jeanne] Shaheen (D-NH) do her energy efficiency bill.
Don't let [Sen. Mary] Landrieu (D-LA) have her win on a minor energy issue."⁶ Political incentives to reflexively oppose are perhaps especially strong on proposals championed by the marginal members whom
a party most hopes to defeat—the members with the strongest political
incentive to build a reputation for bipartisanship.

Through calculations such as these, the zero-sum logic of electoral
competition encroaches into the legislative process. To the extent that a
party in power benefits from legislative successes, in a two-party system
the party with less power and responsibility for outcomes will perceive
political gains from legislative failures.

The Constitutional System and Message Politics

Up to this point, I have explored only in broad-brush terms how the allocation of institutional power and political responsibility affects calculations about the relative priority to place on messaging and legislat-

TABLE 3.1. **Priority of legislating versus messaging under different configurations of power**

Condition	Majority party	Minority party
Unified government	Strongest incentive to produce legislative results. Messaging takes lower priority.	Weakest incentive to produce legislative results. Messaging takes higher priority.
Divided government	Fragmentation of power diminishes incentives to produce legislative results relative to unified government. Both legislating and messaging will be important. Messaging efforts likely to be directed at creating contrasts with the president.	Fragmentation of power increases incentives to produce legislative results relative to unified government. Both legislating and messaging will be important. Legislative efforts likely to be directed at supporting the president's initiatives.
Divided government with a divided Congress	The most fragmented of the configurations, diminishing both parties' accountability for governance. The president's party (as majority in one chamber and minority in the other) has stronger incentive to prioritize legislating so as to give the president a reputation for competence and policies for which to claim credit. The party not controlling the presidency has stronger incentive to focus on messaging; the party controlling the presidency has stronger incentive to focus on legislating.	

ing. But it is important to recognize that the US system divides power in ways that are far more complex than "party in power" versus "party out of power."

Table 3.1 lists the different configurations by which party power can be distributed across US national institutions. Obviously, power is rarely concentrated in the hands of one party in the US system. In fact, no US political party commands the kind of power that theories of responsible party government call for. Given the Senate minority's ability to deploy the filibuster, a party cannot aspire to govern without some constructive participation from the opposition party unless it simultaneously controls the presidency, a majority in the House of Representatives, and at least sixty seats in the Senate.

Still, it is possible to rank US parties along a continuum of being "in power." If we assume as a rule of thumb that, all else being equal, a lack of institutional power increases the incentives for messaging over legislating, table 3.1 offers a few remarks about the likely relative importance of messaging and legislating to each party under different configurations of party power.

Minority Parties

A minority party under conditions of unified government (top-right cell) has the strongest incentives of any party to prioritize messaging over legislating. A minority party in unified government is least able to achieve its party's policy objectives relative to any other position a party can hold in the US system. A party in the "deep minority" (Green 2015, 83, 115) does not even stand in good position to win policy victories by sustaining a presidential veto. Because its actions have the least consequences for policy outcomes, such a party is also the most free to focus on messaging. "As I told my colleagues, we don't have enough votes to legislate," said House Minority Leader John A. Boehner (R-OH) during unified Democratic control in 2009. "They ought to get the idea out of their heads that they are legislators. But what they can be is communicators" (Hulse 2009b, A9). Of course, a minority party's actions are never entirely devoid of policy consequence in the United States, given the number of veto points in the system. Nevertheless, a lack of power liberates a party to denounce and oppose with relative abandon, without offering much, if any, constructive participation.

Assessing the relative importance of legislating and messaging is more complex for minority parties under conditions of divided government (middle-right cell). A minority party under these circumstances lacks the power to set the congressional agenda and thus has less responsibility for congressional performance than does a majority party. It will want to define contrasts and set up issues to aid its case for retaking a congressional majority. Nevertheless, its messaging is constrained by its party's control of the presidency. "The congressional party cannot have a unique message from the president," said one former longtime Senate staffer. "The Congress is diffuse. No matter how hard they try, they're still diffuse."[68]

Unlike in unified government, the congressional minority party under divided government is inhibited by the need to offer legislative assistance to a president of its own party. Public perceptions of a president affect his copartisans' electoral fortunes in Congress (Abramowitz and Segal 1992; Campbell 1993; Kernell 1977). "Life is different when you have a president of your own party in the White House," said another former Senate aide. "It's better in some ways, more constrained in others. You can't just throw roundhouse punches."[69]

Rather than merely "throwing roundhouse punches," divided government incentivizes the minority to engage constructively with the majority, at least at times, in order to yield the president some desirable results. These incentives to cooperate are strongest on "must pass" legislation necessary for the government to operate or to avoid crisis. Minority Leader Robert H. Michel (R-IL), for example, explained how he painstakingly courted both parties for votes in support of the debt-ceiling increase requested by the Reagan administration: "I told the Republican conference, 'We don't want to politicize the issue'" (Arieff 1981). The same incentives are present on many presidential agenda items. For example, Minority Leader Nancy Pelosi (D-CA) did not want to see President Obama denied the trade promotion authority that other presidents have enjoyed, but she also did not want to force Democrats to take a tough vote on a difficult issue for the party. Trying to induce Republicans to pony up the needed votes to carry the bill without Democratic help, she told a journalist, "It's [Boehner's] responsibility. Every time we had a bill under my speakership, you said it was a test of my leadership. It's a test of his leadership" (Dumain 2015). At the same time, however, Pelosi was engaging behind the scenes to find a deal on trade adjustment assistance that a sufficient number of Democrats could support to ensure passage. "She is caught between a caucus that naturally gravitates toward no . . . and loyalty to a White House that is expecting her to get to yes," said a senior House Democrat (Dovere and French 2015).

As one last example, then-Minority Leader Boehner recalled the intense cross-pressure he endured under divided government while managing the George W. Bush administration's highly unpopular Wall Street bailout in 2008. Boehner had to negotiate with the leaders of the House Democratic majority while simultaneously trying to coax votes in support of a Republican administration from within his own conference. "It was the Texas two-step every day!" he said (Cottle 2009, 23). With constituent calls to congressional offices running as much as 30 to 1 against the bailout (Herszenhorn 2008), a member's most politically advantageous position was to vote against the proposal but to have it pass anyway. As long as the legislation passed, members who voted no could denounce the bailout while avoiding blame for any negative policy consequences. One Boehner aide reportedly sent an e-mail to colleagues suggesting that Republicans should just decline to cooperate and blame the whole thing on the White House and the Democrats. "We're going to let them have this turd," he wrote (Kaiser 2013, 136). On the initial House vote, only 34 percent of House Republicans voted in favor of the bailout. But after the bill went down to defeat and the Dow lost more than seven hundred points in one day, an additional twenty-six Republican members voted in favor on the second House vote. In the end, Boehner brought along the votes of just under half of the Republican Party's rank and file to support the Bush administration's request. By contrast, 73 percent of the majority-party Democrats voted in favor. Had a single party held unified control at the time, it seems likely that the out party would have washed its hands of the whole enterprise and thereby better exploited the bailout's stark unpopularity for its messaging purposes.

In weighing trade-offs between legislating and messaging, minority parties generally have less reason to prioritize legislating over messaging than majority parties. However, control of the presidency (and a desire not to embarrass one's own administration) gives a minority party under divided government more political incentive to offer constructive participation than a minority party under unified government.

Majority Parties

Given that majority parties bear a greater burden of expectations to deliver on legislation, they are likely to give greater priority to legislative success over messaging. This is especially true under conditions of unified party control, where party responsibility is most undiluted.

Unified party control (top-left cell) puts significant pressure on a congressional majority party to work productively with the executive branch to produce results—at least if members care about their own party's reputation for effective government. "When a president of your party is in charge, and you have a majority, there is not supposed to be a gulf between the two ends of Pennsylvania Avenue."[70]

The burdens of cooperating with an administration can come at significant cost to a majority party's ability to message effectively. For example, one longtime Senate aide described the difficulties the Republican majority faced when trying to explain the George W. Bush administration's budget to outside constituencies: "We spent months trying to get people to accept what we were able to do on the deficit. Everyone would like to see a zero deficit. But it's hard for members to press for more deficit reduction than where the president was, and cutting the deficit in half (not to zero) was the administration's goal. But this is not good enough for base voters, and it's hard to defend."[71] A deficit merely cut in half is hardly an excellent message to take to voters, much less to a Republican base that had been fed a steady diet of outraged rhetoric about the need for a balanced budget all through the Clinton presidency. But a deficit cut in half is what the administration was able to achieve while balancing its other priorities. In such circumstances, a congressional majority party has no good option: it can neither disavow its president nor easily defend its own performance.

Carrying the administration's water thus complicates a congressional party's messaging. As another example, Democrats discovered that the 2010 Affordable Care Act (ACA), which lacked the "public option" favored by so many liberal groups, presented few credit-claiming opportunities to take to the Democratic base in the 2010 elections. Given how far the legislation fell short of the Democratic Party's ideal, it was not easy for Democratic members of Congress running for reelection to even talk about the ACA. "No matter what we tried around the Affordable Care Act, we never could get traction," recalled one senior Democratic Senate staffer of the legislation's postpassage politics.[72] Actual policy making involving compromise and trade-offs often entails substantial messaging downsides such as these.

A majority party in unified government frequently has to bear the political costs of letting its base voters down at least to some extent if it wants to advance the party's policy goals and gain a reputation for effective governance. By contrast, a party freed from pressure to deliver the doable is in a much better position to message on zero deficits, Medicare for all, and other attractive but difficult-to-achieve policies.

Under conditions of divided government (middle-left cell), a majority party's incentive to engage in messaging increases. In particular, the congressional majority party under divided government needs to build a record of opposition to the president if it intends to make a strong case for retaking the presidency. Presidential popularity will constrain the use of this strategy, of course. But a congressional majority facing an opposition party president should be expected to actively look for the president's political vulnerabilities and exploit any profitable opportunities that arise to resist his leadership. Congressional majorities in divided government will thus be tempted toward "blame game" politics (Groseclose and McCarty 2001) of passing appealing-sounding bills with the intention of provoking presidential vetoes. As one interview subject said, "When your party has a majority in divided government, you often seek to create veto moments. . . . The goal is to draw contrasts, to try to set up what you would do with power if you had the chance."[73]

A majority party under conditions of divided government will not be quite as free to oppose the president across the board as a minority party under unified government, because its actions are far more consequential. Under divided government, the congressional majority must cooperate with the president just for the basic functioning of government—otherwise, it courts some share of blame for itself. But a majority party's cooperation with the president under conditions of divided government is often dangerous for its messaging. "Under conditions of shared power, you always have trouble explaining what you do to your friends," said one longtime Senate staffer.[74] He pointed to the success Republicans had in making nearly all the Bush tax cuts permanent under a fiscal deal with President Obama in 2012, and yet "so many Republican groups saw [the deal] as a defeat, even though in policy terms, it was a victory."

Majority parties in Congress, regardless of whether they control the executive branch, will not neglect party messaging. Even in unified government, a congressional majority party can sometimes derive political value from legislative defeats. A House majority party may occasionally prefer to pass legislation on a party-line vote, even if doing so will harm (or perhaps destroy) the bill's prospects for supermajority support in the Senate, because party votes work better for clarifying its image relative to the opposition. Unsuccessful party-line cloture votes in the Senate can also effectively communicate what a congressional majority party stands for, even when they achieve nothing in policy terms.

In weighing trade-offs between legislating and messaging, a majority party under unified government has the greatest ability to achieve its party goals and the most responsibility for delivering results. As such, a majority party under unified control has the strongest political incentive to focus on legislating rather than messaging. By comparison, a majority party under divided government is less accountable for results and less able to achieve its policy goals. As such, it has more scope for messaging relative to legislating.

Divided Congresses

Power in the US system is most fragmented under the (relatively rare) conditions of divided government where there is also a divided Congress, meaning one chamber controlled by Democrats and the other controlled by Republicans (bottom cell). As under divided government more generally, this fragmentation of power is likely to incentivize messaging activity relative to legislating.

Messaging incentives under these circumstances are probably greater for the minority parties of both chambers than for the majority parties. For example, former Speaker Foley (Biggs and Foley 1999, 142) recalls the budget summit of 1986, when a Republican-controlled Senate, a Democratic-controlled House, and a Republican president needed to strike an agreement to prevent the across-the-board budget sequestration that would otherwise take effect under the Gramm-Rudman-Hollings Deficit Reduction Act: "When I raised the issue whether we shouldn't have some greater participation of the minorities in both chambers, [Sen.] Pete Domenici (R-NM) said to me, 'Don't do it. They have nothing to offer. We are the managing parties of the Congress. Democrats control the House. We control the Senate. We're responsible for outcomes that are productive and effective. The minority doesn't care about that. All they thrive on are failure and defeat, obstruction and objection.'" In Domenici's view, the majority parties of each chamber carried a greater burden to deliver results to keep the government functioning than the minority parties. As such, those in the majority would be more willing to negotiate constructively. Meanwhile, those in the minority could just refuse to grapple with the difficult choices and then criticize whatever the majorities did. Indeed, just as Domenici predicted, the 1987 budget passed the House with only majority party Democratic votes, despite having been negotiated with a Republican Senate. Rep. Trent Lott (R-MS), the minority whip, reportedly said to his colleagues, "You do not ever get into trouble for those budgets which you vote against" (Price 2004, 138).

Comparing the majority parties of the House and Senate under conditions of a divided Congress, it is likely that the chamber majority that also controls the presidency carries the heavier burden of governing, in terms of public expectations. As a consequence, leaders of the president's party should be more likely to want to work constructively across party lines to give the president some credit-claiming opportunities and bolster the public standing of the administration and the party. Members of the president's opposition likely have stronger incentive to engage in messaging, in that the president's perceived failures will redound to their party's benefit in a two-party system.

House versus Senate

Senate rules complexify the US system of government even further. The Senate's supermajority rules have a two-fold effect on party responsibility in that chamber. On the one hand, they dilute a Senate majority party's accountability for governance, at least when it does not hold enough seats to invoke cloture on its own. A Senate majority party can thus point to the rules of the chamber and blame the minority party for obstructing its efforts at governance. In the House, by contrast, "the majority is not helpless and impotent," said former Speaker Foley (Biggs and Foley 1999, 95). Because a Senate majority party can be blocked by a minority party's filibuster, a Senate majority party has less power and thus less responsibility for governance than a House majority party. As one long-time former Senate aide put it, "In the Senate, the majority leader gets to decide what is called up. But the minority controls what can pass."[75] This diluted responsibility gives a Senate majority party more scope for buck-passing and messaging compared to a House majority party.

On the other hand, the Senate minority is never quite as free to oppose across the board as is the ineffectual House minority, because its behavior has more consequences for outcomes. Under its institutional rules, the Senate minority party must participate constructively to some extent for the Senate to function at all. "Governance in the Senate is a partnership between the two parties," said another veteran Senate aide. "A constructive minority is necessary for that partnership to function. In the House, it's the majority party versus the vanquished. In the Senate, it's the majority along with the junior partner."[76]

Clearly, however, a Senate minority party can exploit Senate rules to great effect, to win both messaging and legislative success simultaneously. A Senate minority party has the capacity to engineer the failure of a Senate majority's initiatives and then to denounce the majority party for its lack of leadership. A House minority can and will excoriate the performance of the majority party, but it cannot obstruct it legislatively, assuming the majority is able to hold its ranks together. A Senate minority party, by contrast, can wield a veto over the majority party's agenda. Along these lines, then-Minority Leader McConnell (R-KY) described how Senate Republicans could both thwart the Democrats' agenda and concurrently gain a messaging advantage: "We have a new president with an approval rating in the 70 percent area. We do not take him on frontally. We find issues where we can win, and we begin to take him down, one issue at a time. We create an inventory of losses, so it's Obama lost on this, Obama lost on that. And we wait for the time when the image has been damaged to the point where we can take him on" (MacGillis 2014). In short, Senate supermajoritarianism has complex effects on how parties weigh the strategic choices between messaging and legislating. The lack of party responsibility in the Senate both encourages and discourages messaging in different ways. It reduces the majority's burden of governance, because a Senate majority can blame the opposition for blocking, giving it more freedom to focus on messaging compared to House majorities. At the same time, supermajoritarianism increases a Senate minority's responsibility for outcomes, conscripting it in governance to a greater degree than a House minority party.

When a Senate minority perceives itself as likely to be held responsible for the Senate's failures, it will feel pressure to participate constructively and strike deals to allow the institution to function. Nevertheless, if a Senate minority calculates that a failure of the Senate to act will primarily harm the majority party, it may opt to shun constructive participation and then use the institution's failures as "exhibit A" in its case against the majority's continuation in power.

The Senate majority bears a greater burden than the Senate minority. But compared to the House majority, a Senate majority's policy responsibility is attenuated, and compared to a House minority, a Senate minority party is never completely off the hook. Beyond these observations, it is not possible to offer sweeping generalizations about how either majority or minority party senators will rate the likelihood that their party will be held accountable for policy outcomes in any particular case. The key point is that the Senate's supermajority rules make senators likely to weigh the trade-offs between messaging and legislating somewhat differently than House members.

The Effect of Intensified Party Competition

This chapter draws upon a range of first-person perspectives on party messaging and its relationship to legislating. The clear picture that emerges is that members of Congress generally believe it is necessary to define and dramatize party differences in order to energize their supporters and to persuade undecided voters to prefer their party to the opposition. Drawing partisan differences, however, stands in tension with successful legislating for a variety of reasons. Most importantly, the bi-partisanship typically necessary to legislate in a separated system with many veto points fundamentally undercuts efforts to clarify how and where the parties differ. When faced with such trade-offs, members must make choices about their priorities. Where parties stand in the separation-of-powers system (e.g., as majorities or minorities, in control of the presidency or not) is likely to affect the relative weight they will place on legislating versus messaging. But, as the interviews and per-spectives consulted for this chapter reveal, the quest for partisan major-ities inhibits legislative cooperation across party lines, particularly for parties dissatisfied with their share of institutional power.

Intensified competition for party control of Congress after 1980 and 1994 makes the trade-offs between legislating and messaging more acute. Competition focuses members' attention on the pursuit of par-tisan political advantage. During a period when party control of Con-gress appeared a settled fact of political life, trade-offs between legislat-ing and messaging were less salient. Indeed, members had little reason to consider how they might affect their party's chances of winning or holding control when majority status was seemingly not in doubt. As one staff veteran of the House in the 1960s and 1970s observed, "The era of maximum [bipartisan] cooperation was when Democrats had an over-whelming majority. Under those circumstances, they could afford to give amendments to Republicans, to make concessions. [But] this kind of co-operation only prevails when the minority is resigned to minority sta-tus."[77] On the other hand, as Rep. Vic Fazio (D-CA) observed in 2002, "I'm afraid that when your majority is so small, if you were to overlook the priority of the next election, you would be derelict in your duties" (Nather 2002, 1922).

In the contemporary Congress, neither party is resigned to being a permanent minority. As such, members of both parties are likely to carefully weigh their choices between focusing on politics and focus-ing on policy—between messaging and legislating. In this context, Sen. Joe Manchin (D-WV) has bemoaned what he perceives as an excessive focus on winning partisan advantage. "Politics rules the day," he said. "Don't worry about policy; don't worry about good government, just worry about politics: who has 51 [in the Senate] and who's got 218 [in the House]" (Everett 2014).

CHAPTER FOUR

Emerging Strategies of Confrontation, 1976–94

If you act like you're the minority, you're going to stay in the minority. We've gotta challenge them on every bill. — Rep. Kevin McCarthy (R-CA), House Republican chief deputy whip, 2009[1]

I wouldn't be opposed to confrontation if I thought it would be successful. But you force people in the majority party to stick with their ranks. . . . I can't pass up the opportunity to defeat something or pass something in order to be confrontational. — Rep. Edward Madigan (R-IL), House Republican deputy whip, 1987[2]

Members of Congress ideally seek to enact desirable public policy and enhance their own party's reputation relative to the opposition at the same time. But it is not always possible to do both simultaneously. Bipartisan support is usually necessary to enact public policy, given the many veto points and checks and balances of the US political system (Krehbiel 1998; Mayhew 2005). Bipartisan deals, however, tend to blur differences between the parties, making it harder to communicate why voters should prefer one party to the other.

This politics-versus-policy dilemma is more acute for the party more dissatisfied with its share of institutional power. Bipartisanship is more politically problematic for out parties than for in parties. Indeed, members of parties in power can sometimes benefit from blurring party differences. In particular, majority parties (and presidents) will often want to tout bipartisan support as a testimony to broad acceptance of their legislative enactments. By contrast, unless the majority's initiatives are so unambiguously popular that they are hard to oppose, members of parties seeking to regain power have political incentive to withhold support as a way of criticizing the in party and making the case for their own party's return to power. Rep. Kevin McCarthy (R-CA) articulated this basic logic at an informal Republican strategy session the night of President Barack Obama's inauguration in January 2009 (Draper 2012). To regain the majority, he contended, Republicans should mount unified, across-the-board resistance to "every bill" proposed by the Democrats and then take that message to the voters in the 2010 election campaign. In other words, Republicans should stick together in opposition and resist any temptation to collaborate with the majority Democrats in policy making by exchanging their supportive votes for policy adjustments.

Pursuing a strategy of differentiation, however, comes at a cost of a minority party's policy influence, at least in the present moment. To succeed legislatively, a minority party must have some support from the majority party to either pass its own proposals or defeat the majority's. A minority party's best bet in winning cross-party support is from electorally vulnerable members of the majority party—precisely the incumbents it most needs to defeat in order to retake the majority. Enabling the majority party's marginal incumbents to build a reputation for working across party lines cuts against the minority's campaign to capture their seats. When a minority party pursues a confrontational strategy designed to draw clear partisan lines, it is not seeking to win support from the majority party. Advocating such a strategy, Minority Leader Gerald Ford, for example, tried to persuade his fellow Republicans to stop cooperating with Southern Democrats and thereby force them to take "votes that will hurt them in their home congressional districts." He acknowledged that doing so would come at a policy cost: "We won't win as many legislative fights as we could if we resorted to the old coalition tactics, but it's the Big Prize that counts."[3] More generally, a minority-party strategy of confrontation tends to repel, rather than attract, the support from the majority party necessary for a minority party to prevail on legislative questions. Rep. Edward Madigan, quoted above, was not prepared to accept the loss of policy influence just "to be confrontational."

Minority parties that cooperate with the majority party in policy making are likely to get better policy in the near term, judged by their preferences. But if the minority's contributions are, in effect, just improving the majority party's policy outputs, their very successes cut against their long game of winning institutional control. As Jones (1970, 24) observed, "The minority party may be creative and responsible and not only remain the minority party but even ensure the continued success of the majority party."

In short, minority parties can emphasize the short game of policy making or the long game of winning majorities. The short game is often very attractive, particularly to ranking minority members on committees. Public policy matters, and members have constituents and interests to serve. But when the battle for party control is more competitive, a minority party's time horizon shortens, and its long game and short game collide. Members of such a minority party are more likely to throw bombs, sharpen the differences, and let substantive policy making wait for the day when they're no longer just making contributions at the margins. They look toward the future when their party wins the majority and can drive the legislative agenda instead.

This chapter argues that the trade-offs minority parties face between politics and policy became more acute once competition for majority party control of Congress intensified after 1980. When they no longer felt they had to content themselves with minority status, more minority party members embraced the perceived partisan advantages to be gained from confrontational tactics designed to highlight party differences and make the case for change. This post-1980 calculus contributes to the partisan polarization so familiar today.

As evidence for these claims, this chapter analyzes partisan activity in the Senate and House in the years preceding and following the elections of 1980. The analysis centers on the extent to which members and party leaders pursued strategies of confrontation aimed at highlighting the differences between the parties. To gain insight into such strategic thinking, it is necessary to consult first-person perspectives, because only the actors themselves can offer direct evidence as to their intentions, perceptions, and expectations. To that end, I sought interviews with current and past members and staffers who served in the lead-up to or aftermath of 1980, as well as veterans of the internal battles over Republican Party strategy in the House of Representatives through the 1980s. Beyond these interviews, I draw upon a wide range of additional historical sources and congressional memoirs.

The 1980 elections emerge as a key moment in the development of a more confrontational style of party politics in Congress. In the aftermath of losing their majority, Senate Democrats begin to organize themselves to offer a more forceful contrast to Republicans. In a departure from their behavior while in the majority, Senate Democrats started to meet regularly in caucus after 1980 and to stage and publicize roll-call votes designed to highlight partisan differences. At the same time, the 1980 elections raised Republican expectations on the House side of the Capitol and provided momentum to a small cadre of activist junior members who believed that a Republican House majority was in reach. Over the course of the 1980s, this group increasingly persuaded party colleagues that it was possible for House Republicans to wield committee gavels like their Senate counterparts, if Republicans would just do a more effective job of communicating the alternatives to voters.

In emphasizing the importance of renewed two-party competition as a driver of more confrontational party politics in Congress, my account does not stress either the "Republican Revolution" of 1994 or the influence of Rep. Newt Gingrich (R-GA) as a uniquely transformational leader (Theriault 2013). Although Gingrich and the 1994 elections are undoubtedly very important for understanding future developments, the more confrontational partisan style typical of the contemporary Congress began to take root earlier. Developments in the Senate are especially instructive. Once in the minority after 1980, Senate Democrats adopt distinctly more confrontational strategies in their efforts to retake the majority. Unlike Gingrich, however, congressional observers have never described Sen. Robert C. Byrd (D-WV) as especially visionary or innovative as a party leader. Instead, Byrd was a Senate institutionalist known to say, "The Senate is my life" (Schram 1981). There were unsuccessful challenges to his leadership in both 1984 and 1986, because Senate Democrats were worried about his ability to articulate policy alternatives on behalf of the party (Dewar 1984; Schwerzler 1986). Nevertheless, Byrd led his party toward a tougher, more combative style of partisanship long before Gingrich rose to Republican leadership in the House. The political logic behind a confrontational strategy was sufficiently obvious that even an institutionalist like Byrd apprehended the need for an out party to unify itself in opposition in order to make a case for its return to power. Both parties began to adjust their strategies under pressures of intensified competition for majority control. The story of changing strategic behavior is no less important in the Senate than in the House.

House and Senate Party Strategies before 1980

The 1980 Senate elections shocked almost everyone. As discussed in chapter 2, few journalists or activists speculated about a change of party control in Congress in advance of that election. As Davidson and

Oleszek (1984, 638) observed in a retrospective, "The Republican take-over of the Senate caught almost everyone by surprise—political pundits, scholarly observers, and certainly the vast majority of senators and their aides." With Democrats holding 58 Senate seats and 277 House seats in the 96th Congress (1979–81), the party seemed to have ample cushion to sustain its majorities even through a tough election year.

The Senate Democrats, so long in the majority and feeling invulnerable, did little in preparation for their coming relegation to the minority. There is more to report about partisan efforts among Republicans of this era, though congressional Republicans by no means pursued a strategy of across-the-board confrontation during the administration of President Jimmy Carter. In line with the expectations detailed in chapter 3 (see table 3.1), minority status under Carter's unified Democratic government freed Republicans from the responsibility the party had carried in divided government under Presidents Nixon and Ford when serving as a congressional minority in search of votes in support of a Republican president. As a minority party in unified government, Republicans focused more on messaging and less on legislating. They had their choice of targets and were able to seek politically advantageous battles with a Democratic president who was growing increasingly unpopular over time.

Nevertheless, in an environment when party control of Congress seemed to be in little doubt, minority-party Republicans had not embraced a systematic strategy of partisan differentiation in either the House or the Senate. Instead, playing the short game, Republican ranking members collaborated with Democratic chairmen on legislation, and a Democratic president received critical support on a number of key issues from Republican leaders. Much of the partisan skirmishing that occurred in the Congress of the late 1970s was engineered by a small group of New Right members, especially centered in the recently founded Senate Steering Committee, not under the auspices of the Republican congressional leadership.

Democrats as the Perceived "Permanent Majority"

There is no evidence of congressional Democrats engaging in collective action in advance of 1980 in efforts to avert their losses in that year's elections. The memoirs of Senate Majority Leader Byrd (2005) and House Speaker Tip O'Neill (O'Neill and Novak 1987) fail to mention efforts on the part of Democratic leaders to forestall electoral disaster in 1980. In the election lead-up, there were no Democratic Party retreats or public party-agenda documents and no prominent media events designed to burnish the Democratic brand. There was still some internal organizational ferment among Democrats in the aftermath of the reforms of the mid-1970s, but as in those earlier efforts, Democrats were preoccupied by power struggles between liberals and conservatives within their party, not with guarding against a Republican threat to their majorities (Sinclair 1995). The Democrats' congressional campaign committees spent paltry sums in support of their party's candidates: less than $250,000 in 1978, and around $1 million in 1980—in each case, a mere fraction of the Republican congressional committees' expenditures (Ornstein et al. 1996, 105–6). In retrospect, it is understandable that Democrats failed to countenance the need for collective party enterprises aimed at maintaining Democratic majorities given that the party had held unbroken control of both chambers of Congress for more than twenty-five years and of the Senate for all but four years since 1932. Hindsight is 20/20.

Instead, the Democrats of the 96th Congress leave an overwhelming impression of disunity and constant infighting, both within Congress and between Congress and President Carter. Democrats' party unity scores between 1977 and 1980 plumb some of the lowest depths the party ever recorded (Ornstein et al. 2008, 149). According to the 1978 *CQ Almanac*, "the House continually teetered on the brink of chaos and occasionally fell over . . . la[ying] bare a growing schism among House Democrats and [bringing] out a new unity within the Republican party." The 1979 *CQ Almanac*'s description was similar: Even though Carter "enjoyed a strong Democratic majority in both House and Senate . . . [he] did little to alter the 'disharmony and total separation' [between the branches] during his term." As one example, the Democrats' House leadership was unable to hold the party's ranks together in the early fall of 1979 to carry a series of must-pass bills, including a budget, appropriations, and a debt-limit increase. "This was probably the worst legislative week that any speaker has suffered in the twentieth century," concluded Peters (1990, 229).

Republicans as the Perceived "Permanent Minority"

Partisan collective action among House Republicans in the lead-up to the 1980 elections was not extensive, albeit clearly superior to the Democrats' showing. The Republican leader was John J. Rhodes (R-AZ). Rhodes had been elected leader in 1973, with the support of the conservative wing of the party. Although an inspirational speaker, he would step aside in 1980 due to dissatisfaction with his leadership among Republicans. Rhodes did not embrace a confrontational strategy in dealing with the Democrats (Fenno 1997, 15–16). Describing his resignation from leadership, he said he did not agree with those Republicans who wanted everyone to "rally in Statuary Hall . . . march out on the floor, and do battle with those 'bad Democrats'" (Green 2015, 28).

More generally, Republican Party unity in the late 1970s was only slightly higher than that of Democrats (Ornstein et al. 2008, 149). Nor was there much organizational effort devoted to elevating Republican cohesion. Republican Rep. Mickey Edwards (R-OK) described the House GOP's lack of energy and initiative to a convention of Young Republicans in 1977. He lambasted congressional Republicans for failing to meet to plan strategy or to forcefully confront the opposition, singling out Republican ranking members for working and voting with Democratic committee chairmen. "We are in Congress a party without leadership, with a caucus that never meets, with no official party positions on any major piece of legislation before Congress, with few real alternatives on anything, with no regular spokesman on the House floor, with floor managers who look like, sound like and vote like the floor managers for the Democrats" (Cohen 1977). Edwards was not alone among junior Republicans in the late 1970s demanding more forceful leadership. There was a small group of notable partisan activists. Rep. Bob Walker (R-PA), elected in 1976, stood out as an energetic bomb thrower, as did Rep. Bob Bauman (R-MD), elected in 1972. However, Walker and these other junior members were still very much at the "vanguard of the House, the group of members who were fed up with being in the minority," observed a former House aide of the era.[4]

The Republican leaders on committees during this era were generally even more accommodating and willing to engage in cross-party collaboration than top Republican Party leaders. The so-called "minority party mentality" (Jones 1970, 18) was most evident on committees. "There were a lot of Republicans who were very comfortable being ranking minority members," recalled one staffer with experience working for the House Republican leadership in the late 1970s.[5] If Republicans and Democrats could work out disagreements in committee before bringing bills to the floor, it was more likely that the House would approve the legislation, allowing Republicans to have input and to claim personal credit for the passage of provisions they had gotten into the bill. Rep. Dick Armey (R-TX), who had a PhD in economics, used an academic metaphor to describe the pattern he saw: "I used to call it the dissertation syndrome. You live a crucial, critical part of your life where the most important person in the world for you to please is your dissertation adviser or supervisor. If he's not happy, you're dead. That's what the Democratic chairmen were to a lot of our more senior guys" (Garrett 2005, 53). "The [Republican] ranking members . . . voted for the bills," another Republican aide from the period recalled. "They were getting their goodies, of course. On the occasions when we held the whole Republican Party together on a vote, *any* vote, it felt like a moral victory."[6]

In advance of the 1980 elections, the chair of the National Republican Congressional Committee (NRCC), Rep. Guy Vander Jagt (R-MI), led the most notable House Republican efforts on behalf of the party. He stepped up candidate recruitment, training, and other in-kind campaign assistance to Republican aspirants. He tremendously expanded NRCC fundraising, and the committee went from spending $330 thousand in support of Republican candidates in 1976 to $1.3 million in 1978 to $2.3 million in 1980. More controversially, he recruited and funded challengers to Democratic incumbents who had not previously shown themselves to be vulnerable, including an attempt to target Speaker O'Neill. Rhodes was reportedly shocked by the breaking of the norm against direct challenges to the other party's leader: "It's not with my sanction. There's no way I'd be against Tip O'Neill. I don't agree with him on the time of day, but I love him. He's a great member of the House" (quoted in MacNeil 1981, 73). Despite some agitation among junior Republicans for a more combative stance toward Democrats, the leaders of the House Republican Party had not embraced a strategy of partisan confrontation before 1980.

The same muted partisanship was characteristic of Senate Republicans as well, though Senate Republicans had begun to show some renewed vitality under recently elected Republican Leader Sen. Howard Baker (R-TN). Even though Baker had distinctly emerged from the moderate wing of the party, he pressed his fellow partisans to better define contrasts with Democrats. He assembled a number of party task forces to develop alternatives to Carter's agenda, and these plans provided talking points for Senate Republican candidates in both 1978 and 1980 (Annis 1995, 104). In addition, "Baker began to use [the weekly conference lunches] to rally his caucus around floor strategies designed to create difficult issues for Democrats," remembered a Democratic Senate leadership staffer of the era.[7] "There was the Kemp-Roth tax cut—an across-the-board tax cut of 30 percent. And they began to use the debt limit for this purpose."

Senate Republicans also reorganized their Policy Committee in 1977 to develop policy alternatives to the Democratic administration (Rich 1977). Republican Policy Committee chair Sen. John Tower (R-TX) brought on a new committee staff, headed by Max Friedersdorf, and charged it with the task of developing Republican Party policy. According to a contemporaneous report (Malbin 1977), their goal was "not to produce a package that will be adopted in all its details, but to rally around a common set of principles that will allow them to build a record they can take to the public in the next election."

There are a few other indicators that the Senate Republican Party of the late 1970s was getting better organized to challenge the Democrats. First, during the Carter presidency, congressional Republicans began to hold party retreats. These early party retreats were convened by Sen. Bob Packwood (R-OR), held at the Tidewater Inn in Easton, Maryland, and included House as well as Senate Republicans (Calmes 1986). Second, Republican Senate leadership offices began to bring on board their first professional public-relations staffers in 1977. Third, the National Republican Senatorial Committee (NRSC) began building its fundraising capabilities in the late 1970s (Bailey 1988, 51). For the 1980 election, the NRSC spent $5.4 million, twice as much as it had spent in 1978 and vastly more than the tiny sum ($113,976) it had spent in 1976 (Ornstein et al. 1996, 105).

Despite some efforts to strengthen their party in advance of 1980, however, Senate Republicans did not systematically oppose Democrats on their top agenda items. Rather than harsh denunciation of the president's legislative program, the Republican leader "adopted a relatively detached view toward Carter's domestic centerpiece, his energy bill" (Annis 1995, 108). Along with Carter, Baker also favored the creation of a federal Department of Education (Annis 1995, 129). In addition, Baker worked with the Carter administration on a deal to sell F-15 fighter jets to Saudi Arabia (Annis 1995, 125).

Most importantly, Baker provided President Carter critical and likely decisive support in ratifying the 1977 Panama Canal treaties (Schiller 2012). This was no minor matter in partisan political terms. The Carter administration's transfer of control over the Panama Canal was one of the most galvanizing issues for the Republican base during that period. "If there was one issue more than any other that gave impetus and unity to the conservative movement, it was the Panama Canal," recalled conservative activist Richard Viguerie in 2006 (Clymer 2008, 55–56). Opposition to the Panama Canal treaties had substantial cross-over appeal to moderates and swing voters in a climate of worry about declining US influence abroad. Polls rarely showed even one third of Americans approving of the treaties (Roshco 1978). The issue was "like manna from heaven," said Howard Phillips, another key New Right activist (Clymer 2008, 56).

Despite the partisan advantage the issue offered and strong pressure from the base of his party, Baker determined to support ratification of the Panama Canal treaties after obtaining two amendments clarifying US rights (Annis 1995, 111–21). Support from the Republican leader and a key bloc of Senate Republicans gave Democrats political cover and weakened the potency of the Panama Canal issue for Republicans' partisan purposes.

Congressional Republicans staged a notable media event two months before the 1980 elections. Fully 150 House and Senate Republican candidates gathered on the steps of the US Capitol with presidential nominee Ronald Reagan. In a remarkable foreshadowing of the roll-out of the Contract with America fourteen years later, Republicans in 1980 pledged themselves to a five-point "solemn covenant." They promised to shrink legislative branch expenditures, cut "waste, fraud, and abuse" in government spending, reduce income taxes across the board, encourage more private investment in the central cities, and pursue a more assertive military policy. Although the event attracted little press attention at the time (Garrett 2005, 34) and has been widely forgotten since, it was an innovative effort to present Republicans as a unified national team. "The crowd was mostly congressional aides who did not exactly bubble over with spontaneous enthusiasm," wrote *Washington Post* reporter Helen Dewar (1980, A3). But Dewar took note of "the novelty of such an endeavor between presidential and congressional tickets, a feat that the more divided Democrats are unlikely to attempt to duplicate."

In short, congressional Republicans of the late 1970s had stepped up their messaging, fundraising, and electioneering efforts on behalf of the party. Furthermore, Republican exertions were considerably more substantial than any made by the Democrats, who seemed to have no appreciation whatsoever of the vulnerability of their majority status. Nevertheless, one could not characterize the Republican Party of the late 1970s as having adopted a strategy of partisan confrontation. In an environment when not even Republican Party leaders found much cause for optimism about winning control of Congress, there was less incentive for the party to systematically prioritize messaging over policy negotiation.

Conservative Activists in the Lead-Up to 1980

The most salient efforts to force confrontations with Democrats in the late 1970s were initiated not by Republican Party leaders inside Congress but by leaders of the New Right, both inside and outside the institution. These activists undertook strategies on their own volition and not in coordination with the leadership of the Republican Party in Congress. Sen. Jesse Helms (R-NC) was the most important inside activist. Outside activists included direct-mail pioneer Richard Viguerie, Howard Phillips's Conservative Caucus, Paul Weyrich's Committee for the Survival of a Free Congress, and Terry Dolan's National Conservative Political Action Committee (NCPAC).

The New Right's goal was to advance the cause of conservatism, not the Republican Party per se. Indeed, many of these activists, including Helms himself, had ambivalent attitudes toward the Republican Party. Helms had once even flirted with the idea of founding an independent conservative party (Link 2008, 147). Helms worked with Sen. James McClure (R-ID) to found the Senate Steering Committee in the mid-1970s, an informal organization of Senate conservatives that met weekly to plot legislative strategy. At its inception, the Senate Steering Committee was designed to bring together conservatives regardless of party (see Helms 2005, 66–67). As one longtime Senate Republican staffer explained, "It was not a Republican organization. This was by definition. . . . It's the *Senate* Steering Committee. . . . Its goal was to take conservative issues to the floor, to force votes on them. . . . The Steering Committee was not loved by the Republican leadership."[8] In his memoir, Helms (2005, 97–104, 114–15) never mentions any interest in helping Republicans win control of the Senate, though he does extensively discuss his efforts on behalf of Ronald Reagan, especially in the intraparty nomination battle of 1976. He explicitly distinguishes himself from "people who were more interested in power than principle" (115).

Helms and other New Right senators, such as McClure and Paul Laxalt (R-NV), innovated ways of exploiting the Senate floor to force issues that could then be used to mobilize external constituencies. "I learned that my greatest ally in changing the Senate was the Senate itself," recalled Helms (2005, 65). "The rules of the Senate made it possible to bring to the floor issues that most Senators would just as soon have ignored." "I thought, and I will forever believe," Helms continued, "that people should be 'on record' about things that really matter to most Americans (e.g., for starters, school prayer, spending the people's money on obscenities, killing unborn children, raising taxes)." Helms's amendments rarely prevailed, but in offering them, he did not expect to legislate. Dismissing his "detractors" who saw losing votes as "failures," Helms explained, "I *wanted* senators to take stands and do it publicly. I was willing to leave it up to their constituents what would happen next."

New Right organizations then trumpeted the issues Helms and his allies forced onto the Senate roll-call agenda. These controversies constituted the centerpiece of the direct mail solicitations and broadcast commercials that were so important to conservative fundraising, movement building, and electioneering in the late 1970s and throughout the 1980s. Direct mail, in particular, relies upon the use of emotion-laden issues, clearly defined. Helms was "the generalissimo of our movement," according to one antiabortion activist, who obtained "what we wanted: recorded votes" (Link 2008, 255). The Steering Committee explicitly coordinated with New Right organizations. As a veteran Senate staffer explained, "On Tuesday mornings, the staff of the Steering Committee would meet with advocates, lobbyists, think-tank advocates, outside liaisons. The idea was that if McClure or Helms or someone working with the Steering Committee was going to do a vote on the floor, they'd want to provide a heads-up to the affected groups who can then use the issue." The Steering Committee itself "was never intended to be public. It was never focused on communications. It has no letterhead. Doesn't do press."[9] But the Steering Committee's goal was to highlight issues that would mobilize conservative constituencies outside the institution.

In terms of direct impact on the 1980 elections, NCPAC was the most important of these New Right groups. NCPAC was the first organization dedicated to funding and waging independent third-party campaigns in congressional elections (Bailey 1988, 36). NCPAC was also new because of its national reach, the exclusively negative tone of its ads, and the coordinated effort singling out a specific "hit list" of Democratic senators.

Senate Democrats targeted by NCPAC in 1978 and 1980 included Dick Clark (D-IA), Floyd K. Haskell (D-CO), Frank Church (D-ID), Alan Cranston (D-CA), John Culver (D-IA), George McGovern (D-SD), and Birch Bayh (D-IN). One Senate Democratic leadership staffer of the era recollected, "In terms of understanding the loss of the Senate [in 1980], NCPAC is a very important part of the story. . . . These were the first independent expenditures. They drew up a hit list and went into states. Completely blindsided many people. They were direct attacks on individuals. . . . What NCPAC did, going into the states, hitting [incumbents] in ways they'd never been hit before—that was new."[10] Of the senators on NCPAC's hit lists, all but Cranston were defeated. NCPAC's approach—of which the most important elements were the use of third-party expenditures and negative messages—became a model for future outside expenditures (Powell 2010, 30). NCPAC's advertisements may seem rather tame by contemporary standards, but they were downright shocking in the much less nationalized congressional campaign context of 1978 and 1980.

In short, it is difficult to make the case that Republican leaders in Congress or their party organizations made much concerted effort to bring about the Republican Senate sweep in 1980. To the contrary, it seems they had simply not conceived of the full possibilities of the 1980 political moment. The outcome of the 1980 elections far exceeded even the hopes and expectations of Republican leaders themselves (see Mac-Neil 1981).

More consequential were the exertions of the New Right activists working together inside and outside the Senate and at more than an arms' length distance from Republican Party leaders and organizations. Their efforts extend beyond the scope of this book in many ways, because the New Right is better understood as an ideological movement seeking to reshape both Congress and the Republican Party than as a set of party organizations. But looking forward from 1980, the New Right's innovations unquestionably constituted an important influence on the strategies and tactics that party organizations would themselves deploy in future years, most notably the self-conscious use of floor votes to develop and drive party messaging, as well as routinized liaison between congressional parties and outside groups. In an ironic twist of history, culture warrior Jesse Helms is, in many ways, the father of contemporary congressional party messaging.

Party Strategies and Institutional Developments after 1980

The watershed elections of 1980 disrupted internal politics in both the Senate and the House minority parties. After 1980, both House and Senate minority parties had more reason to believe that majority status was in reach than had been typical for the minority Republicans in the decades before 1980. Senate Democrats certainly did not see themselves as destined for a lengthy stay in the minority. Seeing their Senate Republican colleagues holding committee gavels and conservative icon Ronald Reagan in the White House, House Republicans also took new heart that a Republican House majority might be attainable.

In the Senate, minority status induced Democrats to begin to meet regularly in caucus to plot party strategy. Senate Democrats began to systematically force roll-call votes designed to highlight the differences between the parties. They staged media events to criticize the opposition and fan the flames of scandal. They dramatically stepped up party fundraising. On the House side, the 1980 elections bolstered Republicans advocating a more confrontational stance toward the Democratic majority. This internal Republican Party battle over strategy would continue throughout the 1980s. The confrontational faction would not gain the upper hand until the late 1980s and the election of Rep. Newt Gingrich (R-GA) as whip. Nevertheless, a more combative style of partisanship was emergent in House politics long before the landmark elections of 1994, when Republicans finally overturned the long-standing Democratic House majority.

Senate Democrats' Response to 1980

What we need is a solid record of opposition to Mr. Reagan, built brick by brick, piece by piece. . . . I told my colleagues . . . that they should go out there and offer their alternatives, even though they knew they would be voted down. . . . What looked like defeat after defeat in 1981 would look differently a year and a half down the road. — Senate Minority Leader Robert C. Byrd, 1982[11]

Rejecting pessimism and complacency, the post-1980 Senate Democrats soon began to look with hope toward upcoming elections. "A year ago it would have been inconceivable to think that the Democrats might become the majority again in 1982," observed Byrd in March 1982. "It is not inconceivable now, although I don't think it's likely" (Gailey 1982).

In their quest to give voters reason to return them to power, Senate Democrats began to reorganize their party to offer clear contrasts to Republicans and the Reagan administration.

The Democrats' shift in strategy did not happen overnight. Senate Democrats of 1981 were confused and demoralized in their minority-party status at first. Only three Senate Democrats at the time had ever served in the Senate minority.[12] "When we lost control in 1980, we didn't initially know what to do," recollected a former Senate leadership staffer. "After we lost control, we met endlessly with Sen. Byrd trying to figure out what we would do. . . . We were in the midst of an identity crisis. *What do we do now?* It took us a year to get our footing. And then we began to focus on how to get the Senate back."[13]

One of the first notable shifts was that the Senate Democratic caucus started to meet regularly. In its long years of post–New Deal majority status, Senate Democrats rarely met in formal caucus. A Senate leadership aide remembered, "Byrd saw no need for caucuses before 1980. Democrats would just meet once a Congress. 'Why bring them together?' he'd ask. 'They might throw me out!'"[14] Another former Senate leadership staffer recalled an encounter on his way to Reagan's inaugural address: "Sen. [Daniel Patrick] Moynihan (D-NY) bangs me on the chest, 'Do you think the Policy Committee will ever meet?' 'No, senator,' I replied."[15] But in 1981, Byrd reversed his long-standing policy, and Democrats instituted weekly caucus lunches under the auspices of the Senate Democratic Policy Committee, modeling them after Senate Republicans who had begun using their weekly lunch meetings to organize around "Republican positions" in the late 1970s (Liberatore 2008).

Senate Democrats met at a West Virginia resort in the summer of 1981 for their first party retreat, a practice that subsequently became routine. At that meeting, pollster Peter Hart counseled the senators: "One, raise some issues that make the Republicans bleed a little. Secondly, realize you can be innovative and different without the constraints of governance" (Hunt 1981). Consistent with expectations laid out in table 3.1, the gavelless Senate Democrats of 1981 were freed to focus on messaging, having moved from a position of greater governing responsibility with unified Democratic control under President Carter to Senate minority status in a Republican administration. Quick to perceive the political opportunities in the shift, Hart advised the assembled Senate Democrats to seize the new freedom they enjoyed being out of power and instructed them to find some issues on which they as a party could

visibly oppose the Republicans. It did not take long for Senate Democrats to begin to deploy oppositional strategies against President Reagan
and the new Republican majority.

"We knew we had to spend more time attacking Republicans," recalled a former Senate leadership aide of the period. Democrats began
to plot strategy to raise issues to put Republicans on the spot. "There
were seventy to eighty roll-call votes per session that we orchestrated,"
he recalled. "We packaged these [votes] together in a publication enti-
tled *Democratic Alternatives: A Look at the Record*. We put it out in
1981, '82, '83, and '84; perhaps it was also done subsequently."[16] This
publication begins by offering a summary overview of the major policy
issues or controversies on which at least two thirds of Senate Democrats
took a position opposite to that of at least two thirds of Senate Republicans. It then provides a detailed record of how every senator voted on
each of these roll-call votes. Each of these volumes, hundreds of pages in
length, was assembled for the explicitly stated purpose of documenting
how "on many occasions, the actions of Senate Democrats on issues of
major importance to the nation and its citizens were at substantial variance with the actions of the Republicans who controlled the Senate as
its majority party."[17] The goal was to "give Democratic challengers some
things to talk about. It was opposition research being done in the Senate."[18] It is worth underscoring that Senate Democrats had not compiled
volumes trumpeting the party-line votes that occurred when they had
been in the majority before 1981. But once in the minority, they found
party-line votes to have increased public-relations value as a means of
making a case for change.[19] Senate Democrats went on to put together
the *Democratic Alternatives* volume every year while they were in the
minority throughout the 1980s, discontinuing the practice after retaking
the majority in 1987.

Many of the roll-call votes assembled in these volumes did not arise
simply in the normal course of Senate business. It was no mere accident
that Republicans and Democrats were winding up on the opposite sides
of so many issues that Democrats wanted to highlight. Many of these
votes were deliberately staged by Democrats for the purpose of communicating partisan differences to external constituencies. "I remember
[Sen.] Don Riegle (D-MI) forced the Republicans to vote on cutting Social Security five or six times via amendments," recalled a former Senate leadership staffer from the period. "It was just like the many Obamacare repeal votes they took in the House over the last [113th] Congress.

It made the Republicans crazy, and it had an impact in 1982."[20] Riegle "was one of our big bomb throwers. He'd stop by the Democratic Policy Committee, stick his head in the door, and ask, 'Got any Social Security Amendments I could offer today?'"[21]

By late 1981, journalists began to take note of Senate Democrats' new level of organization and unity. "Early this month, an unusual sight was seen in the U.S. Senate," wrote journalist Al Hunt (1981): "Democrats, of all philosophical stripes, uniting on a series of important votes." Democrats had devised a series of amendments to a Defense Appropriations bill that would have increased spending for a variety of purposes, including ammunition procurement, army modernization, and additional tankers. From the start, Democrats understood that Senate Republicans would have to vote against these amendments to keep intact the Reagan administration's overall defense plan. But taken together, the failure of these amendments would allow the Democrats to make a case against Republicans for stinting on military preparedness. "They'll have a hard time explaining away their votes against readiness," chuckled one Senate Democrat (Wilson 1981, A4).

This partisan losing-to-message approach was a sufficiently novel floor strategy in 1981 that journalists felt the need to explain it to their readers: "If the Democrats didn't achieve legislative victories, they won important political points. . . . This message is likely to be cited frequently by liberal as well as conservative Democratic candidates in 1982" (Hunt 1981). Even Sen. Majority Whip Ted Stevens (R-AK) expressed his admiration for the maneuver: "One of the most delightful and strategic tactics I have seen on the floor in a long time" (Wilson 1981). It is hard to imagine a senator making such a comment in the contemporary Congress, where partisan messaging strategies have become pervasive and routine, but the Senate Democrats' coordinated partisan amending campaign against the 1982 Defense Appropriations bill stood out as innovative in 1981. Like a windows-based computing environment, party cooperation to lose on the floor, on purpose, in order to advance partisan messaging, was novel in 1981.

For example, Sen. Ernest Hollings (D-SC) earned plaudits from his party in 1982 for proposing a one-year freeze on federal spending in lieu of the Reagan administration's tax cut. As noted in a *National Journal* update, "The [Hollings] plan has little chance of being enacted, but it scored some points for Hollings, even among some Democrats who don't like the idea, simply because he offered an alternative to President Reagan's proposed budget" ("Washington Update" 1982). Put differently, liberal Democrats who would not normally support an across-the-board cut in federal spending nevertheless favored Hollings's proposal as a way to give the administration a black eye, as long as it had no chance of becoming law.

Marshalling Senate Democrats to back partisan alternatives was no easy feat in the early 1980s. The party's conservative Southern wing was still strong, including many senior senators long accustomed to wielding committee gavels. Byrd assembled task forces to develop Democratic alternatives to Republican initiatives and the Reagan administration (Schwerzler 1986). According to a Byrd-era leadership staffer, "When we said to Russell Long (D-LA) that we needed a Democratic alternative to Kemp-Roth [the Republicans' tax proposal], he said, 'You keep saying you want a Democratic alternative. I don't know what a Democratic tax bill is! I always get more Republican votes on my tax bills than Democrats.'"[22] When Long was not willing to organize the Democratic response, Sen. Bill Bradley (D-NJ) was recruited instead. Coordinated partisan efforts such as these were unfamiliar to many senior Democrats who had served for so long in a seemingly invulnerable majority party. When Byrd began to whip votes against the increase in the debt limit sought by the Reagan administration in 1981, the older members, especially those who had been committee chairman, were "aghast" at the "idea that they would participate in political guerilla warfare." "Bentsen (D-TX) said, 'This is folly. We are going to destroy our economy and country over politics?' Russell Long said, 'We are going to do what the Republicans have been doing to us?'"[23] Despite some reluctance, Democrats held their ranks and forced the majority Republicans to produce the votes to raise the debt limit. "One by one, the Republicans voted aye," recounted veteran reporter Hedrick Smith (1988, 459). "Henry 'Scoop' Jackson (D-WA) . . . was so tickled to see Republicans squirm that he danced a jig on the floor." Senate Democrats provided few votes for debt-limit increases as the minority party during the Reagan administration (see chapter 7).

Looking toward the 1982 elections, one Senate Democrat remarked in March, "I already see a lot of Republicans getting nervous about having to defend some of the killer votes they cast last year. I think Bob [Byrd] has done a good job in positioning Democrats for the election" (Gailey 1982, A20). For his part, Byrd himself is quoted taking credit:

"This Democratic record didn't just happen. It was created by design, something to use down the road" (Gailey 1982, A20).

Democrats' efforts to distinguish themselves from Republicans extended beyond floor strategy. They also went on the attack against Reagan administration appointees. Even though in the minority, Democrats raised a furor about executive branch officials whenever possible. "The officials in the Reagan administration who got in scandals or got indicted—Anne Gorsuch Burford, James Watt—a lot of information about them came out of our shop," recalled a former Senate Democratic Policy Committee staffer. "The tougher treatment of nominations," he continued, "we started that stuff. In the '80s there was Tower and Bork."[24] Senate Democrats' more confrontational stance on Reagan's appointments was one element of the party's effort to retake their Senate majorities. Growing out of this more combative approach, the Bork nomination is often viewed as a turning point in the history of rising party polarization over judicial nominations (Epstein et al. 2006).

Senate Democrats also staged media events. One of the most successful and widely reported was the 1981 "Reagan school lunch." Led by Byrd, the forty-six Senate Democrats held a luncheon to which they "invited reporters to watch them eating a barebones meal in which ketchup replaced a vegetable and a tiny meat patty was the piece de resistance" (Tolchin 1981, A4). "Ketchup as a vegetable" became a broader symbol with which Democrats of the 1980s memorably attacked Republicans' fiscal priorities.

The new outward orientation of the Senate Democratic Party was also evident in staffing decisions. Minority Leader Byrd hired his first press secretary in 1981. By 1982, the staff of the Democratic Policy Committee included, also for the first time, employees dedicated to communications. By the end of the 1980s, 20 percent of all staff working for Senate Democratic leadership offices worked in communications.

Finally, the Democratic Senate Campaign Committee (DSCC) dramatically increased its fundraising capabilities after 1980, particularly under the leadership of Sen. Lloyd Bentsen (D-TX) and Alan Cranston (D-CA) for the 1984 cycle and Sen. George Mitchell (D-ME) for 1986 (Kolodny 1998, 144). In 1980, the party committee had spent a mere $1.1 million, about 20 percent of the total spent by the National Republican Senatorial Committee that year ($5.4 million). In 1982, the DSCC doubled its 1980 expenditures (to $2.2 million), tripled them in 1984 (to

$3.9 million) and sextupled them in 1986 (to $6.6 million). By the mid-1980s, the DSCC had significantly closed the gap with the NRSC, going from a 5:1 imbalance in expenditures in favor of Republicans in 1980 and 4:1 in 1982, to 1.6:1 in 1984 and 1.5:1 in 1986.[25] A Senate leadership staffer of the period reflected on the party's increased emphasis on fundraising: "We started out with such an amateur operation. There was just no money we could give them. Candidates had to do all their own fundraising. Cranston, Coelho, they knew we had to do something about it, and maybe that's why they played things too close to the line. But they helped to professionalize the fundraising."[26]

Taken together, all signs point to the conclusion that going into the minority transformed Senate Democrats' strategic behavior. They saw new value in caucusing as a party and began meeting regularly. They used these meetings—along with other party support organizations, including party retreats, task forces, and the Senate Democratic Policy Committee—to highlight differences between the parties. They plotted to systematically force roll-call votes that would elicit party divisions that they believed would help them make their case against Republicans. They then sought to message these differences to external constituencies, including the regular publication of a volume documenting each of the party-line votes that had occurred over the preceding year—no doubt the product of many hundreds of hours of staff labor, given the technology of the time. In short, the quest for a return to power led Senate Democrats of the 1980s to strategize ways to better confront their party opponents and to use these issues in the campaign to retake control. This is true even though Senate Democrats of this era were led by Robert Byrd, an archtraditionalist rarely credited with partisan innovations.

The House Republican Response to 1980

Confrontation fits our strategy. Polarization often has very beneficial results. If everything is handled through compromise and conciliation, if there are no real issues dividing us from the Democrats, why should the country change and make us the majority? — Rep. Richard B. Cheney (R-WY), House Republican Policy Committee chair, 1985[27]

Put most simply, competition for party control of national institutions strengthens minority-party incentives to confront their party opponents so as to generate clear issues for electoral purposes rather than hammer out bipartisan legislative compromises. Further historical evidence in support of this claim grows out of a decade-long intraparty fight among House Republicans in the 1980s. The eventual outcome of this internal party battle reshaped the Republican Party's approach to dealing with the long-standing Democratic majority. Beginning in the late 1970s, a handful of junior Republicans, dissatisfied with their party's minority status, began to vocally criticize their party's leaders in Congress for "putting legislative compromise over partisan gain" (Arieff 1979, 1341). An increasing number of Republicans embraced this critique over time, and the confrontationist faction had prevailed by 1989.

The outcome of the 1980 elections dramatically raised House Republican hopes. "The Reagan tide of 1980 quickened Republican expectations of a full-fledged political realignment," observed one longtime reporter (Smith 1988, 675). Looking to the remarkable twelve-seat shift that had unexpectedly given Republicans control of the Senate for the first time since 1954, House Republicans in 1981 began to "talk optimistically about winning control of the House" (Roberts 1981). "There was even some talk about a coalition Speaker," recollected one Republican leadership aide of the time, in which Republicans and conservative Democrats would coalesce to wrest control of the House away from the Democratic leadership.[28]

In the context of these heightened expectations, the decade of the 1980s stands out as a period of dramatically rising party activity among House Republicans. Figure 4.1 displays data on the number of House Republican Conference meetings held in each Congress from 1951 through 1997.[29] As is evident here, House Republicans rarely met in conference before 1980, at least by the standards of the post-1980 period. In 1977, Rep. Edwards (R-OK) had described the party as one that "never meets," which was a bit of an exaggeration, given that the party met around twenty-four times per Congress through the 1970s, about once a month on average. Even so, Republicans in 1977 met only one-third as frequently as would be typical for the party after 1980. Furthermore, the data exhibit a clear break point at 1980. Before 1980, the number of House Republican Party meetings had been trending upward, but only gradually. After 1980, the frequency of meetings rises at a much sharper rate.[30] House Republicans after 1980 met in conference 3.4 times as often as they did on average before 1980.

Interestingly, the importance of 1980 as a turning point in House party organizational activity is confined to Republicans. House Democrats exhibit no evidence of having perceived a reason to meet more fre-

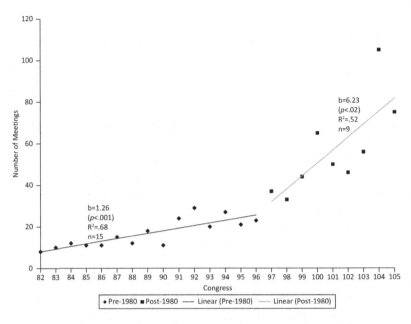

FIGURE 4.1. Number of House Republican Conference meetings, before and after 1980

Note: The shift after 1980 is evident in a regression model of the whole time period: *Number of GOP Meetings* = (1.26)*time* + (−74.27)*post1980* + (4.95)*time*post1980*. All coefficients in the model, including the interaction term, are statistically significant at $p < .01$ ($n = 24$; $R^2 = .86$).

Source: Data on the frequency of House GOP meetings from Forgette (2004).

The number of House GOP meetings increased with time in both the pre- and the post-1980 periods, but the growth in GOP meetings was markedly faster after 1980.

quently after 1980, perhaps reflecting continued confidence about retaining control of the House. For purposes of comparison, figure 4.2 displays data on the frequency of House Democratic Caucus meetings from 1975 to 1999. The time series for the House Democratic Caucus is shorter because of a lack of records before 1970.[31] There is no statistically significant upward trend in the frequency of meetings before 1994. In 1995, the number of Democratic caucus meetings more than doubled (to around forty per year) from the pre-1980 average of around eighteen per year. The much higher frequency of Democratic caucus meetings post-1994 was subsequently sustained through the end of the time series in 1999, with the exception of 1998 (with twenty-six meetings). But during the 1980s, House Democrats did not mirror the growing ferment and activity on the Republican side of the aisle.

House Republican Party politics throughout the 1980s featured a long-running battle between the "Young Turks" and the party's "Old Guard" over how to deal with the long-standing Democratic majority (Connelly and Pitney 1994; Harris 2006; Koopman 1996; Zelizer 2007). The battle was at least as much about party strategy as ideology. The key question was how much to participate in legislative deal making with Democrats versus how much to focus instead on defining clear party differences so that the country grasped the stakes involved in electing a majority party to Congress. Journalist Major Garrett (2005, 53) offered the Young Turk perspective: "Old guard Republicans considered talk of [winning] a majority worse than pointless: it was counterproductive. To pursue a majority meant picking fights with Democrats. Old guard Republicans, by definition, had accumulated seniority and were in a position to vie for some influence with powerful Democratic committee chairmen." House Ways and Means ranking member Rep. Barber Con-

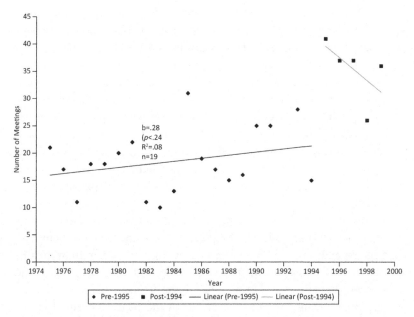

FIGURE 4.2. Number of House Democratic Caucus meetings, 1975–99
Note: Regression models testing for break points in the time series (along the lines of the one shown at the bottom of figure 4.1) do not identify a shift at 1980. With the data extending only to 1999, the shift after 1994, evident visually, does not reach statistical significance.
Source: Data on the frequency of House Democratic Caucus meetings from Forgette (2004).
The number of House Democratic Caucus meetings stays relatively flat through the 1970s and 1980s. There is a sharp jump in frequency in 1995, once the Democrats go into the minority.

able (R-NY) articulated the Old Guard point of view: "I don't like stri-
dency. I don't like game playing. It's more important to try to influence
policy" (Connelly and Pitney 1994, 157). Rep. Tom DeLay (R-TX) took
the other side: "We're having a struggle right now within the Republican party. Basically, it's those who think they're here to govern and those
who think they're here to take over a majority. I am not among those
here to govern. I am here to take over a majority from the Democrats"
(Connelly and Pitney 1994, 62).

In the lead-up to the 1982 elections, this dispute over strategy was
a burning controversy within House Republican ranks. In this context, Gingrich engaged in a remarkable exchange with House Minority
Leader Bob Michel (R-IL) in the pages of the *National Journal* (Cohen
1982a, 316). "The best Republican strategy is to recognize that the Democrats run the House and will do all they can to butcher the budget,"
Gingrich said. "Bob Michel should relax, concentrate on the impotence
of Tip O'Neill and refuse to take up the burden of being Speaker himself." To this, Michel replied, "I don't perceive my role as taking the budget issue to the voters. I have to look at what's achievable for the good of
the country." In short, Michel was focused on the short game of getting
the best policies attainable in the present moment, even with a Democratic majority. He didn't view his role as "taking the budget issue to voters." Gingrich wanted Republicans to withdraw from bipartisan negotiations in hopes of better defining the differences between the parties and
thereby winning the long game of defeating the Democrats in the next
elections. It is difficult to find a clearer statement of the trade-offs minority parties perceive between electoral advantage and participation in
governance.

In 1982, the National Republican Campaign Committee under Vander Jagt's leadership made a major push. The committee more than doubled its expenditures, from $2.2 million in 1980 to $5.3 million in 1982
(Ornstein et al. 1996, 105–6). The NRCC spent 7.6 times as much as the
Democratic Congressional Campaign Committee in 1982.

The Republicans' twenty-six-seat loss in the 1982 midterm elections
was a tremendous disappointment to the party. Nevertheless, undeterred
by the setback, Gingrich founded the Conservative Opportunity Society in early 1983. Every Wednesday, Gingrich and a handpicked group
of young Republican activists met to plot strategy. Once again, the challenge that the Gingrich group posed to the Republican leadership's participation in governing was clear: "The Georgian . . . feels the only way

to increase Republican strength is to confront the Democrats at every turn and draw clear lines between the parties. Many Republican leaders say the party must . . . take on the responsibilities of actually running the government, but to Mr. Gingrich and his compatriots, such talk is heresy" (Roberts 1983). The group would brainstorm lines of attack, with careful attention to specific word choice. "We met every week in the Cannon Building. We'd strategize for an hour—focusing on issues that would help us get control of the House. There was lots of energy, enthusiasm," recalled a former House staffer.[32]

Beginning in 1984, the Conservative Opportunity Society (COS) began coordinating one-minute speeches and special orders on the House floor. These speeches used harsh rhetoric and relentlessly charged majority Democrats with corruption, arrogance, and mismanagement. "We would hold COS meetings at a time in the morning that just preceded [the meeting of] the House and we would literally walk out of the COS meetings and walk as a group over to the House floor and sit down and do our one-minutes on the theme we had decided for that day," recalled Rep. Robert S. Walker (R-PA; Balz and Babcock 1994, A1). These efforts constituted the first sustained, self-conscious partisan message operation on the House floor (Green 2015, 76–77).

As an explicitly partisan organization, the COS was very different from the New Right and the Senate Steering Committee. Although the Steering Committee often raised issues that were useful for Republican campaigns, the purpose of the Steering Committee was to advance conservative causes, both within and outside the Republican Party. The purpose of the COS was to help Republicans win a House majority; like-minded Democrats were not invited to join. The Steering Committee, by contrast, was open to conservative Democrats and early on had cross-party participation. In addition, as one senior Senate staffer explained, "the Steering Committee was more about legislative strategy than the COS. In the House, winning the majority is more of the sole focus of the minority."[33] In defining issues, the COS sought to present a positive vision of what government would look like if Republicans won control. Certainly, that vision was undergirded by a conservative ideology. The "opportunity society" in the group's name was framed as an alternative to the "liberal welfare state" (Weber 1995). But the focus of the COS was on defining party differences aimed at winning a Republican majority.

Many of the party differences the COS highlighted, however, had nothing in particular to do with a conservative philosophy of government. Instead, hard-hitting attacks on Democratic corruption and arrogance were a central theme. COS members charged that the Democratic leadership was abusive and heavy-handed in its management of the House, and they aggressively pursued ethics scandals (Farrell 2001, 626–36; Zelizer 2007). Underlying the approach was Gingrich's maxim, "Conflict equals exposure equals power" (Fineman 1989). When Rep. Mickey Edwards (R-OK) was asked why he had not participated in the Conservative Opportunity Society, he said it was not because of disagreement with its basic ideological goals: "I was an 'opportunity' guy myself. I was a Jack Kemp Republican. But my problem with the COS was that it was just too negative, too focused on attacking the other guys."[34]

Efforts to Rein In the Committees

The battle between the "Young Turks" and the "Old Guard" centered especially on the proper role of Republicans on committees. The willingness of Republican ranking members to negotiate with Democratic committee chairmen was a particular source of frustration to Republicans seeking to present a clearer contrast to Democrats. To Young Turk minds, these ranking members were putting their own personal interests first. As Armey explained, "You watched our ranking guys and what they learned was, 'My best friend, the guy who can help me out with all the reasons that I wanted to be on this committee in the first place, is the chairman.' So they promised the chairman a certain amount of complacency and mob control" (Garrett 2005, 53–54). "There are more rewards for being a good minority legislator than there are for trying to become a majority legislator," said then-GOP whip Newt Gingrich. "The system is biased toward putting the minority member to some extent in a courtier relationship to the majority, especially on the committees" (Connelly and Pitney 1994, 5). Obviously, these "rewards" mean an ability to collaborate in shaping policy, which minority party members lose when their party pursues a strategy of across-the-board opposition.

On a couple notable occasions during the 1980s, elements in the Republican Conference sought to adopt formal party rules that would force their party and committee leaders to stop negotiating with Democrats on key issues.

In 1986, the Republican Conference approved resolutions aimed at imposing party discipline on committee leaders. The new rules would allow the Republican leader to designate "leadership issues" that "require early and ongoing cooperation between the relevant committees and the leadership" (Connelly and Pitney 1994, 49). Furthermore, the resolutions specified that ranking Republicans had an "obligation to ensure that the managerial responsibilities on the floor of the House of Representatives for each measure on which the Republican Conference has taken a position are managed in accordance with such position" (Connelly and Pitney 1994, 49). This effort grew out of rank-and-file Republican anger at Republican members of the Ways and Means Committee who had collaborated with Chairman Dan Rostenkowski (D-IL) on the 1986 tax reform, particularly at ranking member Rep. John Duncan (R-TN), whose substitute legislation closely resembled the Democrats' bill. The Young Turks were also angry at Rep. Jack Kemp (R-NY), chairman of the Republican Conference, for cooperating with Democrats on tax reform after the Republican Conference had specifically voted to oppose the effort. As House Republican Policy Committee Chair Rep. Richard B. Cheney (R-WY) explained, "Leaders accept a certain obligation to the conference at large, and they should try to the best of their ability to support the conference position" (Hook 1986).

In 1988, the House Republican Conference adopted a set of rule changes aimed at forcing their leaders to be more aggressive. They sought to prohibit Republican ranking members from cooperating with the Democrats on year-end catchall spending legislation (Osterlund 1988). They even considered an enforcement mechanism that would strip violators of ranking status (Fuerbringer 1988).

Republican members of the House Appropriations Committee were especially cross-pressured. The Appropriations Committee had a long history of bipartisanship, more robust than on other committees (Fenno 1966, 1973). This tradition rested on a view of the committee's purpose that transcended partisanship: to guard Congress's purse strings and to "cut the fat" from executive-agency requests (Fenno 1966, 104–5). Preserving Congress's independent power over federal expenditures meant appropriators would work out their disagreements quietly in committee (when the rules allowed, in executive session). They would then bring bills to the floor with unanimous or nearly unanimous committee support (and without minority reports) so that Congress would be sure to enact them. When the committee's role is understood this way, as Fenno (1966, 317) observed, "nothing would be more disruptive to the committee's work than bitter and extended partisan conflict."

However, this cozy bipartisan way of doing business on appropriations stood directly at odds with the Republicans' ability to define party differences with Democrats on government spending. Opposition to excessive government spending is a traditional Republican cause, central both to conservative ideology and to making the case for a Republican majority. If Republicans and Democrats disagree so strongly on government spending, how can the two parties' appropriators vote together on all the appropriations bills? If there is no dissimilarity in how Republican and Democratic appropriators behave, then how can the parties say it makes any difference whether Republicans or Democrats control Congress?

Republicans who wanted to establish clearer distinctions from Democrats thus had special reason to focus on trying to change how business was done on appropriations. Republican appropriators came in for regular criticism for forging "unholy alliances" with committee Democrats (Wehr 1987). They were accused of collaborating with Democrats in order to bring home the bacon and enhance their own personal power. No doubt, Republican appropriators did receive concessions in exchange for their support of appropriations bills. One senior Republican House aide relayed an anecdote:

> Vin Weber (R-MN) tells a story about what it was like when he first came to Congress and was appointed to the Appropriations Committee. As a new member, Weber went to the ranking subcommittee Republican—an older woman from Nebraska, I think her name was Virginia Smith (R-NE)—to ask how he could get some things accomplished. She said to Vin, "Well, you just make a list of things that you want. You give it to me. And we'll make sure we put it in the bill."[35]

The well-understood price of having input on these bills was a willingness to support them on the floor and, if necessary, to defend them from hostile amendment. "It really is the club," marveled Weber. "You're expected to operate by consensus" (Wehr 1987).

Maintaining this consensus became increasingly difficult as junior Republicans exploited the open rules typically used for the consideration of appropriations bills to offer amendments designed to force the "government spending" issue. Railing against the budget deficit, these members would offer across-the-board cuts, elimination of particular items, or points of order. Rep. Dick Armey (R-TX), first elected in 1984, organized a group of fifty "Budget Commandos" who would scrutinize appropriations bills and stand at the ready to take targeted action on the floor. He assembled teams of members to take the lead on each appropriations bill. The Chamber of Commerce was enlisted to coordinate other outside conservative and business groups in support of the effort, and the roll-call votes they secured would then be used in the chamber's year-end congressional vote ratings.[36] When self-styled Budget Commandos and other members offered amendments to appropriations bills framed to generate partisan contrasts on government spending, Republican appropriators were caught between a rock and a hard place. On the one hand, there was the long-standing norm of consensus on the Appropriations Committee and the expectation that they would support the bills on which they had input. On the other hand, fellow Republicans were accusing them of failing to do their duty to their party.

One such intra-Republican dispute was aired at length on the House floor in 1987 during the consideration of the appropriation bills for Energy and Water and Interior. Ranking Republican appropriator Rep. Silvio Conte (R-MA) referred to freshman Rep. Fred Upton (R-MI) offering an amendment as a "young slasher."[37] Some Republicans took offense. Freshman Rep. Ernie Konnyu (R-CA) complained, "I just listened a few minutes ago to a ranking Republican member of a committee making what I understood as a personal attack on another member by calling him names. . . . I am wondering if the Republican members on this side of the aisle know what their conference approved job is."[38] Senior Republican appropriator Rep. Ralph Regula (R-OH) responded, defending his committee colleagues, "I think that members who have leadership responsibilities do their cutting in the subcommittee after the hearings" rather than on the floor.[39] A series of Republicans appealed for support of their budget-cutting floor amendments. Among them was Republican Whip Trent Lott (R-MS), who framed the issue as party defining for Republicans: "Now I just want to ask this question. . . . Are there any of us left who are for cutting just a little bit? Are there any Republicans left?"[40]

In response to this public criticism from fellow Republicans, ranking Republican appropriator Bill Green (R-NY) offered an extended defense of the way the committee operated: "The vast majority of the time within the Appropriations Committee we are not working in an adversarial, partisan way. . . . The chairman of [the] subcommittee. . . . is quite open with me. . . . The committee staff is fully available for me for discussions of those problems. I have a very substantial right of input into those discussions and into the resolution. . . . [Republicans] have an opportunity to play a very constructive role in putting these bills together." Concluding, he said, "I think that general spirit of working together that exists within the Appropriations Committee is . . . a desirable one. . . . I certainly do not think it is wise to aggravate those differences or to insist that we try to emphasize the differences rather than the agreements."[41] In the name of preserving that spirit of working together on appropriations, Green asked his fellow partisans to stop looking for ways to play up partisan disagreements.

Even so, a minority party seeking to make its case for a return to power has to show what the differences would be if it won control. The partisan imperative for Republicans to demonstrate the existence of meaningful differences on government spending was particularly strong. Following this showdown on the floor, Republicans met privately to determine how to proceed but reached no resolution (Wehr 1987).

Although bipartisan cooperation on the committees was under pressure throughout the 1980s, it did not break. White's (1989, 15) study concluded that the Appropriations Committee of the 1980s still largely preserved traditional ways of doing business: "The committee remained one of the most nonpartisan on the Hill." However, the internal Republican controversy did not go away either. Party strategy, and the pros and cons of cooperation versus confrontation, continued to be debated. Bipartisanship on the House Appropriations Committee would suffer significant erosion during the 1990s under this strain (Aldrich and Rohde 2000).

Leadership Contests

The battle over party strategy also played out in leadership contests in the House Republican Party throughout the 1980s. Leadership contests in Congress are highly personalized affairs in which members commit to particular candidates on the basis of personal ties, favors, and histories, as well as many other factors having nothing to do with questions of ideology or strategy. Even so, House Republican leadership contests of this era repeatedly featured the choice between members who were distinctly known for advocating either a more or a less confrontational approach to dealing with Democrats (Connelly and Pitney 1994, 54–58; Harris 2006, 193–99; Koopman 1996; Zelizer 2007).

Table 4.1 lists each of the contested House Republican leadership races between 1980 and 1992, including winners, losers, and the vote breakdown in the Republican Conference. For each race where the candidates' stance on party strategy was a dimension of the competition, the name of the candidate with the reputation for preferring a more confrontational approach is shaded. These codings were made based on contemporaneous news reports and profiles. In some cases, members evolved over time in their views on the underlying strategic question.[42] The patterns are stark. First, the question of party strategy was raised in most leadership contests during the period. Out of eighteen contested leadership races, thirteen offered a choice of candidates with differing reputations on the strategic question of confrontation versus cooperation with the opposition party. Second, there is a clear shift toward a more confrontational approach in the late 1980s. Before 1988, every contest pitting the Old Guard against the Young Turks was resolved in favor of the Old Guard. The contests were often close. Confrontationist candidates

TABLE 4.1. **Contested elections for House Republican leadership posts, identifying candidates with reputations for a more confrontational style, 1980–1992**

Year	Office	Winner	Loser or second place	Vote
1980	Leader	Michel (IL)	Vander Jagt (MI)	103–87
1980	Whip	Lott (MS)	Shuster (PA)	96–90
1980	Conf. chair	Kemp (NY)	Rousselot (CA)	107–77
1980	Policy	Cheney (WY)	Holt (MD)	99–68
1980	Research	Madigan (IL)	Walker (PA)	93–74
1983	Research	Lewis (CA)	Coleman (MO)	78–47
1987	Policy	Lewis (CA)	Hunter (CA)	88–82
1987	Research	Edwards (OK)	Gunderson (WI)	93–71
1988	Conf. chair	Lewis (CA)	Martin (IL)	85–82
1988	Research	Hunter (CA)	Bartlett (TX)	100–65
1988	Vice chair	McCollum (FL)	Lagomarsino (CA)	110–50
1988	Secretary	Weber (MN)	McDade (PA)	82–61
1989	Whip	Gingrich (GA)	Madigan (IL)	87–85
1990	Conf. chair	Lewis (CA)	Purcell (MI)	98–64
1990	NRCC	Vander Jagt (MI)	Sundquist (TN)	98–66
1992	Conf. chair	Armey (TX)	Lewis (CA)	88–84
1992	Vice chair	McCollum (FL)	Johnson (CT)	93–70
1992	Secretary	DeLay (TX)	Gradison (OH)	95–71

Note: Candidates are coded as having a reputation for a more confrontational style based on contemporaneous news stories or profiles that identify one candidate in a race as having more of a reputation for working across party lines than the other or one candidate as having more of a reputation as a partisan hard-liner than the other.

Sources: Connelly and Pitney (1995, 54–8), Harris (2006, 193–199), *Almanac of American Politics* (various years), and searches in the relevant issues of *National Journal* and *CQ Weekly*, as well as ProQuest's Historical Newspapers Database.

usually made strong showings, but they failed to win. After 1988, candidates favoring a more confrontational stance toward the Democrats prevailed on all but one occasion that the choice was presented to the House Republican Conference.

The leadership contests in December 1980, particularly the election of Michel over Vander Jagt as minority leader, indicated that House Republicans were not yet on board with a confrontationist strategy. An energetic partisan and party builder, Vander Jagt was "known more for his oratory than for his parliamentary ability" (Arieff 1980a, 3549). "Supporters of Vander Jagt, chairman of the NRCC, contended his polished political style would help elect enough Republicans to give the GOP control of the House," wrote one 1980 roundup ("Washington Update" 1980, 2136). Meanwhile, Michel emphasized the importance of "working during the next two years to enact Ronald Reagan's legislative program" ("Washington Update" 1980, 2136). The vote in the Michel–Vander Jagt race was close (103–87), even though Michel, having served as minority whip since 1974, was next in line of succession. Going into the election, both candidates expected to win. Vander Jagt had sent letters of thanks in advance to the 102 members whom he believed had committed to voting for him (Arieff 1980a, 3549), a majority of the conference. In the anonymous balloting, Vander Jagt did not receive all the votes he had expected to get and wound up being forced to concede the race.

Other leadership races in 1980 presented the same strategic question, albeit less starkly. The former John Birch Society member Rep. John H. Rousselot (R-CA) was seen "in some quarters as a hard-eyed fanatic" (Barone et al. 1979), making Rep. Jack Kemp (R-NY) seem the more willing of the two to reach across the aisle as members chose the party's conference chair. Similarly, Rep. Bob Walker (R-PA) had earned a reputation as one of the House's most aggressive partisans, making Rep. Edward Madigan (R-IL) the better choice as Research Committee chair for those who wanted to prioritize legislative achievement. All the 1980 leadership races were strongly competitive, indicating that the party was divided on this strategic question. In the end, the party opted for candidates who would be expected to focus on legislative achievement during Reagan's first term. "In each case, the winner has shown a greater propensity to work with Democrats on legislative issues," concluded a news report ("Washington Update" 1980, 2136). Immediately after his victory, Michel promised to execute a strategy of bargaining and cross-party collaboration, saying, "We will begin with negotiations with Democrats not only at the top but at the subcommittees" ("Washington Update" 1980, 2136).

The question of strategy was hardly put to rest. The COS got organized and began to demand more confrontation. The issue came to a head again in the leadership races of 1987. The 1987 contest for the Republican Policy Committee chairmanship pitted a traditional legislator and appropriator Rep. Jerry Lewis (R-CA) against Rep. Duncan Hunter (R-CA), an activist in the COS. Lewis, who said, "I am distinctly not a bomb thrower," was narrowly elected as chair, by a vote of eighty-eight to eighty-two (Hook 1987). Interviewed about the 1987 leadership contests, Weber said, "The idea that we could become a majority is a more real prospect [for young members] than it is for older members accustomed to being in the minority" (Hook 1987).

The contests in 1988 signaled that the balance within the party was shifting. That year saw the election of two COS members into lower-level leadership positions. Hunter was elected Research Committee chair. A founding member of the COS, Weber (R-MN), was elected conference secretary. At the same time, however, Lewis was promoted to Policy Committee chair, indicating that Republicans were also ready to promote a leader known for a more cooperative approach. Other 1988 races did not pose the strategic question clearly.

The stakes in the 1989 whip contest between Gingrich and Madigan were high, and the question of party strategy was at the heart of the choice. Gingrich had been advocating for heightening the differences from Democrats since his arrival in Congress a decade before. On the other hand, "Madigan campaigned as a man who knows how to count votes, how to influence colleagues, and how to work with Democrats" (Barone and Ujifusa 1989, 38). "The issue is not ideology, it's active versus passive leadership," said Weber (Hook 1989). The whip slot had opened up when House Republican Whip Richard B. Cheney (R-WY) was nominated as secretary of defense on March 10, 1989. The party's competing factions had to organize on short notice, as the election for Cheney's replacement was held just twelve days later, on March 22 (Koopman 1996, 11). "This was a holy war in the conference. Nothing afterwards really compares to this battle," recalled a former House leadership aide from the time. "The old bulls threw everything at Newt to try to defeat him. But his abilities really showed themselves: his decisiveness, his vote counting, his organization. He blitzed the conference. He had the position sewed up within three or four days."[43] The election was razor close, however, with Gingrich defeating Madigan eighty-seven to eighty-five.

The meaning of Gingrich's victory was well understood at the time. Members had chosen as whip a leader whose primary focus would be on messaging against the Democrats, aimed at building a Republican majority, not on cutting the best available deals with Democrats. Subsequent analysis shows that ideology was only a modest predictor of members' support for Gingrich (Harris 2006, 210–11). Gingrich drew support from across the ideological spectrum in the Republican Conference. "Gingrich had the support of a lot of moderates," one House leadership staffer from the era emphasized in an interview. "Olympia Snowe (R-ME) [was one]. Bill Frenzel (R-MN) seconded Newt's nomination."[44] The outcome of the race turned on a shared belief that Newt's strategic vision deserved a try as much as on any shift in the ideological center of gravity within the Republican Conference. "We had a choice of being attack dogs or lapdogs," said one Republican lawmaker shortly after the vote. "We decided attack dogs are more useful" (Lamar and Gorey 1989). "We want to build for 1992," said Rep. Chuck Douglas (R-NH). "We're not interested in being a better minority. Newt personifies that message" (Hook 1989).

After that 1989 race, with only one exception, each time a contested leadership race posed a question about the candidates' preference for a confrontational or cooperative style, the confrontationist candidate won. The exceptional case was in 1990 when Rep. Lewis beat back a challenge to his continuation as conference chair from Rep. Carl D. Purcell (R-MI). Backed by Gingrich, Weber, and Hunter, the Purcell challenge was specifically driven by members "clamoring for a more aggressive, outward-looking party strategy" (Hook 1990). Even though Lewis turned aside the challenge, he was stripped of his position on the leadership panel that makes Republican committee assignments later that same day. Lewis went on to be defeated by Armey in 1992. "Lewis was very old school, very old school," recollected a former House Republican leadership staffer from the period, "so it had a similar meaning when Armey edged him as when Newt beat Madigan."[45] In 1992, Rep. Tom DeLay (R-TX) was selected conference secretary, further underscoring the party's preference for confrontational leadership.

Despite the changes going on inside the conference, Michel himself held onto leadership until 1995. He was even reelected by acclamation in 1992 at the same time as more confrontationist candidates (Armey,

DeLay, and Rep. Bill McCollum, R-FL) were selected in the contested leadership races (Kuntz 1992). Michel managed to survive as long as he did because he was able to bridge the party's factions. "Michel straddled the two groups," said one longtime House Republican leadership staffer. "Michel was not a guy who just wanted to be a ranking Republican. He was no Stafford."[46] That balancing was on display in Michel's acceptance speech after being retained as leader in 1984. "The most important thing we have done is rid ourselves of that subservient, timid mentality of the permanent minority," he said, acknowledging his acceptance of the need for more confrontation (Granat 1984). "The Republican party in the House is no longer content to go along," he continued. "We want to go for broke" (Granat 1984). But then he immediately qualified that statement: "Sometimes we will confront. Other times we will seek to find out how far the other side is willing to bend" (Granat 1984). Despite this balancing, it was clear by 1992 that Michel was isolated in leadership (Kuntz 1992). Michel announced his retirement in October 1993, with Gingrich as heir apparent.

Explaining the Shift in GOP Strategy

What accounts for the House Republican shift to a more confrontational strategy? The move was not prompted by increased optimism that a Republican House majority was close at hand. Republicans had been stuck at around 40 percent of the House (between 168 and 183 seats) since 1983. Furthermore, the failure to win a Republican majority on the coattails of Reagan's landslide reelection in 1984 had been particularly discouraging. "Gingrich even thought about retiring that year," said one former House Republican aide.[47] There had also been no coattails whatsoever for House Republicans when George H. W. Bush won the presidency in 1988.

Republicans generally explain the shift toward a more confrontational strategy as the result of a growing consensus within the party that the more cooperative approach taken by their leaders had not been helpful in winning a majority. "By that point, people were feeling that you didn't have to agree with Newt on everything to know that it was time to try something new," recalled a former House leadership staffer from the time.[48] After years of debating the question of strategy in the Republican Conference, there was a widespread appreciation that bipartisan deal making was not helpful for majority making. One former Republican leader interviewed by Connelly and Pitney (1994, 155) explained the trade-off that members perceived: "I would divide [the Republican Conference] into those who feel their first and last job is to elect a Republican majority . . . and those who on the campaign trail bash the Democrats but the rest of the week are serious legislators." When asked to explain why Madigan, his favored candidate, had lost to Gingrich, Michel said simply, "There's such frustration on our side about being mired down in the minority" (Lamar and Gorey 1989). In short, after years of narrowly electing leaders who favored a more cooperative, deal-making approach, a majority of House Republicans had come to believe that the strategies that the conference had pursued through the 1980s were unlikely to help win a Republican majority in 1992 or subsequent elections. If the old approach had not worked by now, why would it work in the future?

The shift to a more confrontational strategy can be attributed to two additional factors specific to the political context of the time. First, a more confrontational strategy increased in attractiveness after 1986, when Republicans lost control of the Senate. As laid out in table 3.1, a focus on party messaging becomes relatively more attractive to a party as its power declines. The less power members have, the less they can expect to achieve in terms of their policy goals. Thus, as members' party power declines, the policy trade-offs involved with pursuing a strategy of across-the-board opposition become less severe. No longer in control of either chamber of Congress after 1986, House Republicans could achieve fewer of their policy objectives by cooperating with Democrats than had been possible between 1981 and 1987, when the House chamber was the only institution of national government not controlled by Republicans. With House Republicans less able to obtain desirable outcomes in bargaining with Democrats after 1986, they became more willing to prioritize messaging over legislating. The party's shift toward confrontation is evident in the leadership races of 1988, some of the first contests after Republicans had lost the Senate. In 1988, for the first time, COS members won contested leadership races. A confrontational strategy was even easier for Republicans to embrace following the 1992 election of President Clinton, when House Republicans entered the "deep minority" (Green 2015, 83) as a minority party under a unified government controlled by its opposition. Confrontationists swept the contested leadership races in 1992.

Second, Republican grievances against how the Democrats ran the

House of Representatives had been accumulating. In particular, Republicans felt very unfairly treated by the outcome of a contested election in Indiana's eighth congressional district in 1984. Indiana's secretary of state had certified a Republican challenger as having won the race by 34 votes, and a recount had him up by 418 votes ("House Refuses to Seat Republican" 1985). Citing questions about whether Indiana had thrown out ballots improperly, House Democrats declined to seat either candidate and appointed a task force and the General Accounting Office to do a recount. In the end, the House voted along party lines (230–195) to declare the Democratic incumbent the victor by four votes. In protest, every Republican walked out of the chamber. After returning, they tied up the floor calling for roll-call votes on routine parliamentary matters. Michel himself used COS-style rhetoric excoriating the "autocratic, tyrannical rule of the Democratic majority" (Rohde 1991, 131). "The fight over the 'Bloody Eighth' . . . had a radicalizing effect," recalled a former House Republican leadership aide.[49]

Republicans also began to feel unjustly treated under House procedure. Over the course of the 1980s, Democrats began to make more aggressive use of special and restrictive rules to manage floor debate. A steadily increasing share of measures was considered under rules that limited Republican opportunities to offer amendments, and fewer measures were brought to the floor under open rules (Bach and Smith 1988, 53–61). The trend intensified after 1987 under the speakership of Jim Wright (D-TX; Rohde 1991, 109–13). The Democrats' use of more restrictive procedures partly reflected a Democratic leadership empowered by a more unified caucus to vigorously pursue the enactment of a partisan program (Rohde 1991).

At the same time, the Democrats' greater use of restrictive rules responded to a minority party that had been demanding increasingly more roll-call votes on floor amendments in the wake of the 1970s reforms (Green 2015, 150–53; Roberts and Smith 2003). A couple of the interview subjects for this project referenced the ironic way that the reforms of the 1970s wound up over time redounding to the Republicans' electoral benefit. "The reforms of the 1970s [were] an important precursor" to the strategies pursued by the COS, noted one veteran Republican staffer. By making it easier to force roll-call votes, the reforms made it possible for COS members to "design embarrassing amendments. The votes on them would then be fed to the campaign committees, so you could say, 'Jack voted against the balanced budget,' or something like that."[50] The televising of the House and other transparency reforms of the 1970s were also very useful to a minority party seeking to force its issues into public view.[51] As Republicans seized these opportunities, Democrats adopted more creative procedures to clamp down. In response, Republicans waxed indignant about the Democrats' autocratic rule of the House. The feedback loop worked in favor of the GOP's confrontational faction.

Dating back to the start of the COS in 1983, Gingrich and other Republican activists had made steady use of charges that Democrats "stack[ed] and rig[ged] the game" in their own favor (Farrell 2001, 632–38). Gingrich quickly recognized the effectiveness of these grievances in rallying Republicans. Even Republicans who might disagree with Gingrich and the COS on policy could resent how Democrats ran the House (Farrell 2001, 631–32). The Republican leadership began to come around to Gingrich's point of view. In 1987, Republican staff on the Rules Committee documented how the Democrats' uses of procedure departed from past practice (Bach and Smith 1988, 56), and Minority Whip Trent Lott introduced data on these trends into the *Congressional Record*.[52] In May 1988, House Republicans orchestrated hours of floor speeches about the "inequitable way the Democratic majority controls the House" (Hook 1988). GOP Conference Chairman Dick Cheney (R-WY) published an article in *Public Opinion* (1989) questioning the legitimacy of Democratic procedures. In many other settings, Cheney lambasted the Democrats' "arrogant" management of the House, citing numerous procedural moves by Speaker Wright (Surman 1988). Memories of the Democrats' tactics came up unprompted in an interview with a former Republican staffer of the era. "Jim Wright and Tony Coelho . . . were just thugs, totally brazen, and they treated the Republicans like dirt," he said with some feeling. "This led more Republicans to side with the insurgents."[53] "Gingrich's success among moderates may owe something to Wright," reflected one journalist in 1989. "[Wright's tactics] made moderates more receptive to confrontation politics" (Hook 1989).

In sum, the story of the post-1980 House Republican Party is one of a longtime minority party contentiously debating and then gradually shifting to a more confrontational approach in its quest for majority control. As was clear from the data in figure 4.1, 1980 represented a turning point in House GOP partisan activity, in that the House Republicans dramatically stepped up the frequency of their party conference meetings in the 1980s compared to the party's previous practice. Over the course of the 1980s, a lengthy, fiercely contested battle over party strategy was waged inside the House Republican Conference. The faction of the party more concerned with building a Republican majority tried on multiple occasions to stop other Republicans from negotiating with Democrats. The question of strategy was repeatedly posed in leadership contests. At last, the confrontationist faction finally gained the upper hand in 1989, with Gingrich's election as whip. After that, the question of how the GOP should approach minority-party status was largely settled. The post-1989 Republican Party would not again suffer from "minority-party mentality."

Confrontation and the Quest for Congressional Majorities

If there's no chance of one or the other party taking control, the minority party will just play the hands they're dealt. You become the loyal opposition, instead of the "cut you off at the knees" opposition. — Former Rep. Mickey Edwards (R-OK)[54]

This chapter has presented a detailed analysis of how the minority parties in Congress reacted to the changed competitive circumstances after 1980. The long-standing, seemingly permanent Democratic majorities before 1980 incentivized more "loyal opposition" behavior on the part of the minority-party Republicans. Before 1980, Republicans tended to focus on the short game of influencing policy rather than the long game of winning control. Republicans and Democrats frequently worked together on committees, with Appropriations being one of the most nonpartisan of all. These same persistent Democratic majorities also contributed to complacency on the part of Democrats, who rarely met in caucus, raised little party campaign funds, and had very limited capabilities for imposing party discipline. After 1980, however, a more "cut you off at the knees" style of partisanship began to emerge among both chambers' minority parties, Democrats in the Senate and Republicans in the House. Senate Democrats and House Republicans became newly organized and began to meet more frequently. The minority parties in House and Senate started looking for more ways to message partisan distinctions, force roll-calls that would yield party-line divisions, publicize the partisan controversies, raise more campaign money for their party committees, and make the case for their party to take control.

These analyses put into sharp relief that party conflict in Congress is a result of partisan strategy, not just an accident of the distribution of individual members' policy preferences. In both the House and the Senate of the 1980s, fellow partisans extensively discussed and debated questions of strategy, with the debate being most protracted among House Republicans. Questions of strategy were and remain a perennial subject of intraparty dispute, because members perceive trade-offs between their choices. There is a case to be made on both sides of the dilemma. A minority party's participation in lawmaking yields better public policy from its perspective, even when those gains fall far short of members' goals. But these gains come at a political cost of being able to draw partisan distinctions, criticize the majority's governance, and make a case to retake power. It is clear from the numerous perspectives consulted and quoted here that members perceive and grapple with this fundamental problem in a self-conscious way. It is also clear that the dilemma became a more pressing question once House members and senators recognized greater prospects for change in their majority status after the watershed elections of 1980.

One difference between the post-1980 Senate and House minority parties was that controversy over party strategy was more intense and longer-lasting among House Republicans than Senate Democrats. On this point, it is worth noting that this difference in the two minority parties' behavior is consistent with expectations (laid out in chapter 3) that the trade-offs between messaging and governing are less severe for parties with less power. Between 1980 and 1987, Senate Democrats were a minority party facing an administration of the opposing party. Throughout much of the 1980s, by contrast, Republicans controlled the presidency and the Senate and were a minority only in the House of Representatives. As such, House Republicans perceived a greater likelihood of achieving desirable policy outcomes than did Senate Democrats of the same period. Indeed, House Republicans hoped to see the Reagan administration achieve as much of its legislative agenda as possible. As such, one would expect the House Republicans' institutional position to induce somewhat more cooperation and participation in governing than that of the 1981–87 minority Senate Democrats. The Democrats' weaker institutional position encouraged a more single-minded focus on partisan confrontation and messaging. It is striking that the confrontationist faction only finally prevailed among House Republicans after 1987, once they had been reduced to a full-fledged congressional minority with the Republican loss of the Senate. The confrontationist faction then thoroughly cemented its control over the Republican leadership after the 1992 elections, when Republicans became a minority party in unified

Democratic government under President Bill Clinton. A party's share of power in the constitutional system of separated powers factors into its strategic calculus as it weighs the choice between cooperation and confrontation.

This close look at internal party politics in the 1980s Congress reveals that competition for party control of the institution encouraged both Senate Democrats and House Republicans to seek out and highlight party differences in their quest to win power. It is clear from the analysis that members believe that their party's collective electoral fate, including its majority or minority status, is tied up with their ability to wage this kind of public combat. This chapter documented an array of shifts in partisan strategic behavior in Congress shortly after 1980. Intense competition for majority status in Congress has now persisted for more than three decades. Chapters 5 and 6 will consider the implications of this sustained two-party competition for party behavior and institutions in Congress.

CHAPTER FIVE

The Institutionalization of Partisan Communications

Message is critical. It's been ideas that have brought us to the majority position, and what will keep us there. — Rep. Sam Brownback (R-KS), 1996[1]

My idea is to professionalize our viewpoint and beat them at their own game. — Rep. Mickey Edwards (R-OK), 1984[2]

Inside the Beltway, it is an article of faith that "message is critical." Members, staff, journalists, campaign consultants, and party strategists all believe that messaging matters for a party's ability to win and hold majorities. Although party messaging was not a pressing concern when there seemed little chance for a change in congressional majorities, it became an increasingly important task for party leaders once the prospect of alternation in majorities returned to congressional politics. Rank-and-file members began to expect their leaders to coordinate the party in collective efforts to enhance its image and to undermine that of the opposition.

This chapter focuses on how the parties in Congress have developed and professionalized their messaging capabilities over the course of more than three decades of persistent party competition for control of governing institutions. Subject to these long-standing competitive pressures, the parties in Congress have institutionalized extensive professional messaging operations. The contemporary legislative branch employs a workforce of hundreds of communicators who work full-time on partisan public relations. As will be shown below, this is overwhelmingly a post-1980s development. This chapter presents data documenting the shift in party priorities toward messaging, sheds light on how messages are constructed and disseminated, and takes stock of the types of messages the parties broadcast. As will become apparent, the institutionalization of party messaging has consequences for the allocation of power in the legislative branch, the content of congressional debate, and the atmosphere of relentless partisan invective that characterizes the contemporary Congress.

The Rise of Party Communications

The management of their party's public image has not always been a central feature of party leaders' responsibilities. As a result, earlier scholarship on congressional leaders had almost nothing to say on the subject. To a far greater extent than was true in prior decades, however, contemporary congressional parties have developed as organizations oriented toward communications designed to enhance one party's reputation relative to the other. A large share of legislative party resources is now dedicated to increasingly elaborate efforts to drive partisan messages in the news media.

Recently, scholars have begun to attend to congressional leaders' efforts to affect the parties' news coverage. Scholars have investigated the increased media visibility of congressional leaders (Harris 1998, 2005, 2013; Malecha and Reagan 2012), the development of messaging campaigns (Evans 2001; Evans and Oleszek 2002; Sellers 2010), leadership pressure on members to assist with messaging (Butler and Powell 2014), and individual members' willingness to participate in messaging efforts (Grimmer 2013; Groeling 2010). But there has been little work examining the extent to which the congressional parties' allocation of resources has shifted toward communications relative to the past. Nor has there been any systematic analysis of the types of messages congressional parties send or how such an extensive communications apparatus affects politics and relationships inside the legislative branch.

One way of tracking the parties' intensified focus on messaging is to examine the allocation of congressional staff to party communications functions. Figures 5.1 and 5.2 display the total number of aides working for congressional leadership offices between 1961 and 2015, as well as the share of that total with job titles in communications.[3] The figures are on two axes, with the bars indicating the number of leadership staffers and the lines showing the percentage working in communications. As

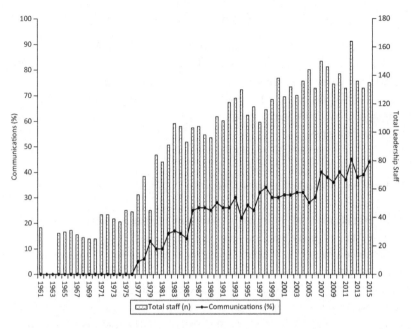

FIGURE 5.1. Total number of Senate leadership staffers and share in communications, 1961–2015

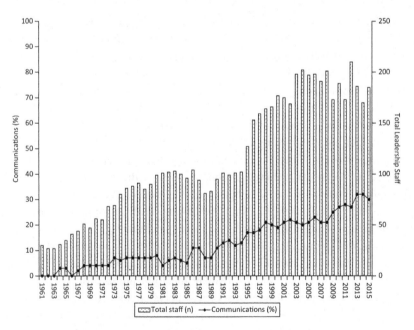

FIGURE 5.2. Total number of House leadership staffers and share in communications, 1961–2015

is evident in these two figures, there has been tremendous growth in the number of staff working for congressional leaders, as well as the share of these employees dedicated to partisan public relations. This increase far exceeds growth in legislative branch staffing overall (Peterson et al. 2010).

As shown in figure 5.1, there were no public-relations aides working for any of the Senate's party leadership offices before 1977. Between 1977 and 1986, the number of leadership staff more than doubled (from 46 to 104), while the share in communications quintupled (from 5 percent to 25 percent). Between 1986 and 1996, communicators held steady at around a quarter of all leadership staff as Senate leaders' total number of aides continued to grow. The share in communications moved up to 30 percent in 1997, remaining at that level until a jump to 40 percent in 2007. By the end of the time series, Senate leadership staff levels were at their highest point to date, and communicators approached half of the total (44 percent).

As shown in figure 5.2, the growth of communications in the House was more gradual, but the trend echoes that in the Senate. In the House of 1975, a grand total of six press aides worked for congressional leaders: one each for the Speaker of the House, the minority leader, and the majority whip, along with two editors and a publisher working for the Republican Conference. The share of leadership staff in communications held steady around or below 10 percent through the early 1990s. Because the total number of staff working for House leadership offices was on the rise, however, the number of party communicators was also steadily increasing throughout the 1980s. Between 1989 and 1999, the number of leadership staff doubled while the share working in communications nearly tripled (from 7 percent to 20 percent). After 2008, the share working in House party communications advanced to a quarter of all leadership aides. After 2013, the proportion of House leadership staff employed as communicators stood at or above 30 percent.

The list of communications job titles in 2015 offers some sense of the extensive specialization and division of labor involved. For example, the Speaker of the House employed a director for communications, a deputy director of communications, a digital communications director, an assistant communications director, two press secretaries, an assistant press secretary, a communications advisor, a director of public liaison, a director of outreach, a digital production manager, and two special events assistants. The office of the House Majority Leader employed a comparable (albeit smaller) array, augmented by a digital coordinator and

a director of external affairs. The Republican Conference employed a
director and deputy director of digital media, a director of coalitions, a
creative director, a design director, and a director of external relations.
House Democrats and Senate leaders were no less generously staffed
with communicators.

The growth in communications capabilities has not been confined to
leadership offices. Contemporary committees also employ communications aides who write and disseminate party talking points on the issues within their committees' jurisdictions. In 1975, congressional committees employed virtually no professional communicators. Among the
584 staffers working for all the standing committees of the House in
1975, there were two press assistants, one employed by the Agriculture
Committee and the other by the Ways and Means Committee. Among
the 489 staff working for the standing committees of the Senate in 1975,
there were no press aides. By 2015, however, every standing committee
in the House except for Ethics employed communicators, as did all the
standing committees in the Senate except for Rules and Administration.
In 2015, 13 percent of all House committee staffers worked on communications, as did 8 percent of Senate committee staffers.

The rise of the communicators signals a shift in Congress's priorities
in resource allocation. Congress has even cut back on other functions
while sustaining ever higher levels of staffing for communications. This
shift is not just a story of the growth of leadership offices, which long pre-
dates the turn toward public relations (Glassman 2012). Party leadership-
staff levels have been on the rise since the 1960s, as is evident in figures 5.1 and 5.2. But before 1980, the increased staffing for party offices
was focused on other purposes, such as enhancing the party's capabilities
to develop policy and to coordinate members and committees internally.
House leadership offices grew by 230 percent between 1961 and 1981, but
only 11 percent of that growth was focused on public relations. Similarly,
Senate leadership offices grew by 154 percent between 1961 and 1980, but
only 16 percent of that increase occurred in the area of communications.
By contrast, if we examine the growth of leadership staff since 1980, the
emphasis tilts far more strongly toward communications. In both the
House and the Senate, the number of people employed by leadership offices more than doubled after 1980. More than half of that total increase
(55 percent of the growth in the House, 61 percent in the Senate) is attributable to expansion of the parties' communications staffs.

Developments in committee staffing reflect a similar pattern. Committee staffs grew markedly between 1950 and 1980, but hardly any of these staffers were hired specifically to do communications.[4] Between 1980 and 2010, however, the overall level of committee staff in House and Senate declined, with House committee staff cut by 32 percent and Senate committee staff reduced by 5 percent (Peterson et al. 2010). Nevertheless, the share of committee staffs devoted to public relations grew during the same period.

Since 1980, members have taken more interest in augmenting their institutional capabilities for partisan communications than in improving their party or committee staffs as repositories of policy expertise. Longtime congressional insiders marvel at the shift. "Back then, we had one and a half people doing press," said one former press secretary who worked for House leadership in the 1980s and early 1990s. "Now there must be fifteen people at least. And I had to do the press back in the district, as well, because [the leader] did not have a separate press secretary who could handle that."[5] One senior committee staffer said, "There are fewer people working on policy for the committee than in the 1990s and more people working on communications. When I first came to the committee, there was a press person. But now there are many more. There are the social media people, the committee's Twitter feed. There is the coalitions director. Every committee now has one of these—someone to manage relationships between the committee and outside groups."[6] "The change in communications has been remarkable to me," said another former staffer. "When I started, the fax machine was whiz bang. We had one press secretary. . . . Now you've got communications directors, whole teams. People doing social media. The whole place is driven by tweeting."[7]

The Messages Parties Send

As discussed in chapter 3, the central purpose of party messaging is to increase the expected party differential (Downs 1957, 39) as a means of convincing voters that they should prefer one party to the other. To gain insight into how parties do this, it is helpful to draw upon concepts from Mayhew (1974). Mayhew argued that as members of Congress seek to promote their own personal reelection, they constantly engage in advertising, credit claiming, and position taking. All these activities are aimed at widening the "expected incumbent differential," meaning the perceived difference "between what an incumbent congressmen is likely to do if returned to office and what any possible challenger . . . would be likely to do" (Mayhew 1974, 39). Despite being developed to explain the behavior of individual members, these three concepts are also remarkably effective tools for analyzing party messaging. Parties continually engage in all three activities as they craft and publicize messages to differentiate their party from the opposition and thereby make the case for their own party's majority status. All these activities have one commonality: they are communications to external constituencies.

Advertising. Any examination of partisan communications quickly uncovers examples of advertising—as in, efforts to "create a favorable image but in messages having little or no issue content" (Mayhew 1974, 49). For example, parties cultivate their reputation by holding "listening sessions" with various constituencies. The Democratic Steering and Outreach Committee organizes such open-ended discussions, such as a March 13, 2013 meeting with fourteen "leaders in workforce development from across the country." Convening a meeting of this kind has advertising value for a party, as does a press release describing it. Similarly, parties offer many statements of their general goodwill toward the American people. House Republicans, for example, held a press conference in front of a sign that read, "Working for All Americans," in order to assure the public that "the House is focused on growing our economy, creating more jobs, and helping hardworking Americans all across the country."[8] Parties hold many such meetings and press conferences. In addition, the congressional parties constantly commemorate and acknowledge events, incidents, and special occasions. House Republicans put out a video paying homage to the contributions of Hispanics to American society for Hispanic Heritage Month (Nicks 2013). All the party leaders disseminated expressions of condolence to those affected by the 2012 massacre at Connecticut's Sandy Hook Elementary School.

Advertising is useful for improving a party's image. It is also useful for tarnishing the opposing party's image. In many cases, the goal is to somehow embarrass the opposition. Minority Leader Boehner, for example, recommended what he called "entrepreneurial insurgency" tactics to all the Republican committee press secretaries, encouraging them to capture Democratic witnesses or members in gaffes on video (Kucinich 2009). The House Republican Conference produced a video ridiculing President Barack Obama for completing his NCAA basketball brackets on time while failing to meet the deadline for submitting a budget to Congress (Slack 2013).[9] House Minority Whip Steny Hoyer (D-MD) wanted to make sure readers saw a selection of editorial cartoons mocking the Republican Party's handling of the government shutdown.[10] Taken together, congressional parties produce a fair amount of public relations content designed to either promote their party image or undercut that of the opposition.

Credit Claiming and Blaming. Partisan communications also seek to disseminate claims that one party is responsible for good policies and the opposing party is responsible for undesirable policies. Credit claiming and blaming are distinct from advertising in that these communications contain more issue content and attribute responsibility for outcomes.

Parties can claim credit for policy much more easily than individual members can. The challenge for individual members is to establish personal responsibility for any outcome amid a Congress of 534 other members (Mayhew 1974, 53–61). Parties, by contrast, do not find it difficult to claim credit for the passage of laws or good policy outcomes, including for far-downstream effects such as lower unemployment, declining deficits, or a growing economy—matters for which no individual member of Congress could credibly assert responsibility. Democratic communications, for example, crowed about any good economic news throughout the Obama presidency.

Parties also make use of a negative variation on credit claiming: blaming. Incumbent members of Congress cannot usually blame their challengers for adverse policy outcomes. Partisan communications, however, lambaste the other party for any and all policy problems for which it might conceivably be held responsible. Republican communications trumpeted every notable bad economic indicator during the Obama presidency, as well as news and reports of problems with the implementation of the Affordable Care Act. House Minority Leader Nancy Pelosi declared that "the GOP earns an 'F' on the first 100 days of Congress" for its "failed leadership."[11] Speaker John A. Boehner wanted it known that President Obama was responsible for blocking the construction of the Keystone Pipeline.[12] One could expand this list of examples, but anyone who follows contemporary US politics is more than familiar with the phenomenon.

Position Taking. Like individual members, parties enunciate "judgmental statements" on political issues (Mayhew 1974, 61). Leaders employ many different means to communicate the party's positions. They put together party-agenda documents, hold press conferences, and stage media events. Aides prepare talking points on most all issues before Congress, along with graphs, videos, and other supporting materials. Leaders force the chamber to take "message votes," which they distinguish from votes that are actually intended to affect policy outcomes (see chapter 6). Senate Republican staffers sometimes track how much time senators of each party have consumed on the floor, and metrics are provided to members during the party's weekly lunches. "We're a competitive lot," noted Sen. John Cornyn (R-TX), "so when you tell Republican senators that we're being out-spoken by Democrats, it gets 'em going" (Parnes 2008). As with partisan credit claiming and advertising, partisan position taking frequently takes a negative form—as in, communications attempting to refute the other party's policy positions.

In sum, advertising, credit claiming, and position taking are all useful activities for parties making their case for majority status. One important difference between communications designed for partisan purposes and those designed for individual members' reelection is that partisan communications are much more focused on the opponent. Individual members say much less about their challengers. In fact, incumbents continually work to enhance the probability of their reelection when they do not know if, when, or where an opponent will emerge. Even after individual members of Congress learn their opponents' identity, they prefer to avoid dignifying challengers by name as long as possible. By contrast, parties seeking institutional control in a two-party system always know their rival's identity: the other party. Given the competitiveness of the two parties in the battle for control of Congress, parties never have the luxury of refusing to "go negative." Like incumbents facing a competitive challenger (Kahn and Kenney 1999), parties in an era of alternating majorities are obliged to draw clear contrasts. The upshot is the production of a steady stream of negative attacks.

The Volume of Partisan Communications

Contemporary party communicators generate an enormous volume of content. This content takes a wide variety of forms: blog posts, press releases, policy notes, links to news stories, annotated photographs, tweets, and reports. Generally speaking, such communications are aimed at steering political dialogue in the party's favor. Most are only a couple paragraphs long. Many could be characterized as "pitches" designed to shape media coverage by encouraging journalists or friendly commentators to write about a particular subject or adopt a favored angle. In some cases, the items are just video clips uploaded with a title and brief description.

Table 5.1 offers a tally of the items released by each House and Senate leadership office during 2013, excluding tweets. The list sums to 3,096 items, which averages 8.5 items a day all year, including Saturdays, Sundays, and congressional recesses. For the offices that generate the most content, such as the House Speaker, House minority leader, and whip, the flow of output is relatively consistent from day to day. The Speaker's

TABLE 5.1. **Tally of public-relations output, House and Senate leadership offices, excluding tweets, 2013**

	Office	Web address	Output
House Republicans	Speaker	www.speaker.gov	613 blog posts and press releases
	Majority leader	www.majorityleader.gov	221 press releases
	Majority whip	www.majoritywhip.gov	53 blog posts and press releases
	GOP Conference	www.gop.gov	222 blog posts
	GOP Policy Committee	www.policy.house.gov	18 press releases
Total			*1,127 items*
House Democrats	Minority leader	www.democraticleader.gov	510 blog posts and press releases
	Minority whip	www.democraticwhip.gov	537 blog posts and press releases
	Democratic caucus	www.dems.gov	78 press releases
Total			*1,125 items*
Senate Democrats	Majority leader	www.democrats.senate.gov	164 press releases and blog posts
	Democratic Policy and Communications Center	www.dpcc.senate.gov	45 press releases, reports, and blog posts
	Democratic Steering and Outreach Committee	www.dsoc.senate.gov	58 press releases
Total			*267 items*
Senate Republicans	Minority leader	www.mcconnell.senate.gov	252 press releases
	GOP Policy Committee	www.rpc.senate.gov	236 policy notes and statements
	Republican Conference	www.republican.senate.gov	89 blog posts
Total			*577 items*
Grand total			*3,096 items*

blog posted two to three items on average each day of the work week. The Hoyer Press Staff Blog on the DemocraticWhip.gov site was only slightly less prolific. The Senate Republican Policy Committee put out a daily "policy note" when the Senate was in session. This continuous production of content reflects the number of staff aides employed specifically for this purpose.

The Content of Partisan Communications

For insight into the types of messages these offices disseminated, I took a stratified random sample constituting 10 percent of all the items released by each leadership office during 2013. Each item was classified into one of six categories: positive advertising, negative advertising, credit claiming, blaming, position taking, and position refuting. The results are displayed in figure 5.3.

Among the output of leadership offices, "blaming" was the single most common type of communication. Fully 33 percent of all the items were efforts to tar the opposing party with responsibility for undesir-

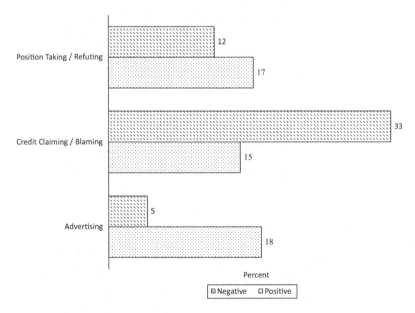

FIGURE 5.3. Content of public-relations items, House and Senate leadership offices, 2013
Source: Stratified random sample (*n* = 336) drawn from items in table 5.1.

able actions or policy outcomes. If one examines all the communications aimed at assigning responsibility for policy actions or outcomes, only 32 percent reflected a party's effort to take credit for positive outcomes, while 68 percent were efforts to attribute negative outcomes to the opposition. Both parties also showed a strong preference for "blaming" over "credit claiming" when the two parties' output was analyzed separately. Perhaps the parties have calculated that messages of blame will be more persuasive to a public that trusts government so little and holds such a low opinion of Congress. Perhaps the emphasis on blame also reflected the limited opportunity for credible credit claiming in the context of 2013, given the sluggish economy and the passage of few major laws. Still, it is fair to conclude from these data that partisan finger-pointing was the primary job description of the communications professionals working in Congress's party leadership offices.

Items classified as "advertising" (22 percent of the total) and "position taking" (29 percent) were each less common than those classified as "credit claiming / blaming" (48 percent). In contrast to credit claiming and blaming, advertising and position-taking messages were somewhat more positive than negative. More of the position-taking items were efforts to affirm one's own party's positions (58 percent) than to refute the opposing party's stances (42 percent). Similarly, both parties' advertising was usually an effort to burnish their own reputation (80 percent) rather than tear down the opposition (20 percent). Unlike with advertising and credit claiming / blaming, where there was no difference between the parties in the percentage of positive and negative items, there was some partisan difference in position taking, in that 79 percent of the Democrats' position-taking items were positive efforts to defend their own party's positions, as compared to only 44 percent of the Republicans' items.[13] Most Republican position taking was aimed at refuting Democratic positions. A presidency controlled by the opposing party afforded a target-rich environment for Republican efforts to shoot down Democratic policy positions. Meanwhile, a party's control of the presidency seems to oblige the president's copartisans to defend the administration's issue stances.

The Role and Function of Party Communicators

Foremost among their roles, party communicators are coordinators. If the goal is to "drive the narrative," they see it as the first order of busi-

ness to get everyone in the party "on message" saying the same things—
repeatedly. "There's a simple rule," said Republican messaging consultant Frank Luntz. "You say it again, and you say it again, and you say
it again, and you say it again, and you say it again, and then again and
again and again and again, and about the time that you're absolutely sick
of saying it is about the time that your target audience has heard it for
the first time" ("Lexington: The War of the Words" 2013).

Message Development and Dissemination

To get everyone on message, it is first necessary for members of a party
to agree upon a message or set of messages to push. Party leaders take
the initiative in message development. They do so in consultation with
pollsters. "Every Monday night," said one Senate leadership staffer, "the
leadership team . . . meets to talk strategy. They bring in pollsters . . . and
they talk about how to set up votes and how to coordinate the floor."[14]
Leaders must confer broadly within the party—with factions, committee
chairs, and interested individuals. "It's a collaborative process," said one
senior staffer of message development. "[There are] lots of discussions
between committee and leadership staff."[15]

It is not always easy to find good issues. "It's fourteen months until
the midterm elections, and we don't have an issue yet!" bemoaned one
Democrat in the lead-up to 1990 (Balz 1989, A6). Another staffer spoke
of a message that misfired: "You can tell a messaging campaign isn't
working when people start making fun of you for it." One Republican
staffer joked about how badly the party's messaging went over one year:
"We really jumped the shark in '06, coming out with Terri Schiavo, then
turning to flag burning and the Balanced Budget Amendment. We were
dying! When [Sen. Dick] Durbin (D-IL) went to the floor to congratu-
late us for tackling such an important issue, that two documented flags
had been burned in the past X years, he was killing us!"[16]

There is widespread agreement among congressional communicators of both parties on the characteristics of an effective party message.
First, messages need to be concise.[17] As an example of just how concise,
one Senate Democrat described the talking points that a political consultant had provided during a closed door party meeting as "Here's our
30-second message, and here's our 10-second message" (Stanton 2010).
Second, a strong message will resonate beyond the Capitol. "Ideally, a
good messaging effort will center around an example, a story that really

illustrates your point, becomes a focus, a symbol of something larger," said another senior staffer.[18] Good leaders, said one veteran staffer, are those who are "highly adept at seeing the intersection of politics and policy. They can look at policy and see what elements will connect with people."[19] Third, a good message will not only get attention; it will also define the differences between the parties in an advantageous way. "One example [of an effective message] was the per-child tax credit," recollected a longtime Republican staffer. "When it was first introduced in Congress, Democrats didn't support it. It created a clear messaging opportunity—a real 'us versus them' exercise. . . . I was telling my colleagues, 'This is awesome. You don't realize how awesome this is. It *defines* who we are.'"[20] "With messaging, the goal is to highlight values," said another experienced communicator. "The values come first, and then you add in the statistics, data, etc."[21]

There are numerous challenges in getting widespread agreement within the party on a message that meets all these criteria. Fellow partisans do not automatically agree on the value of any particular language, issues, or priorities. "Getting everyone in the tent is hard," said Sen. Claire McCaskill (D-MO). "Getting everyone to speak with one voice is near impossible" (Steinhauer and Hernandez 2011). Message development is often a search for the "lowest common denominator," a term that came up in more than one interview.[22] Party meetings are important settings where collective strategy is discussed. "The party lunches are so key each week," said one leadership staffer. "The discussions that happen here really show the direction of the caucus. You see people in a group setting, what issues generate emotion."[23]

The search is for issues that can be embraced across the party's ideological continuum. Asked who is good at message development, one former Democratic staffer said, "Stabenow (D-MI) is not good at it. She thinks she's good at it. But she's too liberal."[24] Asked about the challenges of message development, another communications staffer recommended that I speak with some outside groups skilled at helping the party develop messages that work across the ideological spectrum: "Third Way has been very good on messaging for swing states and red states." To ensure that an issue is working well for message purposes, party communicators monitor whether key factions within the party are refusing to participate in the effort: "What's the uptake on our messaging ideas? We feel it's working if the uptake is widespread and not just limited to senators in safe states."[25]

Once there is agreement on messaging, communicators are enlisted to help with the implementation of the strategy. They line up members to speak on the issue, both on the floor and to media outlets. They assist members with media bookings. They liaise with outside groups, keeping them informed about timing and content. They line up "outside validators" who will testify in support of the party's positions.[26] They prepare documents, videos, talking points, recess packets, posters, and graphs. They advise and encourage members in the use of social media. They promote particular Twitter hashtags. They contrive creative names for bills, such as "Reducing Barack Obama's Unsustainable Deficit Act" or the "Big Oil Welfare Repeal Act" (Simon 2011). They organize events and briefings. They reach out to media and try to sell journalists on the party's favored narratives.

There is a tremendous amount of advance planning involved with message dissemination. Majority parties sketch out a timeline weeks in advance. Coordination efforts extend beyond Congress itself to include outside groups allied to the party. One communicator explained, "You've blocked in the days you'll be doing what. You have to figure out how to loop in the third-party groups. The 'block' dominates your life. In the House, you know the schedule. The Senate, of course, can slip. You get the fact sheets ready. You pull together the press conferences. It's all about driving the message."[27] The minority party has more difficulty with planning, as it lacks agenda-setting power and is usually placed in a reactive role. The minority can't give a lot of advance notice to its own outside groups. "You try to tee up your groups," said one minority-party communicator. "There are many weekly meetings with outside groups—lots of them. . . . [But] we can't control the schedule. . . . We can't tell them: this is what is going to be happening two weeks from today."[28]

It is hard to sustain the momentum behind a messaging campaign. Even after messages are identified and agreed upon, the campaigns often "don't live beyond a press release or initial roll-out. . . . They're just forgettable, and they fall flat." Members' commitment to a messaging effort may "just peter out," and they may fail to follow through on the plan.[29] Members who make a special effort on behalf of the party "are sometimes given an official 'pat on the back' in the caucus meeting for how much they've been out there," noted one senior Senate staffer.[30]

A desired outcome of messaging efforts is an "echo chamber" effect, a term that came up repeatedly in the interviews.[31] An echo chamber is where a party starts hearing its message repeated by others. "With messaging, you want to hear that echo—where your talking points start to come back to you from constituents, on the phones in the office, in the op-eds," explained one senior staffer.[32] Communicators systematically monitor the "metrics." "You track TV hits, coverage on local news media, the number of [Facebook] likes, a good interview during drive time," explained one veteran former communicator.[33] Another staffer said, "You want to be earning media coverage. With earned media, you're not reacting to the press's questions. You're setting the agenda, getting them to talk about the issues you want discussed."[34] The goal is to "move needles," a communicator's term of art.[35] In other words, the hope is that messaging efforts will actually shape the public's views of the issue and the party. "Messaging is successful when you win in the court of public opinion," summed up one former communicator.[36]

Communicators repeatedly emphasized how difficult their job is—how hard it is to have any effect on news reporting or public opinion. "Most of the time [messaging] doesn't work," said one senior staffer.[37] "It's increasingly difficult to break through. People get their news from partisan sources. You just can't cut through the partisanship. And then the public is just tuning out because it's all such a mess," lamented one longtime former communicator.[38] "One of the greatest challenges is the speed of the media cycle, and it's only accelerating," said another communicator. "In order to drive a message, you have to have people constantly bringing it up."[39] "We forget that the minute you get out of town, people just don't know what's been going on up here," reflected another staffer. "It's tough to get away and appreciate what the average person is thinking."[40]

Communications in the Power Structure

Capitol Hill communications has become a profession, and "communicator" is a professional identity. Communicators draw inspiration and use language from private-sector marketing and advertising. Asked why Senate Democrats had merged their "war room" functions with the Senate Democratic Policy Committee in 2010, one communicator explained, "We wanted to have the product-development team integrated with the advertising team. We gather information about what the public is concerned with, drawing on polling data. And we have the policy team directly interfacing with the communications team."[41] Communicators see themselves as possessing specialized knowledge, albeit not about public

policy. Their role is to "give members advice on best practices," said another communicator. "People need to know some policy, but we don't
hire policy specialists."[42] Communicators have their own professional
jargon. "Our effort will work to help build dynamic, multi-layered,
outside-the-Beltway coalitions that will help the Republican Conference
explain the value of our policies," stated one newly hired coalitions director (Kucinich and Palmer 2009, 3).

Communicators are not merely low-level functionaries in the power
hierarchies on Capitol Hill. It is never easy to measure influence or prestige in an organization. But the rise of the legislative-branch communicator is significant not just for what it reveals about the increasing importance of communications to members of Congress. Many of these
communicators are themselves influential staffers. "Back in the 1980s,
senators would have a press secretary, often some young woman with no
influence in the office who would answer press queries," noted one former leadership aide. "But those are big jobs on the Hill now, some of
the biggest jobs up there."[43] Another staffer acknowledged the existence
of power struggles between policy and communications staff. "When
you hear policy people complaining about hiring all those communicators . . . legislative folks bristle at the elevation of communicators in decision making," said one senior Senate staffer. "Communicators are now
at the management level. They are in the room and they make decisions.
It's different now."[44]

One gauge of communicators' influence can be obtained from *Roll
Call*'s "Fabulous 50" list of the most influential staffers on Capitol Hill.[45]
The list is compiled by the reporters and editors at the newspaper based
on "their institutional knowledge of what positions hold the most power"
(Wolfensberger 2014). Such a measure should obviously be taken with a
grain of salt as a measure of influence itself. It is nevertheless useful as
an indicator of perceived influence. *Roll Call* is a Capitol Hill newspaper, and its reporters and editors interact closely with members and staff.
A list of influential staffers that did not track with conventional wisdom
on the Hill would not be accepted and would surely generate sufficiently
negative feedback for the newspaper to end the practice or modify the
rankings. The newspaper has been publishing the list for decades now.

Figure 5.4 displays the percentage of the "Fabulous 50" list employed
as communicators. "Communicators" encompasses those with titles in
communications, as well as those who head up organizations primarily devoted to party communications, such as the directors of the congressional

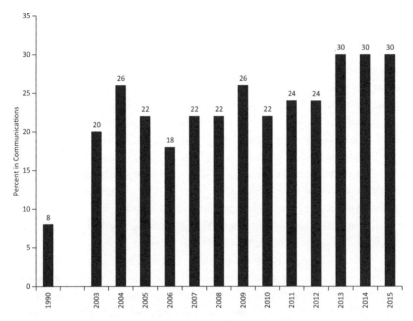

FIGURE 5.4. Communications staffers on *Roll Call*'s "Fabulous 50" list

campaign committees, the Republican Conference, and the Senate Democratic Policy and Communications Center. Nearly a third of the staffers
on the "Fabulous 50" list hold jobs centered in political communications.
Furthermore, the share of the top fifty staffers in communications has
been rising. In 1990, only 8 percent of the list was communicators, while
the bulk was staff directors for standing committees. By the first decade of
the twenty-first century, communicators constituted just over 20 percent
of the list. Since 2013, communicators have made up 30 percent.

The interviews conducted for this project pointed to some systematic sources of conflict between policy and communications functions in
many Capitol Hill offices. "There is a tension between the messaging
people and the policy people," acknowledged one senior Senate staffer.
"The tension exists everywhere in offices all over the Hill. It's in personal offices. In committee offices, the tension is even more pronounced
because you have so many real policy experts on the committees."[46]
When I asked for the source of conflict, one staffer explained, "Communicators sometimes will burn the people that you need to do deals
with. . . . Bad communications can torpedo potential deals."[47] "Commu-

nicators want the sharpest message," said another staffer, while "policy people are more conservative, more deliberative."[48]

For their part, communicators complain that policy staffers are politically naive. Speaking of the policy experts on committee staffs, one aide remarked with some feeling, "Of all the people on the Hill, [the policy staffers on committees] are probably the biggest believers that the 'legislative utopia' exists—that we can just all sit down together and hash out the issues. They are often blind to the larger political realities that members have to deal with. It's a comfortable and lovely job if you don't have to worry about such things."[49] Communicators also complain that policy experts fail to understand how hard it is to message effectively. "Although people have their criticisms of messaging, it's difficult to do it well," said another senior aide. "You can't have anything extraneous. You have to be disciplined. You can't use an eight-page memo—the sort of thing our policy analysts will produce. It has to be a sentence."[50]

The senior aide explained the tension between communications and policy staffers as stemming from messaging's tendency to oversimplify in either defending or criticizing public policies negotiated in the legislative process. "Sometimes you hear policy people say that the communicators are 'dumbing things down.' . . . But you can't message exactitude. You can't message nuance." One endemic frustration for policy-oriented staff is that the party's overall messaging strategy does not permit credit claiming for the compromises and policy adjustments that a minority party successfully negotiates in legislation. "You can't say nice things about a bill you're going to oppose. So even if your policy person got some good things in the Medicare prescription drug bill, you can't get credit for it. If you're opposed to the bill, you're opposed to it. You can't message that there are forty-five bad things in the bill, but a couple of good things, too. You can't get credit for some little part of it." The same constraint applies to messaging around legislation a party is going to support. A message cannot concede that there are downsides to a package a party nevertheless advocates. "The employer mandate in the Affordable Care Act (ACA) was not a Democratic proposal. This was forced on us by Max Baucus (D-MT) in his effort to win support from Olympia Snowe (R-ME). The idea was to keep businesses from dropping their health-care coverage and foisting them off onto Obamacare. . . . And then we had to go out and defend this aspect of the ACA, even though we hated it."[51] Messaging is a blunt instrument. Fine distinctions cannot be drawn in partisan messaging campaigns. The simplicity of messaging stands at odds with the complexity of public policy—a continual source of friction between messaging and legislating in Capitol Hill offices.

In sum, not only do communicators account for a much larger share of congressional staff; they are also seen as important and influential in the Capitol Hill hierarchy. Their perspective is not infrequently at odds with those specializing primarily in policy. Party messaging drives an "us versus them" narrative that stands in tension with the "half a loaf" outcomes inherent in the legislative process. Nevertheless, there is consensus that communicators are much more influential in Congress than they used to be. As one veteran former staffer said, "These days, communications seem to be driving policy more than in the past, rather than the other way around."[52]

Drivers of Institutional Change

One cannot attribute all the growth in the public-relations capacities of congressional parties to the increased competition for control of Congress. The growth of congressional parties' public-relations apparatus has not occurred in a vacuum. The shift is hardly confined to partisan offices alone. The contemporary Congress as a whole is much more oriented toward outside audiences than the Congress of the 1950s and 1960s (Harris 1998; Malecha and Reagan 2012; Sinclair 1989, 2006). Similarly, the job of press secretary has proliferated in individual member offices, reflecting a preference for professional communications work throughout the legislative branch (Cook 1989; Hess 1991).

The rise of the congressional communicator, in turn, mirrors changes inside and outside of government more broadly. The public-relations professional has become a fixture of all large organizations. One study estimated the cost of public relations and advertising among seven cabinet-level agencies at $1.6 billion over thirty months between 2003 and 2005 (US General Accountability Office 2006). Congressional parties are not alone in spending huge sums on flacks.

The twenty-four-hour news cycle undoubtedly places tremendous demands on Congress to supply material and cope with journalists' queries in an increasingly fast-paced media environment. Interview subjects referenced the changing media environment as a factor driving enlarged staffing for communications in Congress. "Technology and the pace of media have changed so much," said one staffer. "You stay silent on Twitter at your peril. You have to have people doing communications all the time to respond to the twenty-four-hour news cycle. There is so much ground to cover."[53] A former staffer marveled at the contrast between the present and his experiences in the 1980s and 1990s: "I remember during the late 90s, we would get together in ___'s office in the morning to watch the clips from the night before. We would watch the three networks. That's all you looked at! You didn't need to keep track of anything during the day, at all."[54] Now, said another former staffer, "[with] the explosion of news sites, the 24/7 nature of news, the rise of blogging . . . everything moves so much faster—[and it's] only accelerated further with Twitter."[55]

Still, though, the content analysis above revealed that congressional communication is by no means primarily reactive in nature. It is not just aimed at providing information in response to journalists' queries. Journalists do not ask for all the spin being churned out by congressional party organs. Instead, the goal of partisan communications is to affirmatively influence news reporting so as to shape public perceptions. Parties want to drive the coverage, to "win the day." They want to generate "earned media" where they are "not reacting to the press's questions."[56] They aim for an echo-chamber effect. A staff presence designed only to respond to questions from the media would be substantially smaller than the one Congress employs. After all, the size of the Washington press corps—encompassing all media outlets with a presence in DC—declined after the mid-1990s (Pew Research Center 2009), while the number of communicators in Congress continued to expand.

The argument being advanced here is that the intensification of party competition for control of Congress fuels the growth of partisan communications. In a media environment that has seen so much change since the 1980s, it is not possible to say precisely how much of these developments have been driven by competition. Nevertheless, the analysis above establishes that much of this communication is explicitly partisan in nature, in that it consists of efforts to promote the image of one's own party and harm the opposition's. A less competitive environment would generate fewer incentives to draw such contrasts. If one party held a dominant congressional majority and its opposition perceived little or no opportunity to regain control, one would expect a reallocation of legislative branch resources away from partisan communications to other purposes. In addition, the task for communicators would likely devolve more toward answering media queries without attempting to drive a partisan message aimed at competitive advantage.

Analyzing the pace and timing of staff changes permits some additional leverage on the role of party competition in contributing to the rise of partisan communications in Congress. First, it is notable that public-relations professionals arrived relatively late to congressional leaders. Looking to individual member offices, the growth of professional communications occurred in the 1960s and 1970s, well before the explosion of public-relations capabilities documented here among congressional leaders. By the time the congressional parties first began hiring communicators, nearly every senator and the vast majority of House members already had press secretaries (Cook 1989; Hess 1991). If changes in the media environment alone were responsible for the shifts, it is not clear why the congressional parties would be so much slower than personal offices in bulking up their communications capabilities.

Second, both news accounts and interview subjects point to minority parties seeking to regain power as a source of innovation in messaging. "Desperation breeds innovation," reflected one senior House staffer. "We had seen the success of what the Republicans had done [in winning the majority in 1994]. They were able to do it because they had to be creative" in drawing the differences between the parties.[57] Casting about for a new approach following the landmark 1980 elections, for example, House and Senate Democrats convened a high-level strategy meeting in 1981 with the goal of coordinating around a set of themes for the 1982 elections. Democrats had not held a meeting like this for decades, but the outcome of the 1980 elections was a wake-up call that sparked rethinking. "Our common thread today," said Rep. Charles B. Rangel (D-NY) at the gathering, "is that we're losers. In the past, we've never had to get along; we've been able to get by just tolerating each other. Now we've reached the point we have to figure out what we do agree on" (Broder 1981, A4). Rangel explicitly points to the loss of power as a motivation for party members to get better organized, to find points of agreement, and to do more than merely "tolerate" one another.

A minority party may have stronger drive to innovate as it looks for a path back to power (see Klinkner 1994). In Congress, losing parties seem to feel special pressure to reform and enhance their messaging operations. It is not unusual to encounter news stories documenting how a new minority party is now "overhauling" its message operation (Kahn 1995). "In the face of stouter Democratic majorities," begins a typical report, "House Republicans have bulked up their press operations to try to steer the Beltway dialogue their way" (McPike 2009).

Figure 5.5 displays separately for each party the percentage of staff in communications for each year between 1961 and 2012. One of the most notable patterns is that minority-party House and Senate Republicans began devoting staff resources to communications well before the majority-party Democrats. Indeed, House Republicans devoted a share of their small leadership staff budget to public relations all through the 1970s.[58] Senate Republicans hired their first communications specialists in 1977. Reporters at the time observed that Republicans were reorganizing their staffs to develop policy alternatives to "take to the public in the next election" (Malbin 1977).

Senate Democrats, by contrast, only began to escalate their spending on public relations after losing the majority in 1980. Newly in the minority, Democratic Leader Robert C. Byrd (D-WV) hired a small communications staff for the Senate Democratic Policy Committee for the first time. He appointed the high-profile Greg Schneiders, a former aide to President Jimmy Carter, as communications director in 1981. Schneiders "now regularly supplies reporters and Democratic offices with multicolored materials filled with the alleged failures of the Reagan administration," noted one report the following year (Cohen 1982b).

After 1980, both Senate parties drastically escalated expenditures on public relations. Democrats first caught up to Republicans in their share of staff devoted to communications in 1988, just after they had resumed control of the Senate in 1987. Between 1988 and 1996, the two Senate parties allocated roughly equal shares of their leadership staff to public relations (around 25 percent). After the Republican take-over in 1994, however, the new minority-party Democrats intensified their communications efforts until they began to substantially outspend Republicans in 1996 (at 37 percent of their leadership staff). Democrats continued to outspend Republicans between 1996 and 2012. After the disappointing outcome of the 2004 elections, Senate Democrats under Minority Leader Harry Reid (D-NV) established a "war room," organized to churn out rapid response to Republican claims and coordinate the Democratic Party message (Grove 2005). Then, following the 2010 elections, when Republicans failed to win control of the Senate despite a highly favorable political environment, Senate Republicans stepped up

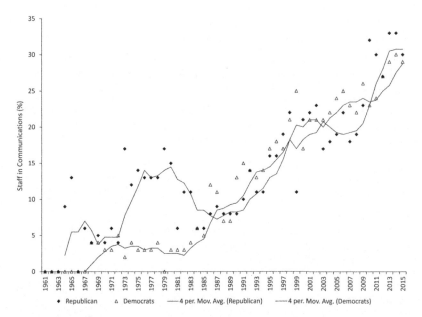

Panel A: House Parties

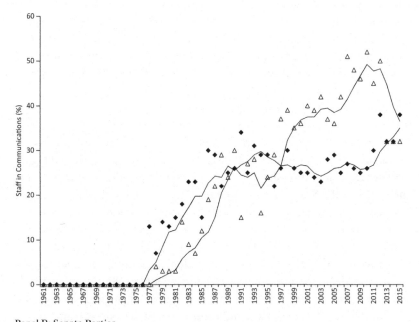

Panel B: Senate Parties

FIGURE 5.5. Priority on communications in party staff allocations, 1961–2015
Note: Trend lines are four-year moving averages.

expenditures on communications (from 26 percent of leadership staff in 2010 to 42 percent in 2012). After 2012, Senate Republicans and Democrats stood at rough parity in their allocations on public relations.

Patterns in the growth of partisan communications in the House bear similarities to the Senate. The discrepancy between the two parties was rather wide during the 1970s, when House Republicans had begun using the Republican Conference to publicly promote the party while House Democrats had no comparable leadership office devoted to communications. House Democrats only began to prioritize public relations after the 1980 elections. In 1979, none of the top leaders of the Democratic Party even employed a press secretary; by 1983, all the top leaders of the Democratic Party had press secretaries. Speaker Tip O'Neill (D-MA) hired Chris Matthews as his press secretary in 1981 (Cohen 1982b) and assumed a higher level of visibility on television news than any previous House Speaker (Harris 1998).

House Democratic and Republican expenditures on public relations closely tracked one another as both parties steadily increased the priority placed on communications from 6 percent of their leadership staff on average in 1985 to around 12 percent in the early 1990s. After they lost their House majority in 1994, Democrats revamped and strengthened their public-relations capabilities throughout their years in the minority, going from 14 percent of leadership staff devoted to communications in 1994 to 25 percent in 2006. Following the loss of their majority in 2006, Republicans redoubled their efforts with another expansion of communications staff. After 2008, the National Republican Congressional Committee explicitly advised House Republicans to "hire higher-level communications staffers to match their legislative directors—in terms of talent and pay" (McPike 2009). By 2010, House Republicans had swelled their staff share working in communications to 32 percent. In 2015, like the Senate parties, the two House parties allocated roughly the same share of staff (~30 percent) to communications.

For additional insight into the institutionalization of partisan communications, table 5.2 displays regression models of the priority congressional parties place on communications over time. The dependent variable is the percentage of party leadership staff dedicated to communications in each party in each year from 1961–2015. Model 1 contains a time trend counter, a variable indicating the years *Post1980*, and an interaction term, *Time trend*post-1980*, to test for a shift in the slope of the growth after 1980. Results indicate that the share of staff allocated

TABLE 5.2. **Predicting priority on communications in party staff allocations**

Variables	Model 1	Model 2	Model 3
Time trend	.42***	.65***	.42***
	(.12)	(.05)	(.12)
Party in minority			6.28***
			(1.71)
Post-1980	−2.85		1.02
	(2.52)		(2.64)
Time trend*post-1980	.29**		.29**
	(.13)		(.13)
Post-1994		6.50	
		(.13)	
Time trend*post 1994		−.10	
		(.12)	
Minority*post-1980			−7.69***
			(1.98)
Constant	−1.09		−4.23**
	(1.45)		(1.64)
Observations	220	220	220
R-squared	.76	.72	.78

Note: The dependent variable is the percentage of party leadership staff dedicated to communications in each party (i)—meaning House Democrats, House Republicans, Senate Democrats, and Senate Republicans—in each year (t) from 1961 to 2015. The models are ordinary least squares with fixed effects for the four party units.
$*p < .05; **p < .01; ***p < .001.$
Congressional parties stepped up the rate of growth in their communications staffs after 1980. The 1994 elections do not mark a similar shift in the trend line. Before 1980, minority parties allocated a larger share of their staff to communications than did majority parties. Since 1980, both majority and minority parties have placed similar priority on communications.

to communications grew over the whole period, but the rate of increase in communications was steeper after 1980 than it was before. Model 2 is similar to model 1 but tests for an effect after 1994. Results reveal no statistically significant shift in the slope of the trend after 1994. Put simply, 1980 seems to have been a more important turning point in the development of party communications than 1994.

Model 3 adds in another set of variables, *Party in minority* and *Minority*post-1980,* to ascertain whether minority parties dedicate higher percentages to communications functions than majority parties and, if so, whether that pattern is more or less pronounced after 1980. Taken together, the positive coefficient for *Party in minority* ($p < .001$) and the negative coefficient for *Minority*post-1980* ($p < .001$) reveal that minority parties allocated more of their staff to communications before 1980. Minority parties in Congress allocated almost twice as large a share of their staffs to communications as did majority parties during the pre-1980 period (13 percent for minority parties as compared to 7.4 percent for majority parties). After 1980, however, majority and minority parties brought to parity the share of staff they dedicated to communications.

These results are consistent with the view that 1980 ushered in an era of intensified party competition. Before 1980, the majority-party Democrats perceived themselves as relatively secure in power. Meanwhile, the minority-party Republicans apprehended some (albeit remote) possibility for change and allocated a modest share of their small staffs to communications. After 1980, however, both majority and minority parties placed heavy and growing emphasis on communications. Under these more competitive circumstances, majority parties had reason to worry about the possibility of losing control, and minority parties began to see themselves as potential majority parties. Watching one another closely, members pressed their leaders to improve their party's capacity for communications by citing concern about competitive disadvantage relative to the opposition (see, for example, Bolton 2007). Both ambitious minorities and insecure majorities perceive a pressing need to invest in communications.

In short, the history of how House and Senate parties built their public-relations capabilities over time appears to relate to competition for two-party control. Like all large organizations since the 1960s, congressional parties would almost certainly have increased their capacity for professional communications. But the pace and pattern of this growth also seem linked to the parties' competitive circumstances. Congressional parties were late adopters, in that individual member offices had already developed professional public-relations capabilities before the 1980s. Before 1980, the longtime minority Republicans were quicker to recognize the value of communications. But once alternation in congressional majorities reemerged after 1980, both parties' leaders began employing increasingly large numbers of communicators. Locked in an arms race, the two parties grew their communications capabilities in tandem with one another over the decades after 1980.

Parties as Public-Relations Operations

Since 1980, both congressional parties in both chambers have built elaborate infrastructures to wage continual partisan public-relations warfare against one another. Every day, these organizations generate output designed to improve their party's position relative to its opposition. Like incumbents seeking reelection, they advertise, claim credit, and take positions (Mayhew 1974). Unlike most incumbents, however, parties seeking majorities also constantly attack their opponents. Parties continually engage in blaming, position refuting, and negative advertising aimed at their party opponents.

Parties-as-PR-operations generate a steady stream of communications in pursuit of partisan advantage. The ultimate goal is to shape public opinion in ways favorable to the party's interests. The main task is thus to drive media coverage. To that end, parties seek consensus on a message. They then coordinate the activities of rank-and-file members, prodding them to take prepared talking points to the floor and to all forms of media. Party organizations drum up publicity via events, liaison with outside groups, media outreach, and every other available means. Party communicators hope to hear their own talking points echoing back in public and media discourse.

Whether messaging actually helps parties win additional seats in congressional elections is an open question, though there is some experimental evidence showing that party messaging can affect voters' choices (Butler and Powell 2014). What cannot be doubted, however, is that members believe that these efforts matter. Clearly, congressional parties have not waited for unambiguous empirical evidence that messaging works before sinking considerable resources into the enterprise.

The emergence of parties as PR operations has consequences that go beyond whatever effect they might have on elections. First, they do not elevate the quality or tone of congressional discourse. Party communications aimed at a public audience are simplistic. They are exercises in clear "us versus them" line drawing. When I asked one recently retired Senate staffer of many decades' experience to name one of the most important changes he had observed in the use of the Senate floor, he said, "The quality of debate and deliberation is nonexistent. It's very sad to have seen the trivialization of the Senate over the course of my career."[59] When members are speaking to outside audiences instead of to one another, the quality of deliberation deteriorates. "There's no actual debate," said another longtime House insider. "The quality of debate has changed when members aren't actually engaging each other. The floor has become a campaign stage."[60] As early as the late 1980s, *Washington Post* journalist Dan Balz (1989, A6) reported that "older senators" were worried about party leaders' efforts to strengthen party messaging, because they "believe the changes will debase the legislative process by bringing campaign-style politics—and a growing role for consultants—into the Capitol." Looking back, such worries seem prescient.

Second, the rise of party communications contributes to the hyperpartisan tone that characterizes the contemporary Congress. Competition for majority control of Congress is inescapably zero-sum in nature. In the battle for congressional majorities, any public perception that advantages Republicans necessarily disadvantages Democrats and vice versa. With these power stakes in mind, the political interests of Republicans and Democrats are diametrically at odds. Party communicators wage this ongoing battle daily. No doubt, the existence of an extensive communications apparatus engaged in constant partisan warfare has a significant effect on the general climate of Capitol Hill. Descriptions of the contemporary Congress employ words such as *toxic* and *hyperpartisan*.[61] Such a negative atmosphere is perhaps not surprising when one considers that attacks blaming the other party for some bad outcome or action are the single most common type of message being disseminated by congressional parties.

Put simply, a substantial workforce in Congress is employed for the purpose of devising ways to undermine the party opposition. If one takes the share of staff dedicated to communications as an indicator of priorities, communications has almost reached equal status with policy expertise among the functions of congressional parties. One might characterize the development as one way in which the United States already has public financing of congressional campaigns.

Third, the steady stream of partisan messaging emanating from Washington likely contributes to the rising partisanship of the American voter. The growing strength of partisan feeling in the electorate begins in the 1980s, after having steadily declined during the 1960s and 1970s (Bartels 2000; Hetherington 2001). Compared to their counterparts in the 1960s and 1970s, contemporary Americans are more likely to see important differences between the parties, place Democrats to the left of Republicans, and to rate the two parties as farther apart on a liberal-to-conservative spectrum. Relative to the 1960s and 1970s, American voters have also grown more loyal to parties in their voting behavior, with a marked decline in split-ticket voting (Bartels 2000; Smidt 2015; Stonecash et al. 2003). Levels of partisan bias and anger in the electorate have also increased (Abramowitz 2010; Brewer 2005), even among voters who are ideologically moderate in their views on political issues (Mason 2015). Hetherington (2001, 628) concludes that "elite polarization is driving the impressive increase in party-centric thinking at the mass level" (see also Smidt 2015). In light of the data presented here, it is important to recognize that the parties in Congress have invested considerable resources since 1980 precisely for the purpose of helping voters perceive these party differences. It is not merely that Republicans and Democrats in Congress wind up on opposite sides of roll-call votes more frequently. Parties in Congress work very hard to communicate their differences to external constituencies, and since 1980, they have steadily enlarged their communications infrastructure to do so.

Finally, understanding parties as PR operations also points to the ways in which congressional parties are organizations designed for electioneering as much as for policy making. Just as the quest for reelection encourages individual members of Congress to take positions and advertise themselves rather than do the hard work of building legislative coalitions (Mayhew 1974), parties' quest for majority control incentivizes similar varieties of "cheap talk." Viewing parties as PR operations highlights the ways in which congressional parties may well devote as much effort to communications as to policy making. Given the difficulty of legislating a party program in the complex, divided US system, the passage of legislation probably blurs party lines more often than it clarifies them. Devoting efforts to communications has no such downside for parties.

CHAPTER SIX

The Rise of the Partisan Message Vote

Every vote is about the next election. As soon as the last election is over, those who lost are thinking, "What can I do to get back in power?" And those who won are thinking, "What can I do to stay in power?" — Sen. Lindsey Graham (R-SC)[1]

Leaders are now expected to coordinate the use of the floor to advance partisan messages. Concurrent with the institutionalization of partisan communications, the partisan message vote—meaning a recorded vote deliberately crafted to dramatize party differences— has proliferated. Contemporary members of Congress regularly refer to "message" or "messaging" bills, "message votes," "message amendments," and "show votes." Message votes stand out from other votes not just because they are purposively framed to influence public perceptions. They are also distinct because they are not expected to change public policy. They are aimed at communication, not lawmaking. The goal is to "move the dial." These votes are a form of position taking, as defined by Mayhew (1974, 62): The "position taker is a speaker rather than a doer. The electoral requirement is not [to] make pleasing things happen but [to make] pleasing judgmental statements. The position itself is the political commodity."

Members are quite clear about how message votes differ from other votes that occur as a normal part of the legislative process. For example, during one 2011 colloquy with the Democratic leader discussing an upcoming vote, Republican Leader Mitch McConnell (R-KY) said, "The exercise we are going to have later today has nothing to do with making laws and making a difference. It is about making a point. We both know how to do that. We both know how to make points and make laws. What we are doing later today is not about making laws."[2] Drawing the same distinction in 2006, Sen. Robert C. Byrd (D-WV) said, "Instead of working to pass necessary legislation . . . we are engaged in yet another leadership-driven message dance."[3] "This is not real," stated Sen. Max Baucus (D-MT) in 2004. "It is not real legislation. . . . I am getting tired of message amendments. Mr. President, I want to legislate. I do not want to give messages."[4] On another occasion, Sen. Rick Santorum (R-PA) proposed to senators across the aisle, "We would be happy to give you a vote on your message amendment in exchange for you giving us a vote on something that is actually going to help people."[5] Members of both parties use the "message vote" terminology and distinguish between message votes and actual lawmaking.

This chapter argues that once control of Congress became more inse-cure and two-party competitive, parties sought to make better use of the floor as a platform for communicating partisan campaign messages. This chapter first lays out the strategy and tactics entailed, drawing upon per-spectives from interviews, the *Congressional Record*, and various news sources. Second, the chapter presents an analysis of amendments that re-ceive recorded votes on the Senate floor, one of the most common ways message votes are staged. Examining floor amendments receiving roll-call votes in the Senate between 1959 and 2013, I offer evidence that sen-ators make significantly more use of floor votes for purposes of partisan communications in the post-1980 period than did senators of the 1960s and 1970s. The implication is that there is more party-line voting in the contemporary Congress in part because floor votes have been enlisted as a weapon in the battle for party control of Congress.

How Message Votes Work

The logic behind partisan message votes is simple. A party brings to the floor an attractive-sounding idea with the following characteristics: (1) its members support it, (2) the other party opposes it, and (3) it is not expected to become law. Former Sen. Olympia Snowe (2013, 27) offers a more detailed explanation: "Much of what occurs in Congress today is what is often called 'political messaging.' Rather than putting forward a plausible, realistic solution to a problem, members on both sides offer legislation that is designed to make a political statement. Specifically, the bill or amendment is drafted to make the opposing side look bad on an issue and it is not intended to ever actually pass."

In the lead-up to the 2012 elections, for example, House Republicans sought to dramatize party differences on energy policy by bringing to the floor the "Congressional Replacement of President Obama's Energy Restricting and Job-Limiting Offshore Drilling Plan." Republicans were under no illusion that this bill would gain any traction in the Democratic-controlled Senate or win a presidential signature (Harder 2012). During the debate, Rep. Chris Van Hollen (D-MD) observed, "Here we are for the eleventh time in the past eighteen months wasting valuable floor time on another drill bill that has absolutely zero chance of becoming law."[6]

The failure of the attractive proposal is key to the strategy, because failure is precisely what argues for a change in party control. When the attractive idea is blocked from adoption, it offers a reason voters should elect more members of the proposing party so as to break the logjam. Republicans in 2012 hoped that Americans wanting development of more domestic oil and gas resources would get the message that they needed to elect Republicans. Such bills or amendments will only serve this political purpose when they go down to glorious defeat. If the legislative proposal became actual law, it would no longer be useful for electoral mobilization. "All we are doing today is having what we call message votes, show votes," observed Sen. Jim DeMint (R-SC). "They are set up to fail."[7]

As with the Republicans' 2012 drill bills, a party may opt to take repeated votes on the same basic policy idea. Just as congressional communicators coordinate members in repeating the same message, contemporary parties may stage failed roll-call votes on the same issues over and over. Holding votes on multiple occasions elevates an issue in the news repeatedly. Doing so also allows members to build a roll-call record that would enable a campaign to claim, as one senior Senate staffer explained, that "someone voted against X thirty-seven times."[8] Of the House's thirty-first attempt to repeal the 2009 Affordable Care Act, one journalist (Frates 2012) wrote, "If the definition of insanity is doing the same thing over and over again and expecting a different result, House Republicans are indeed certifiable. . . . But in an arena that rewards repetitive messaging, the laws of sanity don't hold."

Interviews with contemporary staffers confirm that both parties acknowledge the intentional staging of message votes. As one veteran Senate aide explained, "The leadership has spent a great deal of time working on how to control the floor agenda to help our message. . . . Particularly where we are not going to get legislation, we just focus on clarifying the differences between the parties. As part of this agenda, we have forced votes on the minimum wage, paycheck fairness, student-loan reforms, the Hobby Lobby decision. . . . It creates appealing messages for us, and it creates unappealing messages for the Republicans. We are consciously using the floor for this."[9] Discussing the amendments Republicans sought to offer, one Republican leadership aide said, "Those votes can be used against members in ads: 'You voted against this or that.'" He went on to note that these message amendments can cause political difficulty, even if they are tabled or otherwise handled via procedural motions: "The votes used in these [campaign] ads are often on procedural matters, so it doesn't matter how you handle them; they can always cause some trouble."[10] "All they're trying to do is come up with votes designed to make people look bad," said a senior Democratic staffer of the amendments Republicans had recently offered.[11]

Message amendments are not necessarily insincere, even though they are proposed in the recognition that they are not going to pass. One long-time former aide explained his party's message votes as follows: "With respect to the minimum wage, we think it's good policy, and we want to increase it. So we sincerely want to do it. But there are times when you realize it's not going to go forward, so you're holding votes to put people on the record, to embarrass the opponents of it, and to create fodder for the attack ad."[12] In such circumstances, "members aren't trying to legislate, aren't trying to work things out," said one veteran aide. "You're just out there jamming the bad guys. You're not trying to figure out what kind of deal can be done."[13] There are times when a party or a member will bring up bills in hopes of raising the visibility of an issue and building support for its eventual passage. One can use messaging as "a starting point. You raise awareness of a problem; you get people talking about it."[14] As discussed in chapter 3, however, party messaging is generally aimed at drawing clear "us versus them" lines. As such, negotiated legislative language that might potentially be acceptable to both parties does not work well for party messaging. "We're not putting things up there that are legislatively achievable," said another longtime leadership aide. "The hardest votes [for the other side] are often to vote against something moderate, but that's usually not what we're giving them with message votes."[15]

Because message amendments and bills are not expected to pass, there is little need to subject the legislative language to hearings, committee deliberation, or careful scrutiny. As Baucus pointed out during a 2001 debate, "We are in message amendment time. Nobody has looked at the substance. There have been no hearings on this."[16] To serve a messaging purpose, a legislative proposal need not be workable or carefully designed. A messaging bill "can't survive a real legislative process, to say nothing of passing it," said a former House staffer.[17] All that is necessary is that it sound good to constituencies outside Congress and clearly define the differences between the parties. "If your amendment is just to get a vote [and not to shape legislation]," said one former Senate aide, "it's likely to be short, simple, and pointed."[18]

Parties have many ways of staging message votes. Given their control over the agenda, a majority party can simply bring up bills it has no expectation of being able to move through the other chamber and/or get the president to sign (Groseclose and McCarty 2001). Unsuccessful party-line cloture votes in the Senate also effectively communicate what a majority party stands for and dramatize being blocked by the opposition.

The House minority party, however, does not have many opportunities to force message votes. The majority party's control over the House agenda restricts minority members' opportunities to bring matters to the floor. The House majority will screen the specific amendments the minority seeks to offer, disallowing many of the minority's best messaging opportunities. House minority parties can and do use the motion to recommit for messaging purposes, though rarely with much effect (Green 2015).

The Senate's open amending process affords unique opportunities for a minority party to force message votes. Formally, "the Senate's amending rules enable senators to offer any and as many amendments as they please to almost any bill" (Sinclair 2006, 186). Although the Senate majority leader possesses some cumbersome tools to restrict amending activity (Beth et al. 2009), in practice senators' ability to offer amendments is primarily regulated by informal bargaining processes (Ainsworth and Flathman 1995; Rawls 2009; Wallner 2013). Generally speaking, senators who are determined to force a vote on an amendment have both latitude under the rules and bargaining leverage to do so.

Hostage taking is the Senate minority party's primary bargaining chip for influencing the Senate floor agenda. Given the supermajority threshold for cutting off debate in the Senate, a Senate minority party can usually credibly threaten to block a bill the majority wants to consider and pass. In exchange for permitting a measure to clear the needed supermajority for consideration and/or passage, a Senate minority can induce the majority party to permit votes on amendments, even when those amendments will be politically painful for majority senators. Assuming the minority party holds its ranks together procedurally to engage in this kind of collective bargaining, the majority leadership will be forced to give minority-party senators opportunities to offer amendments if it wants to move forward legislatively. This type of bargaining occurs even on must-pass matters, such as appropriations (Hanson 2014a; Rawls 2009, 47–81).

The minority party may even take bills hostage that most of its members support. For example, Democrats demanded many roll-call votes on amendments to the 1995 Congressional Accountability Act, an uncontroversial measure that extended a variety of nondiscrimination rights to employees of the legislative branch. Democrats tied up the Senate for days forcing votes dealing with such matters as an across-the-board congressional pay cut and regulations on congressional frequent-flier miles—message amendments aimed at making the case that Republicans were not serious about ethics reform. None of these amendments were adopted. In the end, the Congressional Accountability Act still passed the Senate with ninety-eight yea votes. In other words, even though Democrats supported the underlying measure, they still forced the majority Republicans to take unpleasant votes on floor amendments that would potentially be useful for Democrats' electoral purposes. If the majority wanted to pass the bill, the minority expected to be compensated. "Hostage taking is baked into the process . . . and it happens day in, day out on the Senate floor," said one Senate staffer.[19]

One might characterize the basic negotiation simply as follows: Whenever the majority wants to bring up and pass bills, the Senate minority party can exploit the occasion as an opportunity to force message votes. In this sense, the Senate minority party imposes a routine political tax on the majority's exercise of power. Virtually any time the Senate majority wants (or needs) legislation, the minority will likely demand the opportunity to offer amendments, and many of these amendments will be designed to cause political pain for the majority. One longtime former Senate staffer said that he and other aides used to call the process "the spanking machine," meaning "all the roll-call votes that the minority is going to demand if you're going to actually get a result." But, he continued, "you're prepared to go through that if you're going to be able to achieve something that you really want to do."[20] In Republican Leader Mitch McConnell's (R-KY) words, "The price of being in the majority is that you have to take bad votes."[21] Democratic Leader Harry Reid (D-NV) concurred with McConnell's characterization: "I agree with the minority leader that the deal around this place is the majority sets the agenda and the minority gets to offer amendments."[22] Meanwhile, Reid conceded that Republicans had devised some "great message amendments, causing a lot of pain over here."[23]

Senate bargaining over amendments may break down. The minority loses its leverage to demand votes on amendments if it will not allow the majority to pass bills. Bargaining will also fail when the majority party deems the minority's asking price too high. The majority leader may, for example, simply opt not to bring regular appropriations bills to the floor so as to avoid the painful amendments the minority will demand (Hanson 2014b). One former Senate aide observed, "As amendments become more pervasively pointed and less substantive, the leadership wants to crack down [by using procedures to limit the opportunity to offer any amendments]."[24] By historical standards, the Senate took few votes on amendments during the 112th (2011–12) and 113th (2013–14) Congresses.[25] In part, the cause was that the Democratic majority was sufficiently worried about losing control of the Senate that it was not prepared to pay a political price for trying to legislate, particularly when the prospects for getting its favored bills through the Republican-controlled House were so dim. "If we spent more time on things that were legislatively possible," one senior staffer explained, "we would also have to give the opportunity to Republicans to force votes, which they would use to damage marginal members. This is a conscious decision on our part."[26]

Bargaining had also broken down because the majority had lost confidence that the minority would ever permit the desired legislation to pass. As one former staffer stated, the majority leader is "not going to give these guys votes on controversial stuff just to see them obstruct the legislation in the end."[27] Or as another staffer put it, "We're not going to take a bunch of crappy political votes just to lose."[28] Despite the possibility that bargaining can break down, the minority's leverage to force amendments makes the Senate floor uniquely porous to message politics.

The Prevalence of Partisan Message Votes

Message votes are by no means a new strategy. As detailed in chapter 4, Sen. Jesse Helms (R-NC) was a pioneer in their systematic use. He would repeatedly force the Senate to take votes on hot-button issues, knowing in advance that he would be unsuccessful but that he and his New Right allies could nevertheless use these votes for purposes of campaign fundraising and political mobilization. Helms, however, was an individual political entrepreneur, not a Republican Party leader. A difference between the Congress of the 1970s and that of the present is that the parties' incentives to use Helms-style tactics themselves grew stronger once the prospect for change in majority control of Congress appeared likely.

These expectations are intuitive. After all, it makes a lot more sense for parties to invest time, energy, and other resources in coordinated messaging when the majority is up for grabs. However, there are many challenges involved in testing these expectations empirically. It is simply not possible to offer a precise count of the number of bills and amendments intentionally framed for partisan messaging purposes. Little about the legislative language itself indicates that a bill or amendment was designed for messaging, with the exception of (increasingly common) bills with partisan taunts for titles, such as "Repealing the Job-Killing Health Care Law Act."[29] Members and leaders will not announce or publicly acknowledge that a particular legislative initiative is intended as a messaging vehicle.

Below, I attempt to gauge the prevalence of the partisan message vote first by turning to perceptions of longtime Beltway insiders. Then I offer a systematic analysis of Senate floor amendments over time that offers evidence consistent with the thesis that partisan messaging constitutes a larger proportion of the Senate floor agenda in the post-1980s era than it did in the 1960s and 1970s.

Perceptions

Hill insiders with long experience uniformly stated that they believed the use of partisan message votes was more common in the contemporary Congress than it had been in the past. Interview subjects specifically cited Helms as an important influence on the development of congressional message politics. "Helms was an innovator. The basic idea is losing to win," recalled a longtime Republican Senate aide. "You hold votes knowing you will not be successful. But then the losses on these key issues . . . you can then use in elections."[30] Another Senate aide with decades of experience also reflected back to Helms as a pathbreaker: "He'd bring up a series of amendments—all hot potatoes. . . . Today there's a heightened state of awareness of this strategy among leaders. It'd be leadership malpractice if you didn't allow some of that."[31] "Virtually single-handedly, Jesse Helms [brought] down the high wall that had separated the Senate from the outside world of partisan warfare," wrote former Senate aide Ira Shapiro (2012, 214).

When interview subjects were queried about the extent of messaging in the contemporary Congress, they saw it as a dominant activity. One senior Senate staffer characterized 90 to 100 percent of the issues that had come to the Senate floor from January through the summer of 2012 as oriented toward messaging.[32] Another former Senate aide said in 2014, "The only type of legislation on the floor these days is message related."[33] A longtime former high-level congressional staffer working as a lobbyist expressed concern that members' legislative skills had atrophied. "I worry about the current crop there," she said. "There's a class of members in there who only know messaging. They haven't had real legislative experiences. They haven't faced the hard choices, and they lose that skill set."[34] Another longtime leadership aide recalled, "Once setting up votes in this way was seen as a clever thing, but it is now a natural or expected thing. It is just routine."[35]

One can find numerous stories in national and Beltway news outlets about the increased use of the partisan message vote.[36] One such story (Kane 2011) quotes former Senate Republican Leader Trent Lott (R-MS). "I guess I did show votes," Lott said, though he indicated that the practice had become much more prevalent by the end of his congressional service. "There were a couple of votes I was actually ashamed of," he said. "I was getting cynical, and that's not my nature." Interviewed by a reporter about the changes he'd seen in Congress over the course of his career (1969–2011), former Rep. David Obey (D-WI) offered a colorful description of the growth in message votes (Rogers 2010): "I always tell people this [place] used to be 50 percent legislative and 50 percent political. Now it's 95 percent political because you didn't have these 'gotcha' amendments. . . . When you turn every damn bill into a gotcha vote, and when the parties are feeding every roll call to the campaign committees within the hour so they can blast facts to people in the marginal districts and distort what the hell the votes were, it just makes members far more ditzy and makes it harder for them to cast rational votes." Another longtime Washington journalist's history of negative campaigning (Mark 2006, 107) describes the emergence of the message vote technique with Helms in the late 1970s and concludes, "Tactics of campaigning-by-legislation are now a permanent fixture of congressional operations."

One other way of gauging the prevalence of messaging is to look for politicians themselves making explicit references to the strategy. Searches in the *Congressional Record* indicate that *message votes, message bills, show votes,* and *message amendments* are relatively new terms. The first example of this usage I was able to uncover via ProQuest's Congressional Publications Database was in 1997 when Sen. Paul Wellstone (D-MN) commented, "This amendment that I have offered isn't going to win. Maybe this is what you call a message amendment."[37] The second occurrence was Rep. Jim Moran (D-VA) in 1998 stating, "We do not need show votes in the Congress. What we need is people who are willing to make the tough choices. This constitutional amendment is not the right thing to do. It is at best a politically expedient 'show vote.'"[38] Note that both of these early references to message votes assume that the audience is already familiar with the terminology. The earliest example of a senator (that I have found) explicitly discussing partisan message votes in news reporting was, ironically, Helms himself, complaining about the amendments that Democrats had been forcing to increase social-welfare spending during consideration of the Reagan budget. "That's just what the Democrats call some of their proposals to increase spending—November amendments. . . . They're walking down the aisle chuckling and saying, 'Well, we've got 'em on the spot'" (Tolchin 1982).[39]

Changing Patterns in Floor Amending

To assess whether an environment of intense competition for control of the chamber has driven a rise in partisan messaging activity, I analyze patterns in senators' success on the Senate floor across an extended time period, 1959–2013. As discussed above, Senate floor amending offers a particularly opportune outlet for the minority party's message purposes.

The expectation is that Senate floor amendments are more likely to be deployed for purposes of partisan messaging during the post-1980 era of intensified competition for majority-party control than had been the case during the 1960s and 1970s. Regardless of the two parties' competitive circumstances, however, one would expect senators to offer amendments for many varied policy and political purposes. Members will use amendments to adjust legislative language in accordance with their policy preferences. They will also offer amendments to cultivate a "legislative portfolio" (Schiller 2000), meaning a personal reputation for activism on particular issues. As senators aggressively pursue diverse personal goals, one might even see a flowering of Senate "individualism" (Loomis 1988; Sinclair 1989). But when majority control is in doubt, one would expect to find far more floor votes framed to advance partisan messages.

Given that partisan messaging is a losing-to-win strategy, its use should result in a higher failure rate, as senators propose amendments for the purpose of showing how their attractive ideas cannot advance in the current legislative context. If this is the case, one would expect to find that amendments offered by the minority party are disproportionately likely to fail in the post-1980 period. To test such a thesis, however, requires that one control for changes in the distribution of senators' policy preferences. Obviously, the polarization of Senate parties along ideological lines would also depress the minority party's success in floor amending. Under conditions of party polarization, the majority party ought to routinely outvote the minority party. The question, then, is whether minority senators in the post-1980 context are less successful than one would expect, after controlling for party polarization.

To test these expectations, I have estimated a multivariate probit model of amendment success. The dependent variable is *amendment success* (coded as 1 when the amendment is adopted, 0 when not). The key control variable in the model, *distance from the chamber median*, is the distance between the DW-NOMINATE position of the amendment sponsor and the chamber median, with the expectation that senators more distant from the chamber median are likely to be less successful on the floor than senators close to the median. This control should adequately account for how ideological polarization depresses the ability of minority-party senators to succeed on the floor. Beyond this, the model also includes a control for seniority, on the expectation that more senior members should have a higher likelihood of success. Two models are estimated: before and after the emergence of two-party competition for Senate control.[40]

The results of these models are displayed in table 6.1. All three ex-

TABLE 6.1. **Analysis of amendment success in the Senate, 86th–112th Congresses**

	Model 1 (pre-1980) 86th–96th Congresses	Model 2 (post-1980) 97th–112th Congresses
Majority party (+)[a]	.13*	.55***
	(.06)	(.05)
Difference from chamber median (–)	–.97***	–.66***
	(.14)	(.14)
Seniority (+)	.08**	.05*
	(.02)	(.02)
Constant term	–.43**	–.85***
	(.12)	(.09)
N	5,172	6,095
Log-likelihood	–2904.65	–3524.26

Note: The unit of analysis is the amendment, with the dependent variable coded 1 when the amendment is successful, 0 if not. Fixed effects are included for Congresses (not shown). Probit models are estimated with robust standard errors, clustering on the senator sponsoring the amendment. The number of clusters is 213 for model 1 and 251 for model 2.

[a] A test of the difference in the coefficients for *majority party* across the two models rejects the null of no difference ($\chi^2 = 24.8$, $p < .001$).

*$p < .05$; **$p < .01$; ***$p < .001$

planatory variables have the expected, statistically significant effect on the success or failure of amendments in both time periods.

Based on these model results, figure 6.1 displays the predicted probabilities that an amendment will be successful in the 1959–80 period by party and across the ideological continuum, along with confidence intervals around the estimates.[41] As is evident here, amendments offered by centrist senators of both parties during this era were markedly more likely to succeed than amendments offered by more ideologically extreme senators. For both parties, centrist senators were more than twice as likely to see their amendments adopted on roll-call votes than were senators in the most extreme category. Party also had a small effect on amending success. Majority-party senators were slightly more successful at equal distances from the chamber median than minority-party senators. However, the confidence intervals around the estimates for the majority and minority party overlap during this period, raising questions about how different the two parties' success rates really were, especially among centrists and extremists for whom the amount of overlap is the most extensive.

Figure 6.2 presents the predicted model results for the 1980–2013 period. The contrast with the previous era is stark. Party has a powerful association with amending success in the contemporary era. Majority-party senators' amendments are 83 percent more likely to be adopted

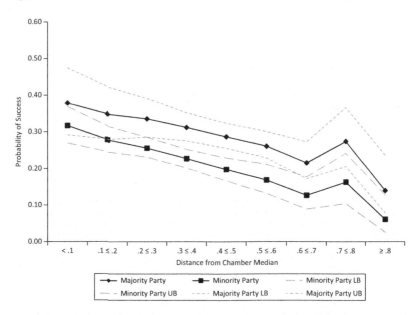

FIGURE 6.1. Pre-1980 majority- and minority-party amending success, by distance from the chamber median

Note: Predicted probabilities calculated based on the coefficients shown in table 6.1 holding all other independent variables in the model at the observed values. Confidence intervals were calculated via statistical simulation.

Majority-party amendments are modestly more successful than minority-party amendments, controlling for the sponsor's distance from the chamber median. But more importantly, centrist senators are more successful than extremist senators, regardless of party.

than those sponsored by minority-party senators, after controlling for the effects of party polarization. As in the previous era, amendments offered by centrists of both parties are more likely to succeed than amendments offered by extremists. But across the full range of ideology, majority-party senators are much more successful than are minority-party senators. Indeed, the most extreme members of the majority party are more successful than the most centrist members of the minority party.[42] To put this result in terms of the 112th Congress, a majority-party senator with the preferences of Bernie Sanders (I-VT) was more successful in the amendments he offered than a minority-party moderate with the preferences of Susan Collins (R-ME). A majority-party senator with the preferences of Tom Harkin (D-IA) was more likely to see his amendments adopted than was a minority-party centrist like Olympia Snowe (R-ME).

These findings comport well with a theory that minority-party senators use floor amendments for different purposes during the contemporary era of competition for majority-party control. In the pre-1980 period, senators' success or failure in amending activity was largely a function of their individual policy preferences, with centrists more likely to succeed on the floor than extremists were. Party had little effect on amending success after *distance from the chamber median* was controlled for. Looking to these pre-1980 Congresses, it is clear why earlier research on the Senate politics of the 1950s, 1960s, and 1970s had identified no consistent pattern in which majority-party senators were more likely to succeed in floor amending (Sinclair 1989; Smith 1989).

In the post-1980 period, minority-party senators are dramatically less successful than majority-party senators, controlling for their individual policy preferences. The analysis reveals that party polarization as mea-

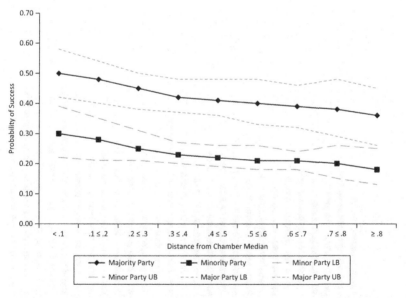

FIGURE 6.2. Post-1980 majority- and minority-party amending success, by distance from the chamber median

Note: Predicted probabilities calculated based on the coefficients shown in table 6.1 holding all other independent variables in the model at the observed values. Confidence intervals were calculated via statistical simulation.

Minority-party amendments are far less successful than majority-party amendments, controlling for the sponsor's distance from the chamber median. The most extreme majority-party members are more successful than the most centrist minority-party members.

sured by DW-NOMINATE cannot account for this shift. But this pattern does make sense in light of the emergence of "message politics" on the Senate floor. As the two parties compete for majority control of the Senate in the contemporary era, a larger share of the minority party's amendments are crafted to highlight the differences between itself and its opponent. In short, minority-party senators' amendments succeed less often, because a larger proportion of their amendments are designed to fail. When the majority party rejects the minority's appealing amendments, the minority party scores political points as it constructs a message to take to the voters in the next election.

The patterns revealed by these analyses have clear implications for the Senate majority party's agenda control. As a window into the overall Senate floor agenda, figure 6.3 displays the share of all amendments receiving recorded votes that had been offered by majority- and minority-party senators.[43] Although recent scholarship has shown that majority parties rarely lose on final passage votes in the Senate (Den Hartog and

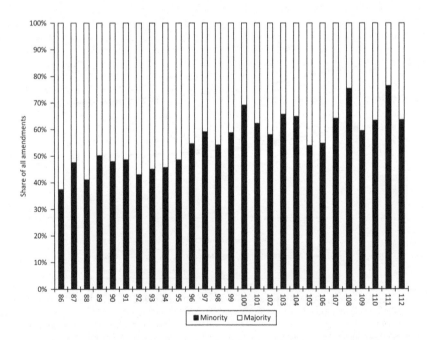

FIGURE 6.3. Share of all Senate amendments receiving recorded votes, by party, 1961–2013
Message politics creates difficulties for the majority party's agenda control. After 1980, a larger share of all the amendments granted recorded votes in the Senate were proposed by minority-party senators than during the pre-1980 period.

Monroe 2011; Smith 2007), the ability of the Senate minority party to extract amendment votes in exchange for permitting the consideration or passage of legislation forces the Senate majority party to allocate a tremendous share of floor time to considering amendments sponsored by the minority party. As shown in figure 6.3, the minority party's share of amendments has grown along with the development of partisan message operations. In fact, the Senate minority party has offered at least 54 percent of all the amendments considered on the Senate floor since the 96th Congress, even though there are by definition fewer senators affiliating with the minority party.[44] In many recent Congresses, the minority's share has exceeded 60 percent or 65 percent of all amendments receiving roll-call votes. Although the majority party is rarely "rolled" on the passage of legislation, it obviously cannot exercise the sort of control a majority party would like to have over the content of the political messages conveyed to the public out of floor debate.

The Permanent Campaign on the Floor

The real question is, how is the Senate going to find a path to move beyond just trying to score points, trying to score political points, and getting to the substantive questions? ... What are you going to do with this hugely important position ... other than scheming to keep it? — Senator Ron Wyden (D-OR)[45]

In the midst of the lengthy "Vote-o-Rama" that concluded the debate over health-care reform in 2010, Sen. Jon Kyl (R-AZ) conceded, "It's very partisan, and it's not fun, and it's not productive." But when a journalist asked why the minority party nevertheless insisted on all those futile roll-call votes, Kyl replied, "You hope for a better day."[46]

The argument advanced here is that members' hope for "a better day" has changed floor politics in Congress. With the emergence of intense competition for majority-party control, an increased share of floor time is consumed with message politics. The intensification of party competition has given members powerful incentive to exploit their institutional resources in the quest for partisan advantage. As detailed in chapter 5, members have beefed up their party's capacities for outreach and public relations. As shown here, they have learned to use floor debate and votes in tandem with their electoral efforts. The interview subjects consulted for this project, along with a variety of other sources culled from the public record and news reporting, testify to the pervasive, deliberate use of the floor for partisan messaging purposes. On all sides, members and staffers concede that votes are explicitly crafted so as to put the other party in a negative light. This strategy turns on staging legislative failures. Parties define themselves against their opponents by inducing the opposition to block their attractive-sounding proposals. In message politics, a party wins politically when it loses legislatively.

These changes in floor politics cannot be explained simply by ideological polarization. Instead, message politics consumes a larger share of the Senate floor agenda in the post-1980 era. With the growth of message politics, minority-party senators have become much less successful than similarly situated majority-party senators. Indeed, the most centrist senators of the minority party have a lower rate of amending success than the most extreme members of the majority party. If contemporary minority-party senators are using floor amendments more for the purpose of communicating partisan differences to external constituencies, then it is hardly surprising that they are less successful in getting their amendments adopted. The whole point of offering amendments for partisan message purposes is to draw a sharp line between the parties, and when the minority party succeeds in doing so, it necessarily loses.

The perceptions and data presented in this chapter also offer insight into the rise of partisan conflict in Congress. Most of the work investigating the causes of increased partisanship in Congress has emphasized ideological changes in the party coalitions. The qualitative and quantitative evidence presented here offer evidence that party strategy plays a key role. If members are staging votes to highlight differences between the parties more frequently in the contemporary era than in the past, then not all the growth in partisan conflict represents genuine ideological polarization, a widening disagreement between the parties on basic questions of public policy. Instead, some share of the increased party conflict is simply an artifact of the changed strategic behavior. Put differently, a substantial amount of partisan conflict in the contemporary Congress is engineered for public consumption. In that sense, not all party conflict is "polarization," a widening difference in the two parties' policy preferences. Instead, driven by electioneering in a more party-competitive context, a considerable amount of party conflict in the contemporary Congress is position taking for partisan public relations.

CHAPTER SEVEN

Governing versus Messaging

The Party Politics of the Debt Limit

Coauthored with Timothy L. Cordova

Politics is not the art of the possible. It consists in choosing between the disastrous and the unpalatable. — John Kenneth Galbraith (1969, 312)

When governing entails Galbraith's choice between the disastrous and the unpalatable, members of parties in and out of power do not stand on the same footing. Bearing responsibility for governance demands policy choices, even when all the options are unappealing. Trade-offs must be managed, competing goods prioritized, and scarce resources allocated. As such, governing constrains messaging, inasmuch as many real-world governing decisions do not make for good campaign messages. Meanwhile, parties not in power are freer to stand aside with clean hands and criticize. Not being responsible for results, they are not subject to the same pressure to accept imperfect compromises. They can message with fewer constraints. They may outbid the in party, proffering attractive, all-gain, no-pain alternatives. They can allow the perfect to be the enemy of the good. In these ways, parties out of power stand to benefit from dissatisfaction with parties in power.

As discussed in chapter 1, "government versus opposition" is an element of party politics around the world. Indeed, it is the dominant form of partisanship in many parliaments, where conflict occurs between members of parties in government and those in opposition, not on left–right lines (Dewan and Spirling 2011; Diermeier and Feddersen 1998;

Godbout and Høyland 2011; Hix and Noury forthcoming; Spirling and McLean 2007). In the United States, the government-versus-opposition dimension of partisan conflict is concealed by the relative lack of party responsibility in a complex political system. Even so, although party responsibility is more diffuse in the US system, it is not altogether absent, in that one party usually has more institutional power and responsibility for outcomes than the other. As such, party politics in the United States also to some extent pits the "ins" against the "outs," as in other democracies.

The overall argument of this book is that intensified competition for majority status focuses members' attention on the quest for partisan advantage. The preceding chapters have contended that congressional minority parties reorganized themselves to adopt a more confrontational strategic posture toward the opposition once competition for majority control of Congress reemerged. Congressional parties then invested steadily more resources in messaging and public-relations operations throughout the post-1980 era. Congressional parties also became more systematic and sophisticated in using the floor to drive partisan messages, staging more roll-call votes for the purpose of highlighting the differences between the parties.

The goal of this chapter is to shed light on how parties weigh the trade-offs between messaging and legislating, particularly under conditions of increased competition for majority control. The task is to analyze how members' behavior is affected by where their parties stand in the constitutional division of power. Grounded in the argument laid out in chapter 3 (and summarized in table 3.1), the expectation is that parties with more institutional power will give greater priority to obtaining legislative results, while parties with less institutional power will tend to prioritize messaging.

Further, this chapter focuses on how the intensification of competition for majority control after 1980 affects the incentives to engage in government-versus-opposition partisanship. Put most simply, party messaging should take on greater importance in circumstances when majority control might conceivably shift. Out parties under conditions of competition should more aggressively exploit opportunities to undercut in parties. As parties in power grapple with difficult decisions regarding budgets, fiscal balance, appropriations, and other policies, parties that hope to retake power have stronger partisan incentives to withdraw from legislative deal making and focus on messaging. By strategically with-holding support, out parties can force the in parties to bear more of the burdens of legislating alone and can better criticize them for the imperfect outcomes they accept. Deprived of cross-party support, a majority party will need to whip its vulnerable members to carry the legislation (Dewan and Spirling 2011). Meanwhile, by keeping their fingerprints off the majority's efforts, the out party stands to capitalize on dissatisfaction with the outcome. In short, under conditions of the "permanent campaign" and fierce two-party competition for control of Congress, one would expect a more parliamentary style of politics to emerge.

The debt limit offers a unique vantage point for an analysis of the trade-offs between messaging and governing. For most issues, it is simply not possible to ascertain how members' position in the constitutional division of power affects their behavior, because the same issues do not recur frequently enough to conduct any such test. The debt limit stands as a marked exception. The need to raise the debt limit has recurred on a roughly annual basis since the 1950s, making it possible to examine how members of Congress deal with the same issue under every configuration of party power. Second, the debt limit is a good issue for purposes of the analysis because the decision to raise (or not raise) the debt limit does not, by itself, implicate ideological questions of left versus right. Increases or decreases in the debt ceiling have no effect on the scope or role of government, the extent of which is defined in law elsewhere (Austin and Levit 2013). Third, the debt limit offers a perennially good party messaging opportunity, because rises in the debt ceiling are highly unpopular with the public at large.

The findings conform to expectations, in that the debt limit is generally a burden of those in power, meaning that majority parties and those controlling the presidency typically have to carry these bills. Meanwhile, out parties exploit these votes as a messaging opportunity. This pattern holds regardless of whether Republicans or Democrats are in power, and it is especially pronounced in unified government. Furthermore, the analysis suggests that government–opposition partisanship on debt-limit votes intensified in the post-1980 period, with the renewal of party competition for control of Congress. Since 1980, in both the House and the Senate, minority parties have tended to withdraw support for debt-ceiling increases relative to similarly situated parties in the 1950s, 1960s, and 1970s.

Government-versus-Opposition Partisanship
and the US Constitutional System

Despite the reasons to believe government-versus-opposition voting occurs in the US system, there has been limited scholarly investigation
of the phenomenon. Prevailing theories of congressional behavior assume that members engage in spatial voting on the basis of their individual preferences (e.g., Krehbiel 1998; McCarty et al. 2006; Poole and
Rosenthal 2011). Compounding the problem, the indicators scholars use
to measure members' policy preferences cannot differentiate between
government–opposition partisanship and voting driven by ideology.
These methodologies, such as NOMINATE and other vote-scaling techniques, can summarize legislative behavior when government–opposition
partisanship occurs. But under such conditions, they measure party discipline, not members' positions on a left–right continuum (Godbout and
Høyland 2011; Hix and Noury forthcoming; Spirling and McLean 2007;
Zucco 2009; Zucco and Lauderdale 2011).

The US system divides power in such complex ways that government–
opposition voting is much more difficult to detect and differentiate from
voting behavior structured by ideology. Indeed, the extent to which
government-versus-opposition dynamics structure congressional politics
is a formidably difficult question to sort out empirically. Despite the difficulties of measurement, however, there is reason to think government-
versus-opposition partisanship occurs in the United States, albeit to a
lesser extent than in parliamentary systems. After all, the United States
has a rigidly two-party system, in which dissatisfaction with a party in
power redounds to the political advantage of a party not in power.

The few studies that directly touch on government-versus-opposition
behavior in Congress have focused on particular policy areas. Work on
trade policy shows that, all else being equal, members of Congress are
more willing to vote for trade liberalization when supporting a president
of their own party, and a subset of members will flip-flop positions depending upon which party controls the presidency (Karol 2000; Keech
and Pak 1995). Kesselman (1961) found that members of Congress were
more willing to support foreign-aid bills when their own party controlled
the presidency. Shared or divided party control of the presidency has
broad-ranging effects on how Congress responds to the president's use
of military force (Howell and Pevehouse 2007; Kriner 2010). A Con-

gress controlled by the president's opposition party is more aggressive in launching and pursuing investigations of the executive branch, particularly in the contemporary era (Kriner and Schwartz 2008; Mayhew 2005, 223–26; Parker and Dull 2013). Although all these cases point toward government-versus-opposition dynamics as Congress interacts with the executive branch, scholars have not systematically considered how these conflicts also play out between the majority and minority parties within Congress itself.

Votes to raise the debt ceiling offer unique insight into government-versus-opposition behavior in Congress for several reasons. First, the need to raise the debt limit has recurred frequently enough that both parties have handled the issue as a congressional minority and a majority party, as well as while controlling the presidency and not controlling the presidency. Every president after Truman has signed at least one bill raising the debt limit.[1] Between 1953 and 2014, there were fifty-four roll-call votes on final passage to raise the debt limit in the Senate and sixty-eight in the House.[2] Second, the debt limit also offers good leverage on this behavior because neither liberals nor conservatives in principle favor higher debts, even if they will both tolerate growing indebtedness to accomplish other goals (such as tax cuts or new spending). Third, votes to raise the debt ceiling are highly comparable to one another over time, because most increases to the debt limit have been passed in "clean" form, meaning that the legislation contains no extraneous provisions (Krishnakumar 2005, 172–75).[3] Finally, the debt limit offers a good vantage point on government–opposition partisanship because the need to increase the debt ceiling presents a perennially good opportunity for an out party to indict and excoriate the in party's performance. Most opinion polls taken on the subject show the public disapproving of raising the debt ceiling by a two-to-one margin.[4] It offers a news hook on which the out party can hang its case that those in power are failing to govern responsibly.

This chapter is not the first analysis of the party politics of the debt limit. Two prior studies have taken advantage of debt-limit votes for insight into how partisanship can structure members' behavior. Asher and Weisberg (1978) analyzed debt-ceiling votes in the House of Representatives between 1949 and 1972 and found that Republicans were more supportive of debt-ceiling increases when a Republican held the presidency. With only one Republican-held Congress during the period (the 83rd), this 1978 study could yield limited insight into how Republicans behave when they are the majority party in Congress or how Democrats behave as the minority. Kowalcky and LeLoup (1993) examined congressional debt-limit votes between 1953 and 1990. Again, with Democrats controlling Congress for so much of the period, there was modest leverage on how members respond to changes in their majority-party status.

Expectations

If members of Congress engage in government-versus-opposition partisanship, then one would expect one key regularity in their behavior over time with respect to the debt ceiling. Members of parties in positions of greater power will be more willing to vote in favor of debt-ceiling increases. Even though such votes are not popular as a matter of political positioning, a party in power would not want to risk bearing responsibility for the negative fiscal or economic consequences of a failure to increase the debt ceiling. By the same token, members of parties with less power feel less obligated to vote to raise the debt ceiling. Not being in a position where they expect to be blamed for negative policy outcomes, such members can afford to take the popular position and use the votes as an opportunity to criticize their partisan opponents for poor fiscal management.

Although the US system divides power in ways more complex than "ins" versus "outs," one might conceive of party power on a continuum, with the extremes appearing under conditions of unified government. A party is least powerful in the United States when serving as a minority party under conditions of unified government and most powerful when serving as a majority party in unified government. In divided-government conditions, the power differential between the two parties is reduced. As such, both parties in divided government share responsibility for outcomes to some extent, but the congressional majority party is in a position to set the congressional agenda and bring up debt-ceiling votes. In that respect, the majority party in divided government bears heavier responsibility for governance. However, the minority party in divided government has a stake in governance so as to prevent embarrassment to a president of its own party.

Under this logic, we posit the following three expectations:

1. Members of majority parties in Congress will be more likely to vote for debt-ceiling increases than members of minority parties.

2. Members of parties controlling the presidency will be more likely to vote for debt-ceiling increases than members not controlling the presidency.
3. Because the differential in party power is greater under unified government, the behavioral differences between the two parties on debt-limit votes should be more pronounced in unified government and less pronounced under divided government.

A First Look at the Data: Descriptive Patterns

As a simple first cut at the data, figure 7.1 displays the average percentage of Republicans and Democrats voting "yea" on debt-ceiling increases when their party is in each of four positions, ranging from least to most powerful: (1) as a congressional minority party that does not control the presidency, (2) as a congressional minority party that controls the presidency, (3) as a congressional majority party that does not control the presidency, and (4) as a congressional majority party that controls the presidency.

A considerable amount of government-versus-opposition partisanship is on display in figure 7.1. First, there is a clear, positive relationship between party power and voting for debt-ceiling increases: generally speaking, the more powerful a party, the more likely it is that its members will vote to increase the debt limit. The difference between the behavior of majority and minority parties under unified government is particularly stark. In both the House and the Senate, minority parties not controlling the presidency provide the lowest levels of support for debt-ceiling increases compared to the behavior of parties in any other configuration of power, while majority parties controlling the presidency provide the highest levels of support.

Second, Republicans and Democrats dramatically alter their behavior on debt-ceiling votes when their institutional circumstances change. When serving as a minority party that does not control the presidency, House and Senate Democrats offer no more support for debt-ceiling increases than do Republicans. But when positioned as a majority party, Democrats, like Republicans, muster high levels of support, most especially when serving as a majority party that controls the presidency.

Third, there are few differences between Republicans and Democrats when they are placed in similar institutional circumstances. There is no statistically significant difference between Republicans and Democrats when situated as (1) the majority party not controlling the presidency or

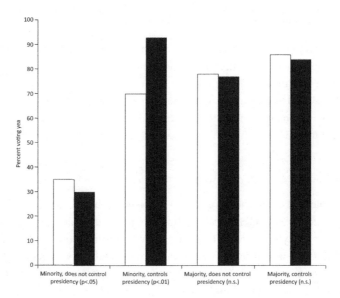

Panel A: Senate Votes

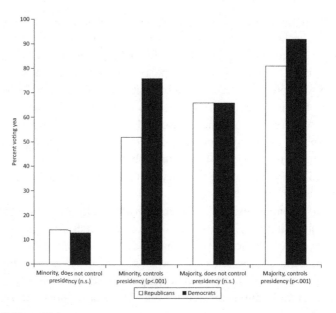

Panel B: House Votes

FIGURE 7.1. Percentage of members voting to raise the debt limit, 1953–2014
The more power members have, the more likely they are to vote for debt-ceiling increases.
Majority parties controlling the presidency provide the highest percentage of votes for
debt-ceiling increases; minority parties not controlling the presidency provide the lowest.
Party affiliation makes little difference.

(2) the House minority party not controlling the presidency. In the Senate, Democrats provide slightly less support for debt-ceiling increases than Republicans when situated as a minority party not controlling the presidency ($p < .05$). In the House, Democrats deliver a modestly higher level of support than Republicans when positioned as a majority party controlling the presidency ($p < .001$).

The one notable difference between Republican and Democratic behavior appears in divided government when serving as a congressional minority party controlling the presidency. Under these circumstances, Democrats put up a larger average percentage of support to raise the debt ceiling than do Republicans when similarly positioned. This difference is the result of the parties' behavior during the Obama presidency, and if these years were excluded, it would not be in evidence. On a few occasions under Obama, the minority-party Democrats provided unanimous or nearly unanimous support for debt-ceiling increases while most majority-party Republicans voted no. Importantly, however, the majority-party Republicans supported bringing these bills to the floor— indeed, nearly every House Republican voted in favor of the rules that allowed the bills to be considered—but most Republicans then refused to support raising the debt ceiling on final passage. These unusual votes provoked some head shaking on the part of Democrats. "This feels like 'Alice in Wonderland,' totally upside down," said House Democratic Caucus Chairman Xavier Becerra (D-CA). "The majority is supposed to be the party that moves it forward because they run the ship" (Costa et al. 2014). These cases illustrate that the majority party in divided government has political leverage to force the minority party to participate in governance so as to prevent embarrassment to the administration. However, it is not clear why majority-party Republicans during Democratic presidencies have been better able to use this leverage to obtain cross-party support for debt-limit increases than majority-party Democrats during Republican presidencies.

Members of out parties exploit these votes as an opportunity to criticize the fiscal record of in parties. Meanwhile, to little avail, members of in parties complain about the opposition's behavior and criticize them as politically motivated. The rhetoric deployed in these debates is not mild. Those voting against debt-limit increases typically call the administration and (in unified government) the whole party in power "irresponsible" and "reckless." Out parties accuse the in parties of burdening future generations of Americans with debt. Then-Sen. Barack Obama

(D-IL) said when he voted against raising the debt limit while serving in the Senate minority during the George W. Bush administration, "The fact that we are here today to debate raising America's debt limit is a sign of leadership failure."[5] The increase may be referred to misleadingly as a "blank check" for the administration. Efforts to dramatize large numbers will be made. Does the listener know how much a trillion dollars is, how high a trillion dollars would stack? The debt already constitutes X dollars for every man, woman, and child in America. Ominous references to foreign bondholders are made.

Perusing the *Congressional Record* underscores that members are sometimes even self-conscious about their party's inconsistent behavior over time. Pointing to a pattern that was obvious to members at the time, Rep. Ed Edmondson (D-OK) said, "The significant point about the record of the other side is that consistently, by overwhelming majorities, the Republicans voted for debt limit increases when a Republican President was in the White House, but they have consistently since that time voted against when a Democratic President was in the White House."[6] In response to such criticisms, Minority Leader Gerald Ford (R-MI) needled the Democrats by listing the large numbers of Democrats who had voted against raising the debt limit during the Republican-controlled 83rd Congress under President Eisenhower. In reply, Majority Whip Hale Boggs (D-LA) conceded, "I did not necessarily say we should have voted that way."[7]

Changes in House procedures used for handling the debt limit over time also shed light on partisan incentives under different institutional configurations. For example, Rep. Richard Gephardt (D-MO)—frustrated by Republican minority-party behavior on the debt limit during the presidency of Jimmy Carter—proposed a successful amendment to the budget process in 1979 that eliminated the requirement that the House have a separate vote on the statutory debt limit. Under this rule, the adoption of a budget resolution would "deem to have passed" an increase in the debt limit as needed to accommodate the planned budget. For the subsequent decade, this rules change reduced the number of debt-ceiling votes taken in the House of Representatives, though separate votes were still needed when the limit was reached before a budget resolution was approved or to adopt a conference report if the Senate had amended the House budget. Once Republicans captured the House majority in 1994, they regularly suspended the Gephardt rule so as to require separate votes on the debt limit and thereby use these votes in efforts to highlight the debt issue under Democratic president Bill Clinton (Krishnakumar 2005). But once the debt ceiling needed to be raised under Republican president George W. Bush, House Republicans reinstated the Gephardt rule and employed it in both 2003 and 2005 (Binder 2013). In 2011, Republicans repealed the Gephardt rule, once again permitting the vote to be used in efforts to embarrass an opposing party administration. Clearly, members perceive that the partisan value of messaging about the debt limit shifts under different institutional circumstances.

Modeling Members' Debt-Ceiling Votes

It is evident from the descriptive data that the institutional position of their parties matters greatly for members' willingness to carry debt-limit increases into law. But it is important to evaluate these differences in light of other individual and electoral factors that are also likely to affect members' behavior. How does holding positions of institutional responsibility (such as party and committee leadership) affect members' decisions? Are freshmen or electorally vulnerable members less willing to vote in favor of debt-ceiling increases? Are centrist members more willing to vote in favor than extremist members? Members may be more inclined to support a debt-ceiling increase requested by an administration when the president has more support in their states or districts. Members' behavior may also vary depending on the size of the majority party's margin of control, given the detrimental effects of large majorities on party discipline (Patty 2008; Smith 2007).

Logistic regression models of members' behavior on debt-ceiling votes are estimated for both the House and the Senate for the whole period, as well as for votes taken pre- and post-1980. Appendix B lists all the roll-call votes used in the study and displays information about the coding of all the variables, as well as the full model results.

Table 7.1 displays the predicted probabilities that a member will vote to raise the debt limit under different institutional circumstances, holding all other variables constant. Broadly speaking, these results confirm that the patterns evident in the descriptive data displayed in figure 7.1 remain robust after controlling for an array of other factors likely to affect members' votes.

In both the House and the Senate, members of parties with more institutional power are markedly more likely to vote for debt-ceiling in-

TABLE 7.1. **Party power and the probability of voting yea on debt-ceiling increases, 1953–2014**

Effect of majority status	House			Senate		
	Minority	Majority	Difference (chi²)	Minority	Majority	Difference (chi²)
Controlling the presidency (+)	.58	.80	.22*** (12.42)	.70	.85	.15*** (9.48)
Not controlling the presidency (+)	.16	.61	.45*** (40.62)	.34	.75	.41*** (51.06)

Effect of controlling the presidency	Does not control	Controls		Does not control	Controls	
On the minority party (+)	.16	.58	.42*** (42.34)	.34	.71	.37*** (24.41)
On the majority party (+)	.61	.80	.19*** (35.61)	.75	.85	.10* (3.46)

Effects of unified and divided government

Controls both presidency and majority	.80		.64***	.85		.51***
Controls neither presidency nor majority	.16		(81.61)	.34		(59.07)
Controls majority but not presidency	.61		.03	.71		.04
Controls presidency but not the majority	.58		(.16)	.75		(.19)

Effect of	Min	Max		Min	Max	
Being a Republican (0, 1) (–)	.61	.50	.11 (3.19)	.68	.66	.02 (.06)
The size of majority party (–)	.67	.47	.20** (9.67)	.67	.66	.01 (.08)

Note: Predicted probabilities from model 1 in appendix tables B.3 and B.4. All other variables held at mean values. Expected direction of effects shown in parentheses next to variable names.
$*p < 0.05, **p < 0.01, ***p < 0.001$

creases than members of parties with less power. Meanwhile, party affiliation has no statistically significant effect. House Republicans have a lower likelihood of voting for debt-ceiling increases ($p = .5$) as compared to House Democrats ($p = .61$), but this difference does not reach statistical significance. In the Senate, the parties barely differ at all ($p = .68$ for Democrats, $p = .66$ for Republicans).

Effect of Majority Status. Consistent with expectations, majority parties in both the House and the Senate are more likely to support raising the debt limit than are minority parties. When controlling the presidency, members of the House majority party are 37 percent more likely to vote in favor of a debt-limit increase ($p = .8$) than are members of the minority party ($p = .58$), and members of the Senate majority party are 21 percent more likely to vote in favor ($p = .85$) than are members of the minority party ($p = .7$). When not controlling the presidency, members of the majority party in the House are 2.8 times as likely to vote for raising the debt limit ($p = .61$) as members of the minority party ($p = .16$). Similarly, when not controlling the presidency, majority-party senators are 1.2 times more likely to vote for raising the debt limit ($p = .75$) as minority-party senators ($p = .34$). Chi-squared tests for these differences indicate that they are statistically distinct from zero at $p < .001$.

Effect of Controlling the Presidency. Members of parties that control the presidency are more likely to support debt-limit increases than members of parties that do not control the presidency. Members of a House minority party that does not control the presidency are 75 percent less likely to vote to raise the debt limit ($p = .16$) as compared to members of a minority party that does control the presidency ($p = .58$). Similarly, minority-party senators whose party does not control the presidency are about half as likely to support increasing the debt ceiling ($p = .34$) as minority-party senators whose party controls the presidency ($p = .71$). Members of a House majority party that controls the presidency are 31 percent more likely to support a debt-limit increase ($p = .8$) than members of a House majority party that does not control the presidency ($p = .61$). Majority-party senators whose party controls the presidency are 13 percent more likely to support debt-ceiling increases ($p = .85$) than majority-party senators of a party not controlling the presidency ($p = .75$). All these differences are statistically distinct from zero at $p < .05$ or better.

Unified Government. Differences in members' behavior are most stark under conditions of unified government. In the House, a member of the majority party controlling the presidency is four times more likely to vote in favor of a debt-ceiling increase ($p = .8$) than a member of the minority party not controlling the presidency ($p = .16$). The effect in the Senate is less pronounced than in the House but still very substantial. Senators in unified government are 1.5 times as likely to support a debt-ceiling increase when serving as the majority party ($p = .85$) than when serving as the minority party (.34). These differences are statistically significant at $p < .001$.

Divided Government. With power divided more equally between the parties under conditions of divided government, parties behave much more similarly. In the House, members of a minority party controlling the presidency are estimated to vote yea at a probability of .58, while the probability for majority-party members not controlling the presidency is .61. In the Senate, members of a majority party not controlling the presidency have a probability of voting yea of .75, while members of a minority party controlling the presidency vote yea at a probability of .71. These differences do not reach statistical significance.

Effect of Majority-Party Size. Majority size makes a significant difference for the behavior of House members but not for senators. The likelihood that a House member will support raising the debt limit declines as the majority's margin of control increases, from .67 at the minimum to .47 at the maximum. The variable has no statistically significant effect in the Senate, perhaps reflecting that chamber's supermajoritarian rules.

Table 7.2 displays the results of the control variables included in the models. Taken together, the effects of the control variables on members' behavior are weaker and less consistent than the party variables displayed in table 7.1. The institutional position of members' parties (e.g., majority or minority, control of the presidency) has a far greater effect on their behavior than individual factors, such as members' leadership roles and electoral circumstances. In many cases, the effects of the control variables are not similar across the two chambers.

Effect of Institutional Position. Members in leadership positions are more likely to vote for debt-ceiling increases. Party leaders in the House are 40 percent more likely to deliver votes in support of debt-ceiling increases than rank-and-file members ($p < .001$). In the Senate, party leaders are 23 percent more likely to vote in favor ($p < .001$). House committee leaders, including both chairs and ranking members, are 14 percent more likely to vote yea than rank-and-file members ($p < .001$); Senate committee leaders are 7 percent more likely ($p < .05$).

Effect of Electoral Context. Members' electoral context has little effect on their behavior. In the House, freshmen members ($p < .001$) are slightly less likely to favor raising the debt limit, but there are no analogous effects among senators. Similarly, retiring House members ($p < .01$), but not retiring senators, are more likely to vote yea. Neither members' margin of victory in the previous election nor the electoral support for the president in their constituencies makes any difference.

Effect of Ideological Extremism. Figure 7.2 displays the effect of ideological extremism on debt-ceiling votes in both the House and the Sen-

TABLE 7.2. **Effects of institutional position, electoral context, and legislative vehicle on the probability of voting for debt-ceiling increases, 1953–2014**

	House			Senate		
	Min	Max	Difference (chi²)	Min	Max	Difference (chi²)
Institutional position						
Party leader (0, 1) (+)	.57	.80	.23*** (45.75)	.66	.81	.15*** (13.53)
Committee leader (0, 1) (+)	.56	.64	.08*** (25.55)	.65	.70	.05** (7.37)
Electoral context						
Margin in last election (+)	.58	.55	.03 (2.49)	.70	.56	.14 (3.71)
Announced retirement (0, 1) (+)	.57	.62	.05** (6.32)	.67	.68	.01 (.09)
Freshman member (0, 1) (–)	.58	.53	–.05*** (7.95)	.67	.66	–.01 (.18)
President's vote share[a] (+)	.55	.61	.06 (1.00)	.67	.67	N.A. N.A.
Legislative vehicle						
Extraneous provisions included (0, 1) (+)	.56	.56	N.A. N.A.	.63	.73	.10* (5.23)

Note: Predicted probabilities from model 1 in appendix tables B.3 and B.4. All other variables held at mean values. Expected direction of effects shown in parentheses next to variable names.
* $p < 0.05$, ** $p < 0.01$, *** $p < 0.001$
[a] Results for president's vote share from model 4 in appendix table B.3.

ate. The predicted probability that members in different institutional circumstances will vote to increase the debt limit is displayed for each percentile of extremism, ranging from most centrist to most extreme. The effects of ideological extremism are dependent upon whether members are part of majority or minority parties. Among majority-party members (as shown with white markers), centrists are less likely than other members of these parties to support debt-ceiling increases, all else being equal. By contrast, among minority-party members (as shown with black markers), centrists are markedly more likely than other members of their parties to support raising the debt limit.

In short, moderate members are not, per se, more "responsible" in backing the Treasury's requests for debt-ceiling increases; their behavior is contingent upon their majority-party status. Moderate members of the majority party are less reliable than other members of the party

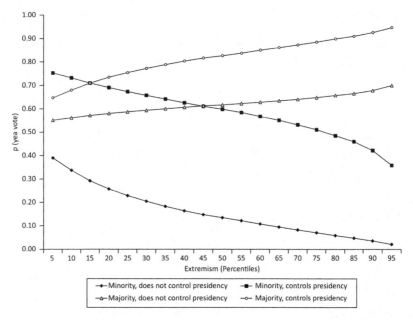

Panel A: Senate Votes

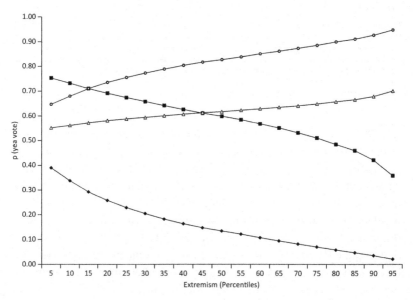

Panel B: House Votes

FIGURE 7.2. Probability of voting for debt-limit increases, by party and ideology, 1961–2014
As members become more ideologically extreme, they are slightly more likely to vote for debt-ceiling increases while in the majority but much less likely to do so when in the minority.

in helping carry debt-ceiling increases; meanwhile, moderate members of the minority party are more likely to cross over and help the opposing party pass the measure. By the same token, extremists are not necessarily more "irresponsible." Although extreme members of minority parties are far less likely than moderate members of their party to approve debt-ceiling increases, extreme members of majority parties are slightly more likely than their party's moderates to help carry the measures.

The Politics of the Debt Limit under Intensified Two-Party Competition

Analyses of House members' and senators' voting behavior on the debt limit reveal a clear pattern of government-versus-opposition partisanship throughout the whole 1953–2014 period. Members of parties in positions of power have to carry these unpopular measures, while members of parties with less power stand aside and vote no.

Although the pattern is evident throughout the data, it is reasonable to expect that the incentives for debt-limit gamesmanship have grown stronger under conditions of intensified competition for majority control. A party that does not believe it has a realistic chance at winning a majority has less motivation to exploit opportunities to denounce the majority party's performance and to strategically withhold support so as to force the majority to take painful votes. By contrast, in an environment of fiercer two-party competition for control of Congress, one would expect members to more aggressively exploit any good partisan messaging opportunity by withholding support.

In order to gauge whether partisan patterns in debt-limit voting are stronger in the contemporary period, we estimate the models of members' behavior on these votes for the pre- and post-1980 periods separately. Figure 7.3 displays the estimated probability for both the House and the Senate that members will support debt-ceiling increases when their party is situated in each condition of institutional power, ranging from least to most powerful: a minority party not controlling the presidency, a minority party controlling the presidency, a majority party not controlling the presidency, and a majority party controlling the presidency. The results are displayed for both the pre- and the post-1980 periods, with confidence intervals around the estimates.[8]

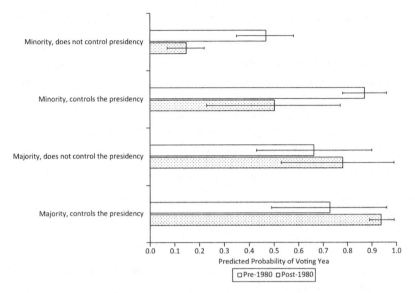

Panel A: Senate

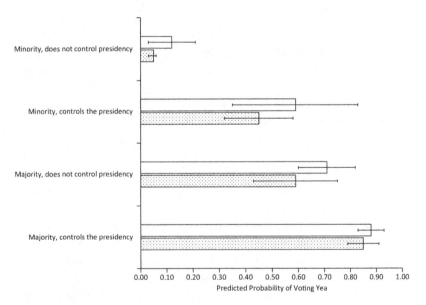

Panel B: House

FIGURE 7.3. Party behavior on debt-ceiling increases, pre- and post-1980

Source: Predicted probabilities and confidence intervals calculated from models 2 and 3 in appendix tables B.3 and B.4. Hausman tests for the equality of the party-control coefficients across the two models reject the null at $p < .001$ for the House (chi^2 = 26.33) and the Senate (chi^2 = 24.87).

Contemporary minority-party members in both the House and the Senate have tended to withdraw support for debt-ceiling increases compared to the behavior of such parties in the past.

In both the House and the Senate, contemporary minority parties have tended to withdraw support for debt-ceiling increases relative to their willingness to support them in the pre-1980 period. In both the contemporary Senate and House, a member of a minority party not controlling the presidency is less than half as likely as a similarly situated member before 1980 to vote yea. Members of minority parties in divided government have also substantially reduced their support for debt-ceiling increases. In the Senate in the pre-1980 period, minority members whose party controlled the presidency voted for debt-ceiling increases at a probability of .87; in the post-1980 period, these senators vote yea at only a probability of .5, a 42 percent decline. Contemporary House members serving in a minority party controlling the presidency are 25 percent less likely to vote for debt-ceiling increases compared to such parties in the pre-1980 period. The gap between the two periods in most cases exceeds the confidence intervals around the estimates.

In the Senate, contemporary majority parties have also stepped up their support for debt-ceiling increases, relative to majority parties of the past. This pattern points to stronger majority-party discipline in shouldering these votes, likely prompted by expanded use of the filibuster. When there is a problem with extended debate, a supermajority is needed to obtain cloture, forcing Senate leaders to marshal even more yea votes. Meanwhile a simple majority is sufficient to carry the measure in the House, so majority parties have little incentive to put up more votes than necessary. In fact, contemporary House majority parties have actually reduced their support for raising the debt limit compared to those of the past, though the confidence intervals overlap.

These pre- and post-1980 comparisons suggest that government–opposition partisanship has strengthened in the contemporary period. The behavioral gaps between members of parties with more and less institutional power are starker than they were in the past.

Conclusion

Analyzing behavior on debt-limit votes from 1953 to 2014 sheds light on government-versus-opposition politics in a complex system of divided powers. Even though raising the debt ceiling is something neither liberals nor conservatives per se want to do, the congressional politics of passing these measures is intensely partisan, with members' willingness to support debt-limit increases heavily influenced by their party's institutional position. Generally speaking, the more power members' parties have, the more willing they are to vote in favor of raising the debt ceiling. Majority-party members are more likely than minority-party members to vote yea, as are members of parties that control the presidency. Meanwhile, members of parties with less power are much less willing to support these measures. In most circumstances, these patterns hold regardless of members' party affiliation. Moderate members are not more likely to vote in favor of debt-ceiling increases; instead, their behavior, like those of other members, reflects their party's institutional position.

Furthermore, there is evidence that government-versus-opposition conflict on the debt limit is more pronounced after 1980. Under conditions of intensified competition for majority-party control of Congress, it is reasonable to expect members to more aggressively seek out opportunities to put the opposition party on the wrong side of public opinion, force its marginal members to take tough votes, and criticize its performance. Throughout the period, the debt limit has always presented partisan opportunities along these lines, but competition for majority control gives members stronger incentive to seize any electoral advantage. Consistent with the thesis, the data suggest that members' votes are more structured by their parties' institutional circumstances in the post-1980 period. Contemporary members of minority parties have withdrawn support for debt-ceiling increases as compared to similarly situated parties in the pre-1980 period.

Although this chapter has focused on members' behavior on the debt limit, there is no reason to assume that government-versus-opposition partisanship is confined to this issue. The debt limit merely offers uniquely good leverage for measuring such behavior, because it recurs so frequently over time, allowing one to observe how members and parties behave on the same issue when situated in different conditions of institutional control. But in principle, this political logic ought to shape many other, nonrecurring issues. Government-versus-opposition partisanship seems especially likely to come into play when leaders need to consider unpopular policy options or impose downsides on particular constituencies. Such trade-offs are especially likely when Congress enacts comprehensive reforms of complex extant policies or sets fiscal priorities under conditions of austerity. Under all those conditions, the in party's available policy options inevitably entail political costs, and an out party

seeking power is likely to perceive political gain from withdrawing cooperation and holding an in party's feet to the fire.

In short, partisanship in Congress is shaped by a politics of the "ins"
versus the "outs," as well as by a politics of left versus right. Even though
lines of party responsibility are much less clear in the US system than
in parliamentary systems, members of parties with more power have
a greater burden of governance, while those with less power are freer
to tout appealing messages. Having power and an expectation of being
held accountable for outcomes forces political leaders to make difficult
choices about trade-offs and the allocation of scarce resources. Meanwhile, a party less accountable for outcomes is better able to criticize, to
exploit any dissatisfaction with the opposition's choices, and to oppose
while not offering specific or workable alternatives. In an environment
when party control of Congress frequently hangs in the balance, one
would hardly expect politicians to eschew such weapons in their quest
for power. Indeed, the evidence presented here points to higher levels
of government-versus-opposition partisanship under conditions of intensified party competition. The implication is that party competition encourages a more parliamentary style of party politics in Congress.

CHAPTER EIGHT

Party Competition and Conflict in State Legislatures[1]

Coauthored with Kelsey L. Hinchliffe

Opposing parties have as a prime objective defeating each other in elections. To do this, each tries to discredit the other, not only during an election campaign but also during the conduct of government. — Alan Rosenthal (1990, 59)

T his chapter departs from the rest of the book's focus on US national government to ascertain whether there is more legislative party conflict in more two-party competitive states. After all, this book's argument ought to apply to other contexts beyond Congress. A party seeking to win or retain power has stronger incentives to establish and clarify differences with its opposition. Such differences constitute the basis of a party's campaign message—the reasons they give as to why voters should prefer their party to the alternative. By the same logic, a lack of competition in one-party-dominant contexts weakens the incentives for partisan line drawing. Parties in less competitive contexts have less motivation to organize themselves to draw party differences, because they perceive a lower likelihood that such efforts would have any effect on which party holds power.

The intensification of two-party competition is one of the most striking changes in the American political landscape. In the 1950s and 1960s, many states were so dominated by a single party that political scientists

1. Material in this chapter was previously published in *State Politics and Policy Quarterly* (DOI: 10.1177/1532440015592240).

referred to them as one-party states (Ranney 1965). "Within a large proportion of states only by the most generous characterization may it be
said that political parties compete for power," wrote V. O. Key (1956, 13–
14). After 1994, two-party competition spread across the remaining historically one-party states (Jewell and Morehouse 2001, 21–46). The vast
majority of states are now two-party competitive, at least to some extent
(Holbrook and La Raja 2013, 88).

A long tradition of scholarship in the field of comparative state politics has viewed close competition between parties as a driver of legislative partisanship and party conflict. "The parties in the most competitive states," wrote Ranney (1976, 59), "are likely to have . . . the highest
cohesion in the legislatures. . . . [Meanwhile,] party cohesion is generally
very low in the one-party and modified one-party states."

Despite the long-standing nature of the thesis that party competition
promotes party conflict, the relationship has never before been subject
to a comprehensive test. Unfortunately, it extends beyond the scope of
this book to try to replicate across the state legislatures the same analyses of partisan strategy, caucus activity, and messaging employed elsewhere in the book. As such, the analysis offered in this chapter relies
on much broader, summary indicators of party competition and conflict.
The measure of party conflict is drawn from new data made available by
Shor (2014). Five measures of party competition are employed: (1) the
number of recent shifts of party control in the legislature, (2) an index of
party competition for state offices, (3) the closeness of presidential elections in the state, (4) the effective number of political parties in the state,
and (5) the ratio of Republicans to Democrats in the state electorate. All
these measures of competition are associated with higher levels of party
polarization in the lower chambers of state legislatures, and most are associated with party polarization in the upper chambers. No measure of
party competition is associated with lower levels of polarization in either
chamber. These results comport well with the inference that competition
for institutional control fosters legislative party conflict more generally.

Party Competition and Partisan Differentiation

The idea that two-party competition promotes legislative party conflict
is central to the literature on comparative state parties, where it is often referred to as the competition/cohesion thesis. This insight dates to

Key's (1949) landmark work *Southern Politics in State and Nation*, in which he found the politics of one-party states characterized by a transient factionalism. States without two-party competition were "no-party states," rather than merely one-party states.

Early scholarship concluded that voting in one-party state legislatures was less structured than in party-competitive legislatures, with coalitions shifting across time and issues (Jewell 1955, 1962; Jewell and Patterson 1973; Patterson 1962). In one of the only longitudinal studies documenting the emergence of party organization in a formerly one-party legislature, Harmel and Hamm (1986) found that after the long-standing minority Texas Republicans elected a governor in 1978 and reached 25 percent of the state legislative seats in 1981, legislative party organization finally began to emerge in the Texas House, and roll-call voting became less factionalized. More recent scholarship reconfirms the pattern. Legislatures without two-party politics have tended to exhibit a relative lack of structure in roll-call voting (Wright and Schaffner 2002). Meanwhile, legislators in two-party competitive states are more reliably partisan (Carroll and Eichorst 2013).

In addition, there is evidence that party competition encourages the two parties to draw starker ideological contrasts in their state party platforms. Coffey's (2007, 2011) content analysis of party platforms between 2000 and 2004 found that "the greater the level of party competition between the state parties, the more conservative the Republican platform and the more liberal the Democratic platform."

It is important to underscore that party differences do not need to be framed around ideological disputes. Valence issues, such as accusations of corruption and incompetence, serve partisan purposes admirably well. In particular, the governor's prestige serves as a rallying point for state legislative parties (Bernick 1978; Jewell and Patterson 1973, 457–60; Morehouse 1998), just as the president's prestige becomes a focus of congressional party activity (Lee 2009). As Rosenthal (1990, 59) writes, "Governors and their programs are prime targets for the opposition. If the governor can be discredited, then the governor's legislative party will suffer as well."

There has been little recent work examining whether state legislatures in two-party competitive states are more party polarized. The main obstacle was difficulty in obtaining data on state legislative roll-call votes.[1] However, some studies examined the relationship between party competition and roll-call voting in handfuls of states, with mixed results (Aldrich and Battista 2002; Jenkins 2006; Shor et al. 2010). One notable recent study drawing on all states from 1999 to 2000 demonstrates that state legislators' voting behavior is more predictably partisan in states where the two parties are more evenly matched in electoral terms (Carroll and Eichorst 2013).

Data and Measurement

The data employed here to measure state legislative party conflict include forty-nine state legislatures for over a decade, with some variation in coverage (Shor 2014).[2]

Measuring two-party competition in state politics presents some challenges. The choice of measure can make a significant difference, in that states may look party competitive according to one measure (e.g., competition in presidential elections) and uncompetitive according to another (e.g., the majority party's margin of control in the state legislature). To deal with these issues, we separately examine five different measures of two-party competiveness in each state.

All the measures we employ gauge the extent of two-party competition for control of state government. We are not focused here on how party competition at the level of the legislative district affects individual lawmakers' voting behavior (Shufeldt and Flavin 2012).[3] We are interested instead in the competitive balance between the parties as they seek to control state political institutions. With this being said, our measures capture both the competitiveness of statewide elections as well as the competitiveness between legislative parties for control of the legislature. Our different measures do not yield identical state rankings, even though they are all reasonable measures of two-party competition.[4] One obvious advantage of this approach is that it reveals whether relationships are robust to alternative specifications.

A second challenge for a study relying on observational data is causal inference. Our expectation is that legislative parties will be more polarized in states with more two-party competition. Multivariate analyses will allow us to control for other factors that drive party polarization and thereby help rule out spurious correlation. But such an analysis nevertheless remains at least theoretically vulnerable to reverse causality.

One way of addressing concerns about reverse causality is to identify measures of party competition that could not plausibly be affected

by the behavior of state legislators. This is one of the advantages of using five different measures of competition. Indeed, it is hard to imagine
that partisan behavior in the state legislature would have any systematic
effect on the competitiveness of the state's presidential elections or the
overall balance of partisan identification in the state electorate. Considering how little voters know about state legislators (Delli Carpini and
Keeter 1996, 78; Rogers 2013), it is not likely that party conflict in the
state legislature would have any effect on voters' behavior at all. In fact,
other research has shown that voters' evaluations of the state legislature
or its performance have little to no influence on state legislative elections (Rogers 2013, 35; Tucker and Weber 1987). Instead, people's votes
in state legislative elections closely follow their vote for Congress and
strongly reflect presidential popularity. Dating back to Key (1956), scholars have raised concerns about lack of accountability in these elections,
because these electoral outcomes seem to hinge on factors that are separate from what state lawmakers do (or fail to do) either individually or
collectively (Campbell 1986; Simon et al. 1991).

A First Look: Bivariate Analyses

The dependent variable in the following analyses is the distance between
the median Democrat and the median Republican in (1) the state houses
and (2) the state senates. Under this measure, lower scores point to a less
party-polarized legislature; higher scores indicate more party polarization. We examine the lower and upper chambers separately.

Frequency of Shifts in Party Control

Our first measure of two-party competition is a count of the number of
shifts of party majority control in the chamber over the preceding decade. Table 8.1 displays the average level of party polarization in state
legislatures between 1995 and 2013 across different numbers of recent
majority-party shifts.

  For both lower and upper chambers, state legislatures where there
were more switches of party control exhibit higher levels of party polarization. For lower chambers that experienced no shifts in party control over the previous decade, the average level of party polarization was
1.28, while for chambers that experienced three or more shifts, the av-

TABLE 8.1. **State legislative party polarization, by the number of shifts in legislative majority party control over the preceding decade, 1995–2013**

Shifts (N)	Lower chambers*		Upper chambers[†]	
	Polarization (mean)	N (state-years)	Polarization (mean)	N (state-years)
0	1.28	495	1.34	465
1	1.52	198	1.39	163
2	1.66	99	1.50	197
3+	1.73	38	1.92	55

*$F = 30.6$ ($p < .001$); [†]$F = 26.4$ ($p < .001$).

Note: For the lower chambers, the overall mean of party polarization is 1.41, with a standard deviation of .48. For the upper chambers, the overall mean of party polarization is 1.4, with a standard deviation of .5.
Legislatures with more recent switches in party control exhibit markedly higher levels of party polarization, for both lower and upper chambers. Comparing states with three or more party switches to those with no switches, the difference is 93 percent of a standard deviation for the lower chambers and 116 percent of a standard deviation for the upper chambers.

erage level of party polarization was 1.73 ($p < .001$). For upper chambers that had no shifts in party control, the mean level of party polarization was 1.34; for chambers with three or more shifts, the average was 1.92 ($p < .001$). The size of this difference is fully 93 percent of the standard deviation in polarization among lower chambers and 116 percent of the standard deviation in polarization among upper chambers. For every year in the dataset taken separately and for both chambers, state legislatures with more recent shifts in party control have higher polarization scores on average than state legislatures with fewer recent shifts in party control.

Effective Number of Political Parties

A second gauge of two-party competition is the effective number of political parties in the state (Aldrich and Battista 2002). Long used in the study of comparative politics (Lijphart 1994), this measure is the reciprocal of the Herfindahl index.[5] In two-party systems, the measure reaches its maximum when the two parties hold equal shares of legislative seats. Figure 8.1 displays scatterplots of the effective number of political parties and the average level of party polarization in each state between 1995 and 2013, with each state labeled.

In both lower and upper chambers, the expected positive relationship is evident. State legislatures where one party dominates tend to be less party polarized than state legislatures where the two parties are more

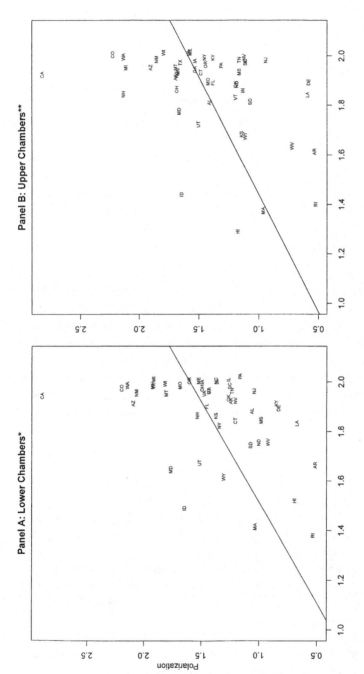

FIGURE 8.1. Mean state legislative party polarization, by effective number of parties in the state, 1995–2013 ($n = 49$)

*b = 1.23 ($p < .01$); R^2 = .19

**b = 1.05 ($p < .01$); R^2 = .16

As the two parties become more equally sized, legislative party polarization tends to increase.

evenly balanced. The relationships are statistically significant ($p < .01$), albeit not tight ($R^2 = .19$ for lower chambers and $R^2 = .16$ for upper chambers). These relationships are not dependent upon the high leverage cases with exceptionally large legislative majority parties, such as those in Massachusetts and Rhode Island.[6]

Competitiveness of Presidential Elections

Voting behavior in presidential elections is often used as a gauge of a state electorate's partisan and ideological balance. Figure 8.2 plots states' average two-party margin in presidential elections against the average level of legislative party polarization between 1995 and 2013. The expectation is that there will be more legislative party polarization in states where presidential candidates win narrowly than in states where they prevail in a landslide. As is evident here, states where presidential elections are close do tend to have more party polarized legislatures ($p < .05$). Lower-chamber legislative party polarization in the "blow-out" states (at the 90th percentile) is estimated at a distance between party medians of 1.20, while party polarization in the battleground states (at the 10th percentile) is projected at a distance of 1.54—a 28 percent increase. Again, although there remains a great deal of unexplained variance, the expected pattern is evident. This relationship is not just an artifact of the high-leverage cases with the least amount of party competition.[7]

Competition for State Offices

A third measure reflects party competition for state offices generally. To create the index of party competition, we averaged over the preceding decade the Democratic Party's proportion of the (1) gubernatorial two-party vote, (2) state house seats, and (3) state senate seats and then "folded" the average by calculating the absolute difference from .5. States where one party dominates state offices have high scores; states that are more two-party competitive have low scores.

By incorporating a measure of competition for the governorship into this measure of competition, we are able to take account of how legislative party polarization might be aimed at retaking or holding control of the governorship. Prior scholarship has shown that the governor's program becomes a focal point for partisan conflict in state legislatures

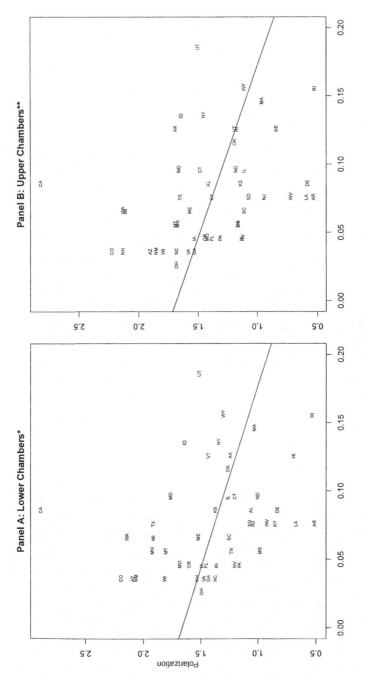

FIGURE 8.2. Mean state legislative party polarization, by competitiveness in presidential elections, 1995–2013 ($n = 49$)

*$b = -3.74$ ($p < .05$); $R^2 = .10$

**$b = -3.97$ ($p < .05$); $R^2 = .11$

As presidential-election outcomes in the state become more lopsided, party polarization in the legislature tends to decline.

(Bernick 1978; Jewell and Patterson 1973, 457–60; Morehouse 1998; Rosenthal 1990). Competition for control of the governorship may be important for state legislative party politics, even in states that are not party competitive, if measured solely by the contest for control of the legislature itself (such as in Illinois).

Figure 8.3 plots the index of party competition against the average level of party polarization. Across both upper and lower chambers, the more two-party competitive states have more polarized legislatures ($p < .01$). This relationship is not fragile after excluding high-leverage cases.[8]

Balance of Partisan Identification

The final measure of two-party competition is the state partisan balance. Drawing upon estimates of state partisanship generated from large national surveys via multilevel regression and poststratification (Enns and Koch 2013), we calculate the ratio of the percentage of constituents identifying with Republicans to the percentage of state constituents identifying with Democrats and then find the ratio's divergence from 1. States in which the electorate is evenly balanced between the two parties will have a score near 0; states where one party's identifiers greatly outnumber the other party's will have high scores.

Figure 8.4 plots state partisan balance against the average level of party polarization. The same pattern is apparent as with the other measures: states that have a closer balance of Republicans and Democrats in the mass electorate tend to have more party-polarized legislatures. According to the model, the most evenly balanced states (at the 10th percentile) have legislatures that are 19 percent more polarized as compared to states most tilted toward one party (at the 90th percentile). Despite a lot of unexplained variance, the relationship is consistent with theory and statistically significant for both lower and upper chambers ($p < .05$). These associations are still present and statistically significant excluding the high-leverage cases.[9]

Multivariate Analyses

Our initial look at the data revealed more party polarization in legislatures in states with higher levels of two-party competition. The question

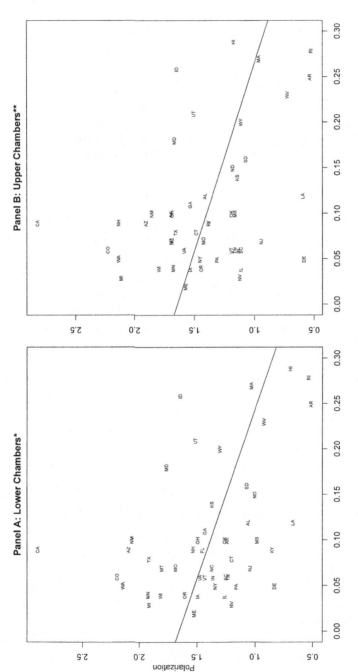

FIGURE 8.3. Mean state legislative party polarization, by index of state party competition, 1995–2013 ($n = 49$)

*b = −2.66 ($p < .01$); $R^2 = .18$

**b = −2.41 ($p < .01$); $R^2 = .15$

Note: The index averages the Democratic Party's proportion of the (1) gubernatorial two-party vote, (2) state house seats, and (3) state senate seats. The average is then "folded" by calculating the absolute difference from .5. Higher scores indicate lower levels of competition.

As a single party wins a larger share of gubernatorial votes and state legislative seats, legislative party polarization tends to decline.

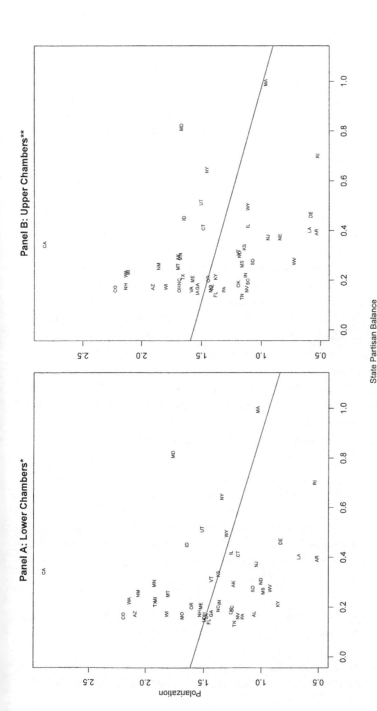

FIGURE 8.4. Mean state legislative party polarization, by balance of partisan identification in the state, 1995–2013 ($n = 49$)

*b $= -.65$ ($p < .05$); $R^2 = .11$

**b $= -.58$ ($p < .05$); $R^2 = .08$

Note: State partisan balance is measured by finding the ratio of the percentage of constituents identifying with Republicans to the percentage identifying with Democrats and then calculating its divergence from 1. Low scores indicate that the electorate is evenly balanced between the two parties. States where one party's identifiers greatly outnumber the other party's have high scores.

As party identification in the state leans more toward one party, legislative party polarization tends to decline.

is whether these relationships hold up after controlling for other factors likely to affect legislative party polarization. These controls include the following:

- *Income inequality.* Some studies have found that rising inequality in the United States correlates with higher levels of party polarization in Congress (McCarty et al. 2006; Garand 2010). Measures of the Gini index by state were obtained from Frank (2014).
- *Legislative professionalism.* The degree of professionalization—referring to a legislature's combination of compensation, full- or part-time status, and staff support—consistently appears as a significant factor affecting state government (Hamm and Moncrief 2013, 163–67). Measures were obtained from Squire (2007).
- *Traditional party organizations (TPOs).* Beginning with Mayhew (1986), scholars have found that political parties in states characterized by a history of patronage-oriented or machine organizations tend to be less ideological. Paddock (1998, 2005) reports that Republican and Democratic Party platforms are less ideologically divergent in such states. States with histories of TPOs exhibit less legislative party polarization (Krimmell 2013; McCarty 2015). The measure of states' history of TPOs is from Mayhew (1986).
- *The South.* The South's long history of one-party dominance and the recency with which it became two-party competitive may affect the extent of legislative party polarization.
- *Urbanization.* Previous work found that more highly urbanized states tend to be more two-party competitive and typically became so earlier (Ranney 1976; Patterson and Caldeira 1984). Data on the percentage of the population living in urban areas were obtained from the US Census Bureau.
- *Chamber size.* The number of seats in the state legislature is included under the supposition that party organizations may be less formal and hierarchical in smaller legislatures.
- *Divided government.* Divided government often forces more bipartisan deal making. The variable is included in case it makes a difference for measures of legislative party polarization.
- *Time.* A time counter is included to capture the trend toward increasing polarization across most states (Shor and McCarty 2011, 546).

The dependent variable is *legislative party polarization*, the difference between the Republican and Democratic Party medians in each state (i) for each year (t) between 1995 and 2013.

We model the relationship between party competition and state legislative polarization using two different approaches.[10] First, we employed Prais-Winsten regression, a method that allows us to include time-invariant independent variables in the model while addressing state effects with panel-corrected standard errors (Beck and Katz 1995).[11] Second, as a robustness check, we employ a more conservative time-series cross-sectional (TSCS) regression model that includes fixed effects for states.

The full results of the models are displayed in appendix C. Every one of the measures of party competition is a statistically significant predictor of state legislative party polarization for both lower and upper chambers in the Prais-Winston regression models shown in appendix tables C.1 and C.2. The results of the fixed-effects TSCS models (displayed in appendix tables C.3 and C.4) generally reinforce these findings. Most of the measures of party competition are statistically significant predictors of party polarization in the lower chambers, and two of the party competition measures continue to have statistically significant effects on party polarization in the upper chambers. Regardless of the estimation approach, the coefficients for the party-competition variables take the predicted directions in all the models.

To provide a better sense for the size of the effects, table 8.2 shows the predicted effects on state legislative polarization across the range between the 10th and 90th percentiles of the independent variables.

Results for Controls

Several of the control variables are highly important in accounting for variation in legislative party polarization across states. States with a history of traditional party organizations have dramatically less party polarized legislatures. Although patronage-based, hierarchical party organizations had broken down by the 1970s if not before, the states where such organizations had been most prevalent—such as Connecticut, Illinois, Maryland, New Jersey, New York, Pennsylvania, Rhode Island, and Delaware—continue to have markedly lower levels of legislative party polarization than states without those histories. The findings reinforce Paddock (1998, 2005), who found that in states with histories of TPOs, Republican and Democratic Party committee members were less ideologically distinct from one another, and party platforms were less ideologically divergent.

TABLE 8.2. **Predicted levels of state legislative polarization**

	Lower chambers			Upper chambers		
	10th percentile	90th percentile	Increase or decrease (%)	10th percentile	90th percentile	Increase or decrease (%)
Party competition measures						
Shifts in legislative party control (+)	1.36	1.49	+9	1.40	1.46	+5
State party competition index (−)	1.54	1.20	−22	1.51	1.29	−14
Presidential party competition (−)	1.45	1.35	−7	1.47	1.37	−7
Party identification balance (−)	1.40	1.34	−5	1.40	1.36	−4
Effective number of political parties (+)	1.28	1.48	+15	1.35	1.46	+8
Controls						
Gini index (+)	N.S.	N.S.	–	N.S.	N.S.	–
Legislative professionalism (+)	1.27	1.50	+18	1.88	1.99	+5
Traditional party organizations score (−)	1.55	1.04	−32	1.57	1.05	−33
The South (−)	1.46	1.23	−16	1.47	1.26	−15
Urbanization (+)	1.30	1.52	+17	N.S.	N.S.	–
Chamber size (+)	1.33	1.46	+9	1.35	1.49	−11
Divided government (−)	N.S.	N.S.	–	N.S.	N.S.	–

Note: Predicted values based on regression results shown in appendix tables C.1 and C.2. Expected effects shown in parentheses next to variable names. "N.S." means that the coefficient for the variable was not statistically significant.

States with professionalized legislatures are considerably more party polarized than amateur legislatures, for both lower and upper chambers. Journalist Charles Mahtesian (1997) theorized that "professionalism, partisanship, and incivility are linked to each other." It is not clear what precisely those linkages are. Nevertheless, the findings here suggest that, even after controlling for a variety of other factors, more professionalized legislatures are more party polarized.

Southern state legislatures exhibit less party polarization. The pattern is clear in models of both lower and upper chambers. These states' relatively short histories of two-party politics may be a contributing factor.

Time takes a positive coefficient in all the models for both lower and upper chambers, reflecting an overall tendency toward increased party polarization across the United States ($p < .001$).

The other controls do not have a strong or consistent relationship with the level of legislative party polarization.

Main Results

After taking account of these alternative sources of variation, two-party competition for control of state government has measurable and statistically significant effects on the level of state legislative party polarization. More two-party competitive states have more party-polarized legislatures.

Of the party-competition measures, the state party competition index stands out as the strongest predictor of state legislative polarization across both chambers. According to the model, uncompetitive states by this measure (including Massachusetts, Rhode Island, Hawaii, West Virginia, Arkansas, and Idaho) had a predicted party polarization score of 1.17 in their lower chambers; meanwhile, highly competitive states (including Michigan, Maine, Nevada, Iowa, Oregon, Illinois, Wisconsin, and Minnesota) scored 1.41, a difference equivalent to 70 percent of the standard deviation of party polarization. Similarly, upper chambers in uncompetitive states by this measure had a predicted party polarization score of 1.27, while upper chambers in party-competitive states had a predicted party polarization score of 1.95, a difference equivalent to 136 percent of the standard deviation for the dependent variable.

Party Competition and Partisan Strategy

Taken together, we find a clear pattern in which state legislatures in two-party competitive states exhibit more party polarization than do legislatures in states where one party is dominant. The findings are consistent across a variety of measures of two-party competition and across both upper and lower chambers. There is no evidence that state legislative parties in competitive circumstances tend to converge.

These findings comport with a theory that party competition for control of governing institutions encourages legislators to seek out ways to distinguish their party from the opposition. In party-competitive contexts, politicians have more reason to care about setting up issues for electoral purposes. As such, legislators will actively look for issues that elicit party conflict so as to dramatize and communicate those cleavages to external constituencies. By contrast, contexts that are less party competitive provide less reason for politicians to foreground party differences. Parties in such legislatures might be strongly at odds with one another on many policy questions, but they have fewer political incentives to pursue strategies designed to communicate those differences to voters and outside groups.

The pattern found here across state legislatures mirrors the documented effect of competition on individual congressional races: candidates in competitive elections are more likely to draw clear issue distinctions from their opponents while candidates in uncompetitive elections prefer to avoid controversy (Kahn and Kenney 1999). Based on these findings, it seems quite likely that message votes are staged in party-competitive state legislatures, just as they are in the contemporary Congress. Future research might profitably delve deeper than the summary measures used here in order to obtain more direct evidence bearing on whether parties in competitive state legislatures systematically pursue more confrontational strategies via message votes and communications.

Taken together, these results offer new evidence in support of a long-standing hypothesis in the literature on comparative state legislatures—that parties will be more internally cohesive and distinct from one another under conditions of party competition. Earlier work on state legislatures had pointed in this direction, though comprehensive data have only recently become available. In the early literature, the pattern was starkest in the state legislatures lacking in two-party competition altogether, in which roll-call voting tended to be factionalized, unpredictable, and poorly structured. Today, however, the range of variation in state two-party competitiveness has narrowed considerably. Most states now are party competitive, at least to some extent. If one were able to extend this study back in time, the relationship would likely be clearer.

Taken together, these results reinforce the central argument of the book: that a party-competitive context creates different political incentives for politicians than a context where one party dominates. When party control is up for grabs, politicians act with an eye to the broader political stakes. Looking toward the next elections, politicians under competitive conditions have stronger motive to exploit legislative debate for purposes of electioneering and partisan mobilization.

CHAPTER NINE

The Perpetual Campaign and the US Constitutional System

After the Republican take-over, Democrats used to ask, "Why can't things be like they were when we were in charge?" And the answer was: because Democrats haven't committed to being in the minority for the next twenty-five years. — Former Republican staff director[1]

Since the long-standing Democratic majorities in Congress were over-turned first in 1980 and then decisively in 1994, neither major American party has perceived itself as a permanent minority. Just after the Republican take-over of the Senate in 1980, the new minority Senate Democrats began to plot their way back to power. At that same time, House Republicans also took renewed hope in their own party's prospects. With Reagan in the White House and Senate Republicans holding committee gavels, a cadre of activist Republican House members began organizing to win the majority, eventually persuading most of their party colleagues to support their efforts. The 1994 elections completed the transition to our present era of partisan parity. Even though it would take Democrats more than a decade to recapture control of the House after 1994, they imagined a return to the majority as early as 1996, and they always stayed in close striking distance. In today's party-competitive context, majority parties cannot afford complacency and minority parties are not resigned to their status. No party suffers from the "minority-party mentality" that plagued Republicans during the long era of the seemingly permanent Democratic majority (Jones 1970).

The argument of this book is that these circumstances of ongoing competition for party control focus leaders' and members' attention on the pursuit of partisan advantage. Angling for advantage in the battle for majority control means continually looking for ways to enhance the public image of one's party and/or harm the opposition's. As such, it entails amplifying the perceived differences between the parties so voters prefer one's own party to the alternative. Cooperating across party lines to legislate bipartisan policy is not an effective way to amplify such differences. Instead, parties draw distinctions with the opposition through two means: (1) media communications and (2) legislative efforts designed to elicit party differences. Both are thought to enable parties to drive their "messages."

To be effective, a party's message must unify its own members, provoke conflict with its opposition, and draw a contrast that makes itself relatively more attractive to voters or key constituencies. As laid out in chapter 3, a party's ability to create effective contrasts and attractive messages is conditioned by its institutional position in the constitutional system. Parties with less power are freer to focus on messaging, because they face less expectation from constituencies to deliver on policy. In order to legislate, parties in power in most cases will need to support the watered-down, compromised proposals that might actually pass in the complex US system, with its many checks and balances. Meanwhile, parties with less power can champion "all gain, no pain" positions, less inhibited by the limits of the doable. In order to achieve legislative results, parties with more power must usually confront and manage trade-offs between competing goods, maintain realism about what is achievable, and tolerate some blurring of party differences in order to clear veto points. More powerful parties thus generally face more constraints on their ability to message, at least if they intend to legislate. Regardless of their party's institutional position, however, members and leaders will attend more closely to their partisan political interests under circumstances of stronger party competition for institutional control. Party messaging takes on greater importance when members and leaders believe the majority is in play.

The high stakes in contention when parties compete for majority status incentivize members to engage in partisan collective action. Legislative parties meet more frequently in caucus. They collaborate in the crafting of partisan messages. They invest in elaborate partisan communications operations. They set up floor votes designed to elicit party conflict so as to drive partisan messages and to clarify for external constituencies the differences between the parties and thus the electoral stakes. The minority party—especially in the Senate—tries to force the majority party to take politically damaging votes virtually anytime the majority needs or wants to move legislation. The upshot of these varied enterprises is a better organized, more confrontational style of partisanship in Congress. A Congress in which members routinely pursue such strategies exhibits higher overall levels of party conflict. These patterns extend beyond Congress in that party-competitive states tend to have more party-polarized legislatures.

Implications for Scholarship on Congress

The argument advanced here suggests at least four important implications for future scholarship on Congress and US politics.

First, it offers additional perspective on the dramatic rise in party conflict in Congress since the late 1970s. Scholars have tended to attribute increased party conflict to ideological polarization, meaning a widening philosophical gap between the two parties. There is no question that the parties in Congress are indeed more ideologically distinct today than they were for much of the twentieth century. The causes of this phenomenon are not fully understood, however. Polarization in Congress does not seem to have been driven by voters moving to the ideological poles, though voters became better sorted by ideology in response to elite cues (Hetherington 2001; Layman and Carsey 2002; Lenz 2013). Regional realignment has unquestionably made the parties both more ideologically cohesive internally and more differentiated from one another. In particular, the realignment of white Southerners into the Republican Party made Republicans more uniformly conservative and Democrats more uniformly liberal. However, the regional sorting of the parties cannot begin to account for the full extent of increased partisanship in Congress, because growing differences between the parties extend throughout the whole country. Republicans and Democrats representing non-Southern constituencies in Congress have also diverged more starkly in their voting behavior (see Barber and McCarty 2015, 26–27). The rise of party messaging under circumstances of intensified competition for majority control offers an additional factor contributing to increased legislative partisanship—one that can help complete scholarly understanding of the phenomenon.

Second, this book invites a more serious consideration of the role party strategy plays in congressional politics. The dominant approach to theorizing about legislative behavior has been to assume that members behave sincerely as maximizers of their policy preferences—that is, individual members vote for policies they prefer and against policies they do not prefer, regardless of collective considerations for their parties. Attending to how party competition for institutional control figures into members' calculations points to ways in which their concerns for policy and politics do not always align. At times, members must make trade-offs between advancing their party's interests and advancing their own individual policy goals. Party-cartel theories (Cox and McCubbins 1993, 2005) have contended that moderate members of the majority party may be willing to trade off their policy preferences in exchange for helping their party maintain a majority and control of the agenda. But theorists have not considered how the trade-offs between politics and policy also figure into minority-party lawmakers' decision making. Minority members are assumed to vote sincerely.

Members have incentives to vote against initiatives proposed by the opposition party even when those proposals may be strictly preferable to the status quo in policy terms. These political incentives are especially strong for out parties seeking a return to power. Voting no allows a minority to define differences between the parties, avoid responsibility for imperfect outcomes, force marginal members of the majority to take tough votes, and capitalize on discontent with the majority's performance. Minority members may even be willing to forego negotiations with the majority party altogether and relinquish potential influence over policy outcomes so as to reap these political advantages. As shown here, members explicitly grapple with this dilemma, and their choices shape battles over leadership, debates in caucus, and behavior on the floor. This book argues for closer attention to the goals and behavior of minority parties in Congress more generally, an understudied subject (but see Egar 2015 and Green 2015). Members of both majority and minority parties are likely to weigh the trade-offs between politics and policy differently when party control is up for grabs.

Third, the book suggests that the level of party conflict in Congress may exaggerate genuine party differences between Republicans and Democrats on questions of public policy. When members set up recorded votes for purposes of party messaging, they provoke party conflict. But message votes do not naturally occur in the normal course of the legislative process. Message votes are deliberately staged for electioneering purposes, a point that comes through clearly from the interviews and other first-person perspectives consulted for this book. As a result, the frequency of party conflict on roll-call votes is not a simple gauge of the actual levels of disagreement between the parties. The amount of conflict on recorded votes also reflects strategic behavior and the extent to which parties believe it is in their interest to communicate their differences to external constituencies. If floor votes are used for party messaging purposes more frequently under conditions of stronger party competition for majority control, the level of party conflict in Congress is not a reliable indicator of the extent of substantive policy disagreement between the parties over time.

Given the pervasiveness of party messaging activity in the contemporary Congress, the observed level of partisan conflict in the institution probably overstates the breadth and depth of genuine policy differences between the parties. This fact may shed some light on the reasons new majority parties often do not attempt to reverse or even substantially revise policies they excoriated while they were in the minority. For example, Democratic leaders enjoying unified party control in the 111th Congress did not try to roll back or substantially rework Medicare Part D, No Child Left Behind, expanded national security surveillance, or the partial-birth-abortion ban, even though when they were in the minority, Democrats vigorously denounced the adoption of these policies. Less-powerful parties often use messaging to gin up discontent with policies adopted under governments controlled (or largely controlled) by their opposition, but such resistance does not necessarily mean that they have feasible and preferable policy alternatives to implement themselves if given an opportunity.

Fourth, the analyses advanced here redirect attention to legislative parties as organizations designed for partisan electioneering as much as for policy making. Political scientists have historically viewed parties as mechanisms of collective accountability for policy. This line of thinking dates back, at least, to the American Political Science Association's (1950) report on political parties, *Toward a More Responsible Two-Party System*. It endures in theories of legislatures that stress the incentive of congressional majority parties to deliver on programmatic legislation as a way of advancing members' policy goals (Rohde 1991) or preserving their party's "brand name" (Cox and McCubbins 1993, 2005). However, the role of legislative success in the quest for majority status is actually rather equivocal. A party does not need to succeed in passing programmatic legislation to engage in messaging aimed at improving its image. It can still advertise, take positions, rebut the other party's positions, and blame the opposition for bad or failed policy. All these tactics of party image making are available even if a party has not achieved anything in terms of legislation.

Instead, legislative failure is often a good political strategy for parties, especially for minority parties and parties not controlling the presidency. Out parties can rarely aspire to enact their favored policies. But they can win political points when the in party votes down their attractive ideas, thus making an implicit argument for their own return to power. Under some circumstances, even majority parties can benefit politically from failed legislative efforts. Failed proposals can allow a House or Senate majority party to take attractive positions that either might entail undesirable political backlash if actually implemented or lack sufficient support for passage in the other chamber or with the president. Considering the difficulty of passing party programmatic legislation in the United States, a party rarely has good opportunity to use legislative achievements to significantly enhance its brand name relative to the opposition. Major legislation tends to have majority support from both parties (Krehbiel 1998; Mayhew 2005) and therefore does little to differentiate the two parties in terms of branding. Given the way the US system stymies parties in their policy aims, today's stronger congressional parties are probably better organized for partisan image making than for realizing legislative success.

Implications for the US System

This book's analyses also have a number of important implications for the operation of US national government. In a decentralized constitutional system with many veto points, neither a simple majority nor one party acting alone is usually able to make the system work. Bipartisan cooperation is generally necessary for US government to function.

Party competition for institutional control reduces incentives to engage in bipartisanship. Bipartisan deals are politically dangerous, because they typically disappoint party-base constituencies. Demoralizing its supporters is the last thing a party seeking to win or retain congressional majorities wants to do, if it can avoid it. Bipartisanship is particularly problematic for a party seeking to win a larger share of institutional power. Bipartisanship blurs the differences between the parties, renders voters less able to perceive the electoral stakes in choosing one party over the other, and therefore makes it harder to mobilize support for change. Bipartisanship confers legitimacy on the status-quo division of institutional power, in that bipartisan deals convey that both parties are able to achieve goals they each support, despite the unequal division of power. Bipartisanship thus implicates a minority party in governance over which it has limited influence. In doing so, it undercuts its ability to exploit dissatisfaction with policy outcomes and the majority's performance—a vital political resource for out parties around the world. A minority party that puts up a solid wall of opposition clearly defines the issues and avoids being tarred with responsibility for imperfect outcomes. Political disincentives to bipartisanship under conditions of intensified party competition for institutional control thus likely contribute to policy stalemate.

Competition for majority control may also be tied to the decline of "institutional patriotism" (Matthews 1960, 101) in Congress. Mann and Ornstein (2006, 146–69) point to a loss of institutional patriotism across a number of dimensions: members' lack of concern for institutional reform, their reluctance to pursue executive oversight when it conflicts with their partisan interests, and their failure to protect Congress's independent power vis-à-vis the executive branch unless it dovetails with their partisan interests. When majority control of Congress hangs in the balance, members have more reason to prioritize their partisan identity over their institutional identity. As members focus on the long game of winning power, they offer less constructive participation in ongoing legislative efforts in the present moment. "There are fewer and fewer people in the Senate who think of it as an institution. They put first and foremost their party allegiance," said Sen. Paul Sarbanes (D-MD) shortly before his retirement in 2006 (Toner 2005). Sen. Susan Collins (R-ME) leveled a similar indictment in a 2012 op-ed: "What has been lost in recent times is a commitment to Congress as an institution, a sense that we are collectively responsible for addressing the issues that confront our country. . . . If I could compress all that has gone wrong in one phrase, it would be 'perpetual campaign.'"

The activities involved in party messaging inhibit bipartisan negotiation. Aimed at drawing clear lines between the parties, messaging is inherently adversarial. Successful legislating requires negotiation, compromise, and bridging differences. Differences can be bridged by both logrolling and a search for common ground, but messaging pushes in the opposite direction, as members look to highlight points where the parties disagree (Gutmann and Thompson 2012). "Campaigning is about talking to win, not to learn or teach," wrote Hugh Heclo (2000, 13). "Techniques of effective campaigning are essentially anti-deliberative." Former presidential speechwriter Mark Lange (2007) advances a similar contrast:

> [Campaigning] is about crystallizing a message and endless repetition. It's long on reductive skill and often short on intellectual honesty. There are no shades of gray. Campaigns are messy, openly divisive, all-or-nothing battles with clear winners and losers.
>
> Making policy is different. It means relentlessly working the politics of inclusion and compromise. . . . It demands suffering fools gladly . . . and engineering outcomes where everyone has to seem to be right and appear to win.

There is no question that congressional leaders and members can engage in messaging and legislating simultaneously. They do so all the time. But a Congress that is more preoccupied with messaging and winning partisan advantage in a battle for majority control probably faces extra barriers to successful legislating.

This book contains extensive evidence that members and staff perceive trade-offs between majority seeking and bipartisan participation in legislation. These tensions even trouble relationships between congressional staffers employed in communications and those specializing in policy, with policy staff complaining about how communicators oversimplify the issues and damage relationships across the aisle. In these respects, messaging and legislating frequently work at cross-purposes. When Sen. Max Baucus (D-MT) was asked why the 112th Congress had accomplished so little, he said, "This place is so partisan—when it's more partisan, it tends to push messaging. . . . I think our country is better served with less messaging and more substance" (Raju 2011).

The congressional parties' relentless messaging wars may well be a factor driving down public approval of the institution as a whole. Such a consequence would be ironic, in that the goal of messaging is to make one's own party more attractive to voters. But the public's esteem for the institution as a whole is undercut when both parties continually engage in the partisan attacks and finger-pointing so central to message operations. Public disapproval of Congress regularly plumbs record depths. Gallup polling has not found public approval of Congress to exceed 20 percent since 2010; it has not exceeded 50 percent for more than a decade. Research has shown that partisan conflict in Congress drives down public evaluations of congressional performance (Hibbing and Theiss-Morse 1995; Ramirez 2009). To the extent that party messaging activity—particularly the deliberate staging of votes to dramatize party differences—drives rising party conflict, it also contributes to the decline of public regard for Congress itself.

The continual party messaging emanating from Capitol Hill also helps explain why voters have grown much better able to perceive differences between the parties in recent decades. American voters today are much more likely than voters of the 1960s and 1970s to believe that there are important differences between the parties (Hetherington 2001). Since 1980, the parties in Congress have invested considerable resources precisely for the purpose of helping voters understand how and why Republicans and Democrats do not agree with one another. It seems likely that these investments have, in fact, paid dividends. Not only do American voters better comprehend party differences; they also exhibit much more party loyalty in their voting behavior (Bartels 2000; Smidt 2015). The relationship between elite and mass partisanship is probably characterized by mutually reinforcing reciprocal cause and effect. The steady diet of harsh partisan invective that elites have fed voters over a protracted era of intense party competition for institutional control probably contributes to voters' rising distaste (even hatred) for the other party (Huddy et al. 2015; Iyengar and Westwood 2015; Mason 2015; Mutz 2015). In turn, the intensity of voters' partisan feeling encourages elites to continue to deploy more tough rhetoric and strategies of partisan confrontation against their party opposition.

The strategic logic laid out in this book also suggests that party competition for institutional control can make it even harder for Congress to deal with complex or challenging policy problems. Congress faces many difficult issues where tough choices involving political risks must be made. Passing budgets and appropriations under conditions of fiscal constraint stand out as the most obvious. Many other public policies entail inevitable downsides or trade-offs among competing goods. When it is necessary to handle such issues, minority parties have always had some incentive to refuse participation, keep their hands clean, and withdraw support so as to hang the majority party out to dry. As then-House Minority Whip Trent Lott reportedly said in 1987, "You do not ever get into trouble for those budgets which you vote against" (Price 2004, 138).

Competition for majority control strengthens these incentives. A minority party hoping to win majority control has more reason to saddle the majority party with responsibility for making difficult decisions and to exploit any resulting dissatisfaction for its own political gain. Chapter 7, on the party politics of raising the debt limit, pointed to increased difficulties of this kind in the post-1980 Congress. It is likely that a similar dynamic plays out whenever Congress is asked to handle politically difficult issues. "The real problem with big issues like Medicare is that both parties have to be brave at the same time. Every pollster will tell you not to do that to get partisan advantage," said Rep. Jim Cooper (D-TN; Nocera 2011). A majority party that cannot secure bipartisan political cover may well prefer to postpone or avoid putting such issues on the agenda at all. These political calculations may shed some light on the contemporary Congress's much lamented tendency to "kick the can down the road" (Blake and Sullivan 2013; Haskins 2014).

It may be that the US system of government functions better when competition for majority control is less fierce—when there is a "sun party" and a "moon party" (Lubell 1965). Although scholars and commentators normally celebrate the virtues of party competition for purposes of democratic accountability, it is possible that the US political system works better when the party competitors are less evenly matched. Lowi (1963) makes precisely this argument. He contends that a party system best suited "to perform the functions we expect of our parties is not a competitive two-party system but a system in which the second party is very weak: that is, a 'modified one-party system'" (575). Under circumstances where the parties are too closely matched, he argues that both parties are too preoccupied with winning advantage via "intensification of existing commitments, tightening of ranks, [and] activation of existing followings" (ibid.). By contrast, a system in which one party is truly out of the running for the moment encourages the out party to engage in serious rethinking and policy innovation. Of course, such speculation extends far beyond the evidence offered here. But it is worth pondering whether it is altogether a coincidence that an outsized share of major postwar legislative enactments occurred between the mid-1960s and mid-1970s (Grossman 2014; Howell et al. 2000; Mayhew 2005)—a particularly low point of competition between the parties for majority control of Congress.

Party competition is undoubtedly vital for the functioning of democratic institutions. Indeed, the presence of open contestation is obviously central to democracy itself (Dahl 1973). Party competition is important for presenting voters with meaningful choices, holding governments accountable to the public, airing failings of those in power, and engaging the interest and involvement of the citizenry in public affairs. But these virtues do not necessarily imply that more party competition is always superior to less. Highly competitive conditions are also likely to keep politicians preoccupied with winning political advantage over their partisan rivals, a preoccupation with clear downsides for bipartisan negotiation and cooperation.

Looking Forward

The contemporary era of party competition for control of Congress has persisted for more than three decades. Under the pressures of this long battle for control, Congress has created new institutions and established new operating procedures. House and Senate parties have built up large staff infrastructures for partisan communications, and these organizations will continue to churn out partisan spin for as long as they exist. Party messaging practices have become routine in both the House and the Senate. Members and leaders of both parties simply assume that a substantial share of roll-call votes will be aimed at winning partisan advantage, and they adapt their behavior accordingly. Fellow partisans meet in caucus at least weekly (usually more) to plot strategy. Only a handful of members can remember what Congress was like before 1980, when party message operations did not exist and members rarely met in caucus. Fewer than 10 percent of the members of the 114th Congress (2015–17) were elected before 1994. Like institutions generally, such practices are probably somewhat "sticky" and may outlast even the conditions that helped give rise to them.

It is not clear how long these highly competitive conditions will endure. According to the thesis advanced here, the existence of a dominant majority party in American politics would undercut partisan incentives. If the party system were no longer as competitive, partisan effort on both sides would atrophy. With majority status not up for grabs, the stakes in elections would be lower. Members would see less reason to invest time and effort in party organization and partisan fundraising. Incentives for fellow partisans to work together as teams would decrease. Members of a minority party that cannot expect to gain majority control in the foreseeable future would take more interest in playing the short game of influencing policy than the long game of trying to win institutional power. Members of a majority party that does not fear a loss of power would have more trouble holding their ranks together, thereby opening up more opportunities for the minority to play a role. Partisan political incentives would not set such a high barrier to bipartisan cooperation. It might be easier for the parties to grapple with difficult policy issues involving political risk if doing so seemed to pose less of a threat to a majority party's continuation in power. However, voters show no sign of entrusting one party with dominance in American politics anytime soon.

It currently appears that Republicans enjoy an edge in retaining control of the House of Representatives. An exceptionally large partisan wave would be necessary to return Democrats to a House majority (Jacobson 2013). A Democratic wave of this size seems unlikely, at least before there is a midterm election during a Republican presidential administration. Increased Republican security in their majority status may over time facilitate increases in bipartisanship, as on a few key issues in the 114th Congress.[2] At the same time, secure majorities may also contribute to the fractiousness that has been conspicuous among congressional Republicans since 2012. Several factions of hardline conservative Republicans, most visibly the House Freedom Caucus (formed in 2015), have seemed more focused on plotting against their own party's leaders than taking on the Democrats. Like the Democrats of the 1970s, a majority party confident about retaining control can better afford to indulge in this kind of infighting. It is notable that schismatic tension has been less pronounced in the Senate, where the Republican majority is more tenuous.

Notwithstanding recent Republican confidence about retaining control of the House of Representatives, one would be hard pressed to claim that the post-1980 era of intense party competition has come to a close. Control of the both the presidency and the Senate stand in strong contention. The balance of party affiliation in the national electorate remains close (Pew Research Center 2015). Activists of both parties usually have ample reason for both fear and optimism as elections approach. An ongoing struggle for power will continue to drive Washington politics and policy making for as long as majorities remain insecure.

Appendixes

Notes on Interview Subjects and Methods

Although interviews were conducted with the promise of confidentiality, it is important to provide as much detail as possible about the interview subjects and process (Bleich and Pekkanen 2013). This appendix provides additional information beyond that incorporated into chapter 1. The Institutional Review Board (IRB) at the University of Maryland College Park determined that this research was exempt from IRB review according to federal regulations (under exemption category 2).

Interviewees

Table A.1 provides a summary description of the interviewees. As is evident here, the sample is reasonably balanced between Republicans (57 percent) and Democrats (42 percent). It is also balanced between those with House (45 percent) and Senate (55 percent) experience.

I sought interviewees with long-term perspective on the institution of Congress. On average, interview subjects had sixteen years of experience working on Capitol Hill, with 79 percent having at least a decade of experience. Beyond the years working directly in Hill offices, many of the staffers and former staffers interviewed had additional years of experience (not tallied here) in private lobbying. All subjects held positions of significant responsibility in congressional offices, with 88 percent having served as chief of staff or its equivalent and the remainder in other senior roles, such as press secretary. Two were former members of Congress, who opted to waive confidentiality.

I was particularly concerned to interview congressional insiders who

TABLE A.1. **Interview subjects**

	N
Party	
Democrats	14
Republicans	19
House or Senate?	
House	11
Senate	18
Both	4
In or out of office?	
In office	12
Out of office	21
Years of service	
At least a decade	26
Minimum	5
Maximum	38
Mean	16
Median	12
Experience with party leadership	20
Experience with committee leadership	10
Chief of staff, staff director, or equivalent	29
Hill experience before 1980	8
Hill experience before 1994	24
Total interviewees	33
Average length of interview	72 minutes

had perspective on the institution before Democrats lost their long-standing majorities in 1980 and 1994: 24 percent of the subjects had experience working on the Hill before 1980, and 73 percent had experience before 1994.

Interview Process

As explained in chapter 1, the interviews were secured via a "snowball" or cluster-sampling approach. Some individuals were cold-called, but in most cases interviews were solicited via referrals and introductions. The standard request letter is below, though the letter would be customized to mention the names of those making referrals.

Dear [Name].
I am a professor at University of Maryland working on a book on how Congress has changed since 1980. I'm writing to request an interview

APPENDIXES   215

with you because of your significant Hill experience and your reputation
for insight.

The interview would be conducted on a not-for-attribution basis, and
I would anonymize any references that would reveal anything about
where or for whom you worked. This is the typical way political scientists
conduct interviews, and it is how I have done all of my interviews so far.

If you have any gaps in your schedule between [time frame], I could
easily schedule a meeting at your convenience.

If you would like to know more about me, here is a link to my website
at University of Maryland, where you can find a profile and a list of my
prior work: http://www.gvpt.umd.edu/facultyprofile/Lee/Frances.

The interviews were open-ended and unstructured. The bulk of the
interviews took place in the summer and fall of 2014, though a small
number were held in the summer of 2012. All were conducted in person,
with notes taken via pen and paper. These notes were then transcribed
immediately after the interviews.

In most cases, interviews became more interesting the longer they
extended. Over time, subjects would typically relax and begin to speak
more candidly. These were lengthy interviews. One interview lasted only
half an hour, but all others extended at least forty-five minutes. The average interview lasted seventy-four minutes, and several went two hours
or longer.

Data, Variables, and Model Results for Chapter 7

TABLE B.1. **Final passage votes on debt-ceiling increases, 1953–2014**

Bill	Date	Yeas	Nays
House votes			
HR 6672	7/31/1953	239	158
HR 6992	6/27/1955	267	56
HR 9955	1/23/1958	328	71
HR 7749	6/19/1959	256	117
HR 7677	6/26/1961	231	148
HR 10050	2/20/1962	251	144
HR 11990	6/14/1962	211	192
HR 6009	5/15/1963	213	204
HR 7824	8/8/1963	221	175
HR 8969	11/7/1963	187	179
HR 11375	6/18/1964	203	182
HR 8464	6/9/1965	229	165
HR 15202	6/8/1966	199	165
HR 10328	6/7/1967	199	209
HR 10867	6/26/1967	217	196
HR 8508	3/19/1969	313	93
HR 17802	6/3/1970	236	127
HR 4690	3/3/1971	360	3
HR 12910	2/9/1972	247	147
HR 15390	6/27/1972	302	35
HR 8410	6/13/1973	294	54
HR 11104	11/7/1973	253	153
HR 14832	5/23/1974	191	190
HR 2634	2/5/1975	248	170
HR 7545	6/16/1975	175	225
HR 8030	6/24/1975	223	196
HR 10049	10/29/1975	178	217
HR 10585	11/13/1975	213	198
HR 11893	2/25/1976	212	189
HR 14114	6/14/1976	184	177
HR 8655	9/19/1977	180	201
HR 9290	9/28/1977	377	17

(continued)

TABLE B.1. (*continued*)

Bill	Date	Yeas	Nays
HR 11180	3/7/1978	165	248
HR 11518	3/21/1978	233	172
HR 12641	5/17/1978	167	228
HR 13385	7/19/1978	205	202
HR 1894	2/28/1979	194	222
HR 2534	3/15/1979	209	165
HR 5229	9/20/1979	200	215
HR 5369	9/26/1979	219	198
HR 7428	5/29/1980	335	34
HR 1553	2/5/1981	305	104
HR 5665	5/22/1984	152	265
HR 5927	6/28/1984	138	282
HR 5953	6/29/1984	201	190
HJ Res 372	12/11/1985	271	154
HR 5395	8/14/1986	216	199
HR 2360	5/13/1987	296	124
HR 3022	7/29/1987	183	230
HR 3024	8/1/1989	231	185
HR 5355	7/31/1990	221	205
HR 5835	10/26/1990	227	200
HR 1430	4/2/1993	237	177
HR 2264	8/5/1993	218	216
HR 3021	3/12/1996	362	51
HR 3136	3/26/1996	328	91
HR 2015	8/5/1997	346	85
S2578	6/28/2002	215	214
S2986	11/18/2004	208	204
HR 3221	7/23/2008	272	152
HR 1424	10/3/2008	263	171
HR 1	2/17/2009	246	183
HR 4314	12/28/2009	218	214
HJ Res 45	2/4/2010	234	187
S365	8/1/2011	269	161
HR 2775	10/16/2013	285	144
S540	2/11/2014	221	201
Senate votes			
HR 11990	6/28/1962	56	34
HR 6009	5/28/1963	60	24
HR 7824	8/20/1963	57	31
HR 8969	11/21/1963	50	26
HR 11375	6/26/1964	48	21
HR 8464	6/16/1965	61	26
HR 15202	6/16/1966	50	17
HR 4573	2/21/1967	39	31
HR 10867	6/27/1967	60	30
HR 8508	3/26/1969	67	18
HR 17802	6/29/1970	64	19
HR 4690	3/12/1971	76	0
HR 12910	3/8/1972	55	33
HR 15390	6/30/1972	73	3
HR 8410	6/27/1973	63	2

TABLE B.I. (*continued*)

Bill	Date	Yeas	Nays
HR 11104	11/27/1973	48	36
HR 14832	6/26/1974	58	37
HR 2634	2/17/1975	70	20
HR 8030	6/26/1975	72	21
HR 9290	9/30/1977	58	30
HR 13385	8/2/1978	62	31
HR 2534	3/27/1979	62	33
HR 5369	9/28/1979	49	29
HR 7428	6/4/1980	67	20
HR 7471	5/30/1980	47	10
HJ Res 569	6/26/1980	54	39
HR 1553	2/6/1981	73	18
HJ Res 265	9/29/1981	64	34
HJ Res 519	6/23/1982	49	41
HJ Res 520	9/23/1982	50	41
HR 2990	5/25/1983	51	41
HJ Res 654	10/12/1984	37	30
HJ Res 372	12/11/1985	61	31
HJ Res 668	8/9/1986	47	40
HR 2360	5/14/1987	58	36
HR 3190	8/7/1987	51	39
HJ Res 324	9/23/1987	64	34
HR 5835	10/27/1990	54	45
HR 2264	8/6/1993	50	50
HR 2015	7/30/1997	85	15
S2578	6/11/2002	68	29
HJ Res 51	5/23/2003	53	44
S2986	11/17/2004	52	44
HJ Res 47	3/16/2006	52	48
HJ Res 43	9/27/2007	53	42
HR 3221	7/26/2008	72	13
HR 1424	10/1/2008	74	25
HR 1	2/13/2009	60	38
HR 4314	12/24/2009	60	39
HJ Res 45	1/28/2010	60	39
S365	8/2/2011	74	26
HR 325	1/31/2013	64	34
HR 2775	10/16/2013	81	18
S540	2/12/2014	54	43

TABLE B.2. **Variables and coding for chapter 7**

Majority party member is coded 1 for majority party members in each Congress, otherwise 0.

Same party as the president is coded 1 for members who share the president's party, otherwise 0.

Majority party's margin of control is coded as the difference between the percentage of the seats held by the majority and minority parties in the chamber.

Republican is coded as 1 for Republican members, otherwise 0.

Extremism is the absolute distance of a member's DW-NOMINATE score from 0. Data obtained from Voteview.com.

Party leader is coded as 1 for the top party leadership of each chamber (Speaker of the House, majority and minority leaders, and majority and minority whips), otherwise 0.

Committee leader is coded as 1 for the chairs and ranking members of all the standing committees in each Congress.

Majorityparty#Samepartypresident is an interaction term to ascertain whether the effect of majority-party status varies depending on whether the party also controls the presidency.

Majorityparty#Extremism is an interaction term to ascertain whether the effect of extremism varies across the majority and minority parties.

Samepartypresident#Extremism is an interaction term to ascertain whether the effect of extremism varies depending on whether the member shares the president's party.

Majoritymargin#Majorityparty is an interaction term to ascertain whether the effect of the majority-party margin varies depending on whether a member is part of the majority party in the chamber.

Margin in the last election is the member's share of the two-party vote in his or her last election.

Announced retirement is coded as 1 if the vote occurred after the member had announced his or her retirement from Congress, otherwise 0. These data are courtesy of David Karol, University of Maryland.

Freshman member is coded as 1 if the member is serving his or her first term, otherwise 0.

President's vote share is the percentage of the vote the president received in the member's state or district in the most recent election. For the House after 1966, these data were obtained from the *Almanacs of American Politics*. Before 1966, we were unable to get a complete set of data that included the president's vote share for all the urban House districts, though we filled in all the results for districts not divided across counties from a dataset compiled by James M. Snyder, Jr. Because of the loss of cases in the early period for the House, we estimated the models with and without this variable.

Part of broader package is coded 1 when the bill raising the debt limit contains extraneous provisions, otherwise 0.

TABLE B.3. **House members' votes on debt-limit increases, 1953–2014**

	(1) All years	(2) Post-1980	(3) Pre-1980	(4) All years
Majority party member (1, 0)	.24	2.35**	−.29	2.50***
	(.75)	(.97)	(.56)	(.87)
Same party as the president (1, 0)	1.49***	3.21***	1.72***	1.46***
	(.54)	(.91)	(.53)	(.50)
Majority party's margin of control	−.01***	−.02***	−.01	.001
	(.001)	(.01)	(.01)	(.01)
Republican (0, 1)	−.62*	−.18	−.51	−.35**
	(.35)	(.37)	(.54)	(.44)
Extremism (DW-NOM distance from 0)	−5.38**	−1.48	−5.58***	−3.69
	(2.33)	(2.52)	(1.74)	(2.71)
Party leader (1, 0)	1.52***	1.58***	1.42***	.92***
	(.33)	(.54)	(.40)	(.35)
Committee leader (1, 0)	.44***	.61***	.37**	.44**
	(.07)	(.13)	(.09)	(.11)
Majorityparty#Samepartypresident	−1.21***	−1.39	−1.31**	−1.84***
	(.47)	(.94)	(.55)	(.58)
Majorityparty#Extremism	6.42***	.78	9.18***	2.66
	(2.15)	(2.40)	(1.57)	(2.56)
Samepartypresident#Extremism	2.64	−1.24	2.06	4.15**
	(1.98)	(2.07)	(1.46)	(1.83)
Majoritymargin#Majorityparty	.002	.01	.001	−.01
	(.01)	(.01)	(.001)	(.01)
Margin in last election	−.002*	.001	−.001	−.004**
	(.001)	(.001)	(.01)	(.002)
Announced retirement (1, 0)	.31***	.35**	.29*	.23
	(.12)	(.14)	(.17)	(.17)
Freshman member (1, 0)	−.28***	−.11	−.38***	−.08
	(.10)	(.09)	(.14)	(.10)
President's vote share				.46
				(.49)
Part of broader package (1, 0)	.06	.02	.17	.03
	(.16)	(.19)	(.27)	(.24)
Constant	.80	−.59	.72	−.68
	(.68)	(.87)	(.46)	(.79)
Pseudo R^2	.21	.19	.26	.28
Observations	28,125	11,349	16,776	13,634

Note: Dependent variable is House members' votes on debt-ceiling increases, with "yea" coded as 1, "nay" as 0. Logistic-regression coefficients displayed, with robust standard errors clustered on the Congress in parentheses.
*$p < .05$, **$p < .01$, ***$p < .001$

TABLE B.4. **Senators' votes on debt-limit increases, 1956–2014**

	(1) All years	(2) Post-1980	(3) Pre-1980
Majority party member (1, 0)	.34	.27	−1.80**
	(.54)	(.96)	(0.71)
Same party as the president (1, 0)	1.48***	2.75***	1.05**
	(0.55)	(0.56)	(0.49)
Majority party's margin of control	0.01	−0.11***	.02
	(0.02)	(0.05)	(0.02)
Republican (0, 1)	−0.10	−0.49*	−1.45*
	(0.43)	(0.45)	(0.77)
Extremism (DW-NOM distance from 0)	−4.69***	−1.39	−7.73***
	(1.11)	(1.18)	(0.51)
Party leader (1, 0)	0.94***	0.73**	1.00*
	(0.28)	(0.31)	(0.58)
Committee leader (1, 0)	0.27*	0.20	0.43*
	(0.10)	(0.15)	(0.14)
Majorityparty#Samepartypresident	−1.00**	−0.40	−1.94***
	(0.41)	(0.50)	(0.85)
Majorityparty#Extremism	5.54***	2.05*	8.20***
	(1.43)	(1.78)	(1.43)
Samepartypresident#Extremism	0.91	−2.71	3.76***
	(1.51)	(1.73)	(1.46)
Majoritymargin#Majorityparty	−0.02	0.14**	0.002
	(0.02)	(0.08)	(0.03)
Margin in last election	−0.01*	0.01**	−0.02***
	(0.003)	(0.003)	(0.01)
Announced retirement (1, 0)	0.05	0.07	−0.05
	(0.17)	(0.27)	(0.36)
Freshman member (1, 0)	−0.08	0.24	−0.35*
	(0.18)	(0.27)	(0.19)
President's vote share	−0.06	−1.42	−0.11
	(0.85)	(1.09)	(1.68)
Part of broader package (1, 0)	0.53**	0.58*	0.95
	(.24)	(0.31)	(0.59)
Constant	0.61	0.69	2.78
	(0.66)	(0.86)	(0.96)
Pseudo R^2	0.21	0.28	0.21
Observations	4,566	2,510	2,056

Note: Dependent variable is senators' votes on debt-ceiling increases, with "yea" coded as 1, "nay" as 0. Logistic regression coefficients displayed, with robust standard errors clustered on the Congress in parentheses.
*$p < 0.05$, **$p < 0.01$, ***$p < 0.001$

Model Results for Chapter 8

TABLE C.I. **Effect of party competition on state legislative party polarization, lower chambers (Prais-Winston regression models)**

	Model 1 B (pcse)	Model 2 B (pcse)	Model 3 B (pcse)	Model 4 B (pcse)	Model 5 B (pcse)
Shifts in party control	.06*** (.01)				
State party competition index		−1.51*** (.20)			
Presidential competition			−.77*** (.24)		
Party identification balance				−.12*** (.04)	
Effective number of parties					.47*** (.08)
Gini index	.12 (.22)	.09 (.24)	.06 (.24)	.03 (.24)	.04 (.25)
The South	−.21*** (.02)	−.23*** (.02)	−.24*** (.02)	−.26*** (.02)	−.25*** (.02)
Professionalism	.99*** (.13)	.86*** (.14)	1.09*** (.10)	1.16*** (.11)	.92*** (.12)
Divided government	−.001 (.01)	−.01 (.01)	−.004 (.01)	−.01 (.01)	−.02 (.01)
Traditional party organizations	−.12*** (.01)	−.12*** (.01)	−.13*** (.01)	−.13*** (.01)	−.13*** (.01)
Urbanization	.01*** (.001)	.01*** (.001)	.004*** (.001)	.01*** (.001)	.01*** (.001)
Chamber size	.001*** (.0001)	.001*** (.0002)	.001*** (.0001)	.001*** (.0001)	.001*** (.0002)
Time	.02*** (.002)	.02*** (.002)	.02*** (.002)	.01*** (.002)	.02*** (.002)
Constant	.75*** (.14)	.97*** (.15)	.87*** (.14)	.80*** (.14)	−.06 (.24)
Rho	.82	.82	.79	.77	.79
R-squared	.67	.69	.65	.62	.66

Note: Prais-Winsten regression coefficients, with panel-corrected standard errors in parentheses. The dependent variable is legislative party polarization. N = 830 (except for model 4, where N = 700 due to missing data on state party identification from 2010 to 2013); 49 states.
*$p < .1$, **$p < .05$, ***$p < .01$

TABLE C.2. **Effect of party competition on state legislative party polarization, upper chambers (Prais-Winston regression models)**

	Model 1 B (pcse)	Model 2 B (pcse)	Model 3 B (pcse)	Model 4 B (pcse)	Model 5 B (pcse)
Shifts in party control	.03*** (.01)				
State party competition index		−.99*** (.26)			
Presidential competition			−.77*** (.21)		
Party identification balance				−.08** (.05)	
Effective number of parties					.22*** (.09)
Gini index	.17 (.24)	.14 (.26)	.09 (.25)	.03 (.29)	.001 (.25)
The South	−.21*** (.03)	−.22*** (.03)	−.23*** (.03)	−.21*** (.03)	−.23*** (.03)
Professionalism	1.37*** (.14)	1.24*** (.14)	1.38*** (.14)	1.39*** (.11)	1.33*** (.14)
Divided government	.01 (.01)	.01 (.01)	.01 (.01)	−.01 (.02)	.004 (.01)
Traditional party organizations	−.13*** (.01)	−.13*** (.01)	−.13*** (.01)	−.13*** (.01)	−.13*** (.01)
Urbanization	.002 (.002)	.003 (.002)	.002 (.002)	.001 (.002)	.002 (.002)
Chamber size	.01*** (.001)	.01*** (.001)	.01*** (.001)	.01*** (.001)	.01*** (.001)
Time	.02*** (.002)	.01*** (.002)	.02*** (.002)	.01*** (.002)	.02*** (.002)
Constant	.82*** (.17)	.99*** (.18)	.95*** (.17)	1.01*** (.19)	.55*** (.22)
Rho	.85	.84	.84	.78	.83
R-squared	.63	.63	.63	.57	.63

Note: Prais-Winsten regression coefficients, with panel-corrected standard errors in parentheses. The dependent variable is legislative party polarization. N = 825 (except for model 4, where N = 697 due to missing data on state party identification from 2010 to 2013); 49 states.
*$p < .1$, **$p < .05$, ***$p < .01$

TABLE C.3. **Effect of party competition on state legislative party polarization, lower chambers (fixed-effects TSCS models)**

	Model 1 B (se)	Model 2 B (se)	Model 3 B (se)	Model 4 B (se)	Model 5 B (se)
Shifts in party control	.03*** (.01)				
State party competition index		−.48*** (.12)			
Presidential competition			−.08 (.12)		
Party identification balance				−.02* (.02)	
Effective number of parties					.13*** (.05)
Gini index	.29* (.18)	.19 (.18)	.21 (.18)	.50*** (.18)	.14 (.18)
Professionalism	.99*** (.21)	.89*** (.21)	.86*** (.21)	.51** (.20)	.82*** (.21)
Divided government	−.0001 (.01)	−.01 (.01)	−.01 (.01)	−.001 (.01)	−.01 (.01)
Urbanization	.003* (.002)	.003 (.002)	.003 (.002)	.003* (.002)	.003* (.002)
Time	.02*** (.001)	.02*** (.001)	.02*** (.001)	.01*** (.001)	.02*** (.001)
State fixed effects	X	X	X	X	X
R-squared	.21	.23	.18	.16	.24
Constant	.61*** (.18)	.78*** (.18)	.75*** (.19)	.64*** (.18)	.80*** (.18)

Note: Fixed-effects regression model coefficients. The dependent variable is legislative party polarization.
$N = 830$ (except for model 4, where $N = 700$ due to missing data on state party identification from 2010 to 2013); 49 states.
$*p < .1, **p < .05, ***p < .01$

TABLE C.4. **Effect of party competition on state legislative party polarization, upper chambers (fixed-effects TSCS models)**

	Model 1 B (se)	Model 2 B (se)	Model 3 B (se)	Model 4 B (se)	Model 5 B (se)
Shifts in party control	.03*** (.01)				
State party competition index		−.24* (.18)			
Presidential competition			−.03 (.18)		
Party identification balance				.003 (.04)	
Effective number of parties					.06 (.06)
Gini index	.66** (.28)	.50* (.28)	.52* (.28)	.64** (.29)	.49* (.28)
Professionalism	.61** (.32)	.55* (.32)	.55* (.32)	.70** (.32)	.55* (.32)
Divided government	.05*** (.01)	.04*** (.01)	.04*** (.01)	.06*** (.01)	.04*** (.01)
Urbanization	−.01** (.003)	−.01*** (.003)	−.01*** (.003)	−.01** (.003)	−.01*** (.003)
Time	.02*** (.001)	.02*** (.002)	.02*** (.002)	.01*** (.002)	.02*** (.002)
State fixed effects	X	X	X	X	X
R-squared	.05	.04	.02	.05	.03
Constant	1.24*** (.28)	1.42*** (.28)	1.40*** (.28)	1.17*** (.30)	1.30*** (.30)

Note: Fixed-effects regression model coefficients. The dependent variable is legislative party polarization. $N = 825$ (except for model 4, where $N = 697$ due to missing data on state party identification between 2010 and 2013); 49 states.
$*p < .1, **p < .05, ***p < .01$

Notes

Chapter One

1. The prevalence of government-versus-opposition voting in Congress cannot be ascertained by vote-scaling methodologies such as NOMINATE (Poole and Rosenthal 1997). These methodologies can be used to summarize behavior in legislatures where this kind of behavior predominates, but such methods do not yield estimates of legislators' policy positions on a left–right continuum. When such behavior occurs, these scores track party discipline instead of ideology (Godbout and Høyland 2011; Hix and Noury forthcoming; Spirling and McLean 2007; Zucco 2009; Zucco and Lauderdale 2011). Similarly, if members of minority parties in Congress reflexively oppose the majority's initiatives along a similar parliamentary logic, the behavior will be captured on the first dimension of NOMINATE and thus will be characterized as "ideological."

Chapter Two

1. The search term used was "(Congress* AND election?)." This search returns all articles about the upcoming elections. I then read the articles to determine whether they included discussion about possible shifts in majority control of either or both chambers of Congress.

2. The Democrats regained control of the Senate in 2001 only as a result of Jim Jeffords's party switch on May 24.

3. Panel, "How Congress Functions: Perspectives and Observations," The First Branch: The Congressional Research Service Centennial Symposium, Library of Congress, Washington, DC, July 16, 2014.

4. Interview 23.

5. Interview 15.

6. Interview 20.

7. Interview 24.

8. Interview 13.

9. Interview 25.

10. Interview 31.

11. Interview 15.

12. Interview 24.

13. Interview 14.

14. Interview 16.

15. Interview 18.

16. Interview 14.

17. Interview 20.

18. Interview 32.

19. Interview 14.

20. Interview 27.

21. Interview 20.

22. Interview 32.

23. Ibid.

24. The Supreme Court overturned the post-2010 congressional districts in Alabama (*Alabama Legislative Black Caucus v. Alabama*, 575 U.S. ___ 2015) and in North Carolina (*Dixon v. Rucho*, 575 U.S. ___ 2015).

25. Interview 5.

26. Interview 3.

27. Interview 11.

Chapter Three

1. Interview 32.

2. Quoted in Hulse 2006.

3. Interview 9.

4. Interview 1.

5. Interview 25.

6. Interview 12.

7. Interview 28.

8. Interview 29.

9. The majority party does not claim the chairs of all legislative committees in some state legislatures, but this practice has been the custom in Congress since the nineteenth century.

10. Interview 19.

11. Interview 30.

12. Interview 1.

13. Interview 28.

14. Interview 19.

15. On average, fifteen articles on "party messages" per year appeared in *Roll Call* and *The Hill* between 1995 and 2012.

16. Quoted in Hallow (1991).

17. Quoted in Farrell (2001).

18. Interview 1.

19. Interview 20.

20. The agenda included a minimum-wage increase, a bill to implement the homeland security recommendations of the September 11 commission, allowance for federal funding of stem-cell research, reductions in student-loan rates, permission for the federal government to negotiate drug prices under Medicare, and a rollback of tax benefits for oil and gas companies to fund research on alternative energy.

21. Interview 20.

22. Interview 1.

23. Interview 32.

24. Interview 7.

25. Interview 20.

26. Interview 28.

27. Interview 27.

28. Interview 30.

29. Interview 8.

30. Interview 20.

31. Interview 3. See also Bai (2005).

32. Interview 19.

33. Ibid.

34. Interview 10.

35. Interview 1.

36. Interview 9.

37. Interview 1.

38. Interview 9.

39. *Congressional Record*, December 15, 1995, S18698.

40. Interview 9.

41. Interview 20.

42. Interview 19.

43. *Congressional Record*, April 9, 1987, H1959.

44. Interview 2.

45. Interview 3.

46. Interview 5.

47. Interview 11.

48. Interview 17.

49. Interview 14.

50. Interview 9.

51. Quoted in Klein (1995, 37).

52. Interview 2.

53. Interview 9.

54. Interview 26.

55. Interview 30.

56. Interview 32.

57. Interview 24.

58. Interview 17.

59. See, for example, "Republicans Hit the Airwaves, Calling for Bipartisan Stimulus," Speaker of the House John Boehner Blog, January 29, 2009, http://www.speaker.gov/general/republicans-hit-airwaves-calling-bipartisan-stimulus.

60. See, for example, House Democrats' positions on the Medicare Modernization Act of 2003 ("Medicare Revamp Cuts It Close" 2004).

61. Interview 27.

62. Interview 18.

63. From the transcript of the Cannon Centenary Conference (US House of Representatives 2004, 111).

64. Interview 14.

65. Ibid.

66. Ibid.

67. Interview 7.

68. Interview 17.

69. Interview 1.

70. Interview 27.

71. Ibid.

72. Interview 8.

73. Interview 27.

74. Ibid.

75. Interview 14.

76. Interview 13.

77. Interview 24.

Chapter Four

1. Quoted in Draper (2012).

2. Quoted in Calmes and Gurwit (1987, 11).

3. Quotes are from a 1967 speech Ford gave at Bowling Green University, reprinted in the *Congressional Record*, May 15, 1967, 12611.

4. Interview 14.

5. Interview 29.

6. Interview 15.

7. Interview 31.

8. Interview 26.

9. Ibid.

10. Interview 25.

11. Quoted in Gailey (1982).

12. These three senators were John C. Stennis (D-MS), elected in 1947; Russell B. Long (D-LA), elected in 1948; and Henry M. "Scoop" Jackson (D-WA), elected in 1953.

13. Interview 25.

14. Interview 31.

15. Interview 25.

16. Ibid.

17. Democratic Policy and Communications Committee staff in 2014 were able to locate in the committee's archives the 1985 and 1986 volumes of this publication, labeled "Part 5 and Part 6," which is consistent with the account that these volumes first began to be assembled in 1981. The statement of purpose appears on the inscription page immediately following the title page.

18. Ibid.

19. On the minority party's stronger interest in forcing votes that result in party-line divisions, see Egar (forthcoming).

20. Interview 25.

21. Interview 31.

22. Ibid.

23. Ibid.

24. Interview 25.

25. Data on campaign committee expenditures are from Ornstein et al. (1996, 105).

26. Interview 25.

27. Quoted in Barnes (1985, 9).

28. Interview 29. See also Farrell (2001, 631) and Arieff (1980).

29. Data were obtained from Forgette (2004).

30. As noted in the footnote to figure 4.1, the post-1980 shift is evident in a regression model that includes a variable interacting *time* and *post1980*. The shift is also clearly visible in the scatterplot.

31. The lack of records reflects the dormancy of the House Democratic caucus for the fifty years before 1969, when reformers revived the House Democratic caucus in their struggle to assert control over conservative committee chairmen (Peters 1990, 152–53).

32. Interview 14.

33. Interview 26.

34. Interview 23.

35. Interview 5.

36. Papers of Richard K. Armey, Legislative Series, Box 46, Folder 7, Budget Commandos, 1985–86, Carl Albert Center Congressional Archives, University of Oklahoma.

37. *Congressional Record*, June 25, 1987, 17402.

38. Ibid., 17404.

39. Ibid.

40. Ibid., 17407.

41. Ibid., 17406.

42. For example, the former Democrat Rep. Trent Lott (R-MS) was seen as more open to bipartisan negotiation than his opponent Rep. Bud Shuster (R-PA) at the time of his election as House minority whip in 1980 (Lott 2005, 78). But Lott maintained close ties to the Conservative Opportunity Society and moved in a more confrontational direction later in the 1980s.

43. Interview 14.

44. Interview 16.

45. Interview 15.

46. Interview 29. The reference is to Robert T. Stafford (R-VT), a moderate Republican who served long tenures in both the House (1961–71) and the Senate (1971–89).

47. Interview 14.

48. Interview 16.

49. Interview 14.

50. Interview 24.

51. Interview 20.

52. *Congressional Record*, September 21, 1987, H7639.

53. Interview 18.

54. Interview 23.

Chapter Five

1. Quoted in Gelbart (1996, 4).

2. Quoted in Granat (1984, 3057).

3. Data compiled from *Congressional Staff Directories*.

4. See tables 5–6 and 6–7 in Ornstein et al. (2013).

5. Interview 21.

6. Interview 5.

7. Interview 14.

8. Video from the press conference was uploaded to the House Republican Conference's blog on April 24, 2013.

9. House Republican Conference, "Budgets or Brackets?," video, GOP.gov, March 19, 2013.

10. "Editorial Cartoons on the GOP Government Shutdown," The Democratic Whip Steny Hoyer Blog, October 3, 2013, http://www.democraticwhip.gov/content/editorial-cartoons-gop-government-shutdown.

11. "Pelosi: The GOP Earns an 'F' on the First 100 Days of Congress," Democratic Leader Nancy Pelosi Blog, April 12, 2013, http://www.democraticleader.gov/newsroom/pelosi-gop-earns-f-first-100-days-congress/.

12. Katie Boyd, "Pressure Mounts on President Obama to Approve Keystone Pipeline," Speaker of the House John Boehner Blog, March 27, 2013, http://www.speaker.gov/general/pressure-mounts-president-obama-approve-keystone-pipeline.

13. This difference of means is statistically significant ($t = 3.6, p < .01, n = 97$).

14. Interview 3.

15. Interview 5.

16. Interview 1.

17. Interviews 20 and 8.

18. Interview 5.

19. Interview 1.

20. Interview 27.

21. Interview 19.

22. Interviews 10 and 19.

23. Interview 30.

24. Interview 19.

25. Interview 10.

26. Interview 19.

27. Ibid.

28. Interview 28.

29. Interview 19.

30. Interview 9.

31. Interviews 8, 29, and 32.

32. Interview 8.

33. Interview 19.

34. Interview 5.

35. Interview 28. The reference is to making a measurable difference in public opinion polls.

36. Interview 19.

37. Interview 8.

38. Interview 19.

39. Interview 10.

40. Interview 30.

41. Interview 10.

42. Interview 28.

43. Interview 25.

44. Interview 9.

45. The idea of using *Roll Call*'s ranking as a measure of perceived influence originates with Wolfensberger (2014), who uses the list to track the rising influence of party leadership staff relative to committee staff.

46. Interview 8.

47. Interview 9.

48. Interview 10.

49. Interview 9.

50. Interview 8.

51. Ibid.

52. Interview 14.

53. Interview 29.

54. Interview 25.

55. Interview 19.

56. Interview 5.

57. Interview 20.

58. The House Republican allocation amounted to three or four communications staffers out of a total staff of about twenty-five to thirty. House Democrats during this period typically had two communications staffers out of a staff of fifty-four to fifty-nine.

59. Interview 13.

60. Interview 14.

61. See, for example, the remarks of Rep. Louise Slaughter, *Congressional Record*, January 1, 2013, H7532.

Chapter Six

1. Quoted in Hulse (2009a).

2. *Congressional Record*, November 3, 2011, S7094.

3. Ibid., August 1, 2006, S8506.

4. Ibid., March 26, 2004, S3217.

5. Ibid., April 1, 2004, S3530.

6. Ibid., August 3, 2012, E1441.

7. Ibid., May 25, 2011, S3342.

8. Interview 27.

9. Interview 3.

10. Interview 30. For confirmation that procedural votes are often used in campaign ads, see Smith et al. (2013).

11. Interview 8.
12. Interview 19.
13. Interview 27.
14. Interview 8.
15. Interview 3.
16. *Congressional Record*, March 17, 2001, S5090.
17. Interview 14.
18. Interview 26.
19. Interview 19.
20. Interview 11.
21. *Congressional Record*, October 6, 2011, S6317.
22. Ibid., S6319.
23. Ibid., S6316.
24. Interview 26.
25. The Senate only took 209 votes on amendments in the 112th Congress and 218 in the 113th Congress, as compared to an average of 400 amendment votes per Congress since 1980 and an average of 440 per Congress since 1960.
26. Interview 3.
27. Interview 19.
28. Interview 9.
29. H.R. 2, 112th Congress.
30. Interview 27.
31. Interview 11.
32. Interview 33.
33. Interview 19.
34. Interview 17.
35. Interview 3.
36. For a few representative examples, see Barbash (2011), Editorial (2014a), Harder (2012), Pierce (2008), Raju (2008), and Stanton (2008).
37. *Congressional Record*, September 10, 1997, S9055.
38. Ibid., April 22, 1998, H6394.
39. Searches in the *Congressional Record* for the term *November amendments* did not yield any hits. I have not been able to identify other synonyms for the tactic beyond those listed here.
40. The models do not include a control for the amendment sponsor's party (Republican or Democrat) in addition to the variables indicating majority or minority status because there are no Republican Congresses between 1959 and 1980. If a party variable is included in the post-1980 models, it has no statistically significant effect and does not change the other model results.
41. Predicted probabilities are calculated holding all other independent variables in the model at the observed value for each case, and confidence intervals were calculated via statistical simulation (Hanmer and Ozan 2013).

42. Amendments offered by the most extreme group of majority-party senators (those with distances from the chamber median of .8 or greater) have a probability of success of .36. Amendments offered by the most centrist group of minority-party senators (those with distances from the chamber median of .1 or less) have a probability of success of .30. This difference is statistically different from zero ($p < .01$).

43. Note that the total number of amendments receiving recorded votes on the Senate floor rose and then fell over the time period examined. The number of amendments considered on the Senate floor increased dramatically over the 1960s and 1970s with the rise of a more activist Senate style (Sinclair 1990; Smith 1989). During the 1980s, however, there was a steady decline in the number of amendment votes back to 1960s levels (Lee 2012, 113–16). The number of amendments receiving recorded votes held steady at 1960s levels through the 1990s and the first decade of the 2000s, before dropping to levels characteristic of the late 1950s.

44. Through an analysis of all Senate amendments offered to landmark legislation (whether or not they received a recorded vote), Madonna and Kosar (2015, 7–8) show that amendments sponsored by minority-party senators have constituted a steadily escalating share of the total amendments offered since the 1970s.

45. "The State of the U.S. Senate: Understanding the Filibuster and the Emergence of the 60-Vote Majority," transcript, Brookings Institution, May 17, 2010, 7–8, http://www.brookings.edu/~/media/Files/events/2010/0517_senate/20100517_wyden.pdf.

46. Quoted in Senior (2010).

Chapter Seven

1. Changes in federal policy are not necessary for federal debt to reach its statutory limit. The total amount of federal government borrowing is specified in nominal dollars so that the ceiling needs to be raised even when the ratio of debt to gross domestic product remains the same in a growing economy. In addition, many factors besides policy changes precipitate the need to raise the debt limit, such as interest-rate increases, economic downturns (that both reduce federal revenues and intensify demand for spending), and demographic changes affecting the share of the population receiving various entitlement benefits.

2. Appendix B lists all these votes in both the House and the Senate.

3. Of the Senate's roll-call votes to raise the debt ceiling, 63 percent were on "clean" debt-ceiling bills. In the House, 60 percent of debt-limit votes were on clean measures. Although the dataset compiled here includes all final passage votes to raise the debt ceiling throughout the 1953–2014 period, the findings re-

ported in this chapter are not altered if the dataset is restricted solely to the sub-set of "clean" debt-ceiling increases.

4. Despite dozens of polls on the topic, searches in the Roper iPoll database yielded not one in which most respondents favored raising the debt ceiling.

5. *Congressional Record*, March 16, 2006, S 2236.

6. Ibid., February 8, 1967, 3015.

7. Ibid.

8. Hausman tests of the equality of the party-control coefficients across the pre- and post-1980 models reject the null of no difference at $p < .001$ for both the House and the Senate.

Chapter Eight

1. Before Shor and McCarty (2011), the only previous effort to compile data on legislative voting behavior across all fifty states was led by Gerald C. Wright, whose dataset covers 1999–2000 and 2003–4 (Clark et al. 2009).

2. Nebraska is not included because of its use of nonpartisan elections. As of the 2014 data release, there are fourteen states covered in 1995, forty-five states in 1996, forty-eight or forty-nine states every year between 1997 and 2008, twenty-seven states in 2009, twenty-eight states in 2010, forty-four states in 2011, forty-four states in 2012, and forty-one states in 2013.

3. Generally speaking, two-party competition at the level of the legislative district has been thought to encourage representatives to adopt moderate po-sitions, and a line of scholarship has found that lawmakers from swing districts tend to be less party loyal than those representing districts that tilt decisively to-ward one party (see, e.g., Erikson and Wright 2000; Griffin 2006).

4. Our interval measures correlate with one another with statistically signifi-cant r coefficients ranging from .61 to .93.

5. Historical data on the composition of state legislatures were obtained from Dubin (2007).

6. Excluding all cases with centered leverage three times the overall mean (HI, MA, RI, and ID), the relationship between effective number of political parties and legislative party polarization holds up for both lower ($p < .01$) and upper chambers ($p < .01$).

7. Excluding all cases with centered leverage three times the overall mean (UT, WY, RI, and MA), the relationship between the competitiveness of presi-dential elections and state polarization holds up for both lower and upper cham-bers ($p < .04$).

8. Excluding the five states with high leverage on the regression line (HI, RI, MA, ID, and AR) yields $n = 42$. Nevertheless, the coefficients remain negative and statistically significant ($p < .05$).

9. Excluding all the cases with more than three times the mean centered leverage (HI, MA, and MD), the coefficient for state partisan balance is −1.08 ($p < .05$) for lower chambers and −1.33 ($p < .01$) for upper chambers.

10. These panel data present some difficult trade-offs with respect to the choice of modeling approach. A number of our control variables do not vary over time (e.g., the South, TPOs) and will thus drop out of any model with fixed effects for states. Nevertheless, we are interested in knowing if these particular controls affect the relationship between party competition and party polarization, because they have been shown in previous scholarship to have systematic effects on state party politics. A second, more serious problem is that there is limited variation with respect to most of the variables in the model. Our key independent variables measuring party competition change only modestly over time. The same is also true for a number of our controls (e.g., legislative professionalism, urbanization). A fixed-effects model is not only less efficient, given the loss of degrees of freedom. It is also very difficult for slowly changing independent variables to survive in a fixed-effects model, because such variables will be highly collinear with the effects.

11. Given the variability of state coverage, there are a small number of year gaps for particular states. Missing cases are handled via pairwise deletion. Results do not substantially change, however, using casewise deletion.

Chapter Nine

1. Interview 22.

2. Examples include the 2015 bipartisan accords on Medicare payments to doctors, trade promotion authority, transportation infrastructure, and a two-year budget framework.

References

Abramowitz, Alan I. 2010. *The Disappearing Center: Engaged Citizens, Polarization, and American Democracy.* New Haven, CT: Yale University Press.

Abramowitz, Alan, and Jeffrey A. Segal. 1992. *Senate Elections.* Ann Arbor: University of Michigan Press.

Ainsworth, Scott, and Marcus Flathman. 1995. "Unanimous Consent Agreements as Leadership Tools." *Legislative Studies Quarterly* 20 (1): 177–95.

Aldrich, John H., and James S. Coleman Battista. 2002. "Conditional Party Government in the States." *American Journal of Political Science* 46 (1): 164–72.

Aldrich, John H., Jacob M. Montgomery, and David B. Sparks. 2014. "Polarization and Ideology: Partisan Sources of Low Dimensionality in Scaled Roll Call Analyses." *Political Analysis* 22 (4): 435–56.

Aldrich, John H., and David W. Rohde. 2000. "The Republican Revolution and the House Appropriations Committee." *Journal of Politics* 62 (1): 1–33.

Allen, Craig. 1992. "Eisenhower's Congressional Defeat of 1956: Limitations of Television and the GOP." *Presidential Studies Quarterly* 22 (1): 57–71.

American Political Science Association, Committee on Political Parties. 1950. "Toward a More Responsible Two-Party System: A Report of the Committee on Political Parties." *American Political Science Review* 44 (3): 1–14.

Annis, J. Lee. 1995. *Howard Baker: Conciliator in an Age of Crisis.* Lanham, MD: Madison Books.

Apple, R. W., Jr. 1968. "Nixon Forecasts Sweeping Victory." *New York Times,* October 16, 1.

Arieff, Irwin B. 1979. "House Freshmen Republicans Seek Role as Power Brokers," *Congressional Quarterly Weekly Report,* July 7, 1339–45.

———. 1980a. "House Democrats, GOP Elect Leaders, Draw Battle Lines." *Congressional Quarterly Weekly Report,* December 13, 3549–51.

———. 1980b. "House, Senate Chiefs Attempt to Lead a Changed Congress." *Congressional Quarterly Weekly Report,* September 30, 2695–700.

———. 1981. "House GOP, Still a Minority, Seeks Peace with Democrats." *Congressional Quarterly Weekly Report*, February 28, 379–81.

Asher, Herbert B., and Herbert F. Weisberg. 1978. "Voting Change in Congress: Some Dynamic Perspectives on an Evolutionary Process." *American Journal of Political Science* 22 (2): 391–425.

Austin, D. Andrew, and Mindy R. Levit. 2013. *The Debt Limit: History and Recent Increases*, Congressional Research Service, RL31976, May 22.

Bach, Stanley, and Steven S. Smith. 1988. *Managing Uncertainty in the House of Representatives: Adaptation and Innovation in Special Rules*. Washington, DC: Brookings Institution.

Bai, Matt. 2005. "The Framing Wars." *New York Times Magazine*, July 17, 38.

Bailey, Christopher J. 1988. *The Republican Party in the U.S. Senate, 1974–1984: Party Change and Institutional Development*. Manchester, UK: Manchester University Press.

Balz, Dan. 1989. "Democrats Grope for Winning Message." *Washington Post*, September 11, A6.

Balz, Dan, and Charles R. Babcock. 1994. "Gingrich, Allies Made Waves and Impression; Conservative Rebels Harassed the House." *Washington Post*, December 20, A1.

Barbash, Fred. 2011. "Divided Government Could Result in Stalemate." *CQ Weekly*, January 10, 96–97.

Barber, Michael J., and Nolan McCarty. 2015. "Causes and Consequences of Polarization." In *Solutions to Political Polarization in America*, ed. Nathaniel Persily. New York: Cambridge University Press, 15–58.

Barnes, Fred. 1985. "Raging Representatives." *New Republic*, June 3, 9.

Barone, Michael, Grant Ujifusa, and Douglas Matthews. 1979. *Almanac of American Politics 1980*. New York: E. F. Dutton.

Barone, Michael, Grant Ujifusa. 1989. *Almanac of American Politics 1990*. Washington, DC: National Journal.

Bartels, Larry M. 2000. "Partisanship and Voting Behavior, 1952–1996." *American Journal of Political Science* 44 (1): 35–50.

Beck, Nathaniel, and Jonathan Katz. 1995. "What to Do (and Not to Do) with Time-Series—Cross-Section Data in Comparative Politics." *American Political Science Review* 89 (3): 634–47.

Berke, Richard L. 1994. "Democrats Glum about Prospects as Elections Near." *New York Times*, September 4, 1.

Bernick, E. Lee. 1978. "The Impact of U.S. Governors on Party Voting in One-Party Dominated Legislatures." *Legislative Studies Quarterly* 3 (3): 431–44.

Beth, Richard S., Valerie Heitshusen, Bill Heniff Jr., and Elizabeth Rybicki. 2009. "Leadership Tools for Managing the U.S. Senate." Paper presented at the Annual Meeting of the American Political Science Association, Toronto, Canada, September 3–6.

Biggs, Jeffrey R., and Thomas S. Foley. 1999. *Honor in the House: Speaker Tom Foley.* Pullman: Washington State University Press.

Binder, Sarah A. 2013. "Reality Check: 'Gephardt Rule' Alone Can't Fix the Debt Limit Crisis." *Washington Post*, October 13, http://www.washingtonpost .com/blogs/monkey-cage/wp/2013/10/13/reality-check-gephardt-rule-alone -cant-fix-the-debt-limit-crisis/.

Black, Earl, and Merle Black. 2002. *The Rise of Southern Republicans.* Cambridge, MA: Harvard University Press.

———. 2007. *Divided America: The Ferocious Power Struggle in American Politics.* New York: Simon and Schuster.

Blake, Aaron, and Sean Sullivan. 2013. "Congress's Addiction to Kicking the Can Down the Road." *Washington Post*, January 22, http://www .washingtonpost.com/news/the-fix/wp/2013/01/22/congresss-addiction-to -kicking-the-can-down-the-road/.

Bleich, Erik, and Robert Pekkanen. 2013. "How to Report Interview Data." In *Interview Research in Political Science*, ed. Layna Mosley. Ithaca, NY: Cornell University Press, 84–108.

Bolton, Alexander. 2007. "Senate GOP Begins Repair of Messaging." *The Hill*, January 17, 1.

Brady, David W., and Phillip Althoff. 1974. "Party Voting in the U.S. House of Representatives, 1890–1910: Elements of a Responsible Party System." *Journal of Politics* 36: 753–75.

Brady, David W., and Charles S. Bullock III. 1980. "Is There a Conservative Coalition in the House?" *Journal of Politics* 42 (2): 549–59.

Brady, David W., Joseph Cooper, and Patricia A. Hurley. 1979. "The Decline of Party in the U.S. House of Representatives, 1887–1968." *Legislative Studies Quarterly* 4 (3): 381–407.

Brewer, Mark D. 2005. "The Rise of Partisanship and the Expansion of Partisan Conflict within the American Electorate." *Political Research Quarterly* 58 (2): 219–29.

Broder, David S. 1981. "Democrats' Policy Session a Big Gamble." *Washington Post*, October 19, A4.

Burnham, Walter Dean. 1970. *Critical Elections and the Mainsprings of American Politics.* New York: Norton.

Busch, Andrew. 2005. *Reagan's Victory: The Presidential Election of 1980 and the Rise of the Right.* Lawrence: University Press of Kansas.

Butler, Daniel M., and Eleanor Neff Powell. 2014. "Understanding the Party Brand: Experimental Evidence on the Role of Valence." *Journal of Politics* 76 (2): 492–505.

Byrd, Robert C. 2005. *Robert C. Byrd: Child of the Appalachian Coalfields.* Morgantown: West Virginia University Press.

Calmes, Jacqueline. 1986. "Gramm-Rudman a Focus of Discussion: House

Members Head for Party Conferences." *Congressional Quarterly Weekly Report*, January 25, 164.

Calmes, Jacqueline, and Rob Gurwitt. 1987. "Profiles in Power: Leaders without Portfolios." *Congressional Quarterly Weekly Report*, January 3, 11.

Campbell, James E. 1986. "Presidential Coattails and Midterm Losses in State Legislative Elections." *American Political Science Review* 80 (1): 45–63.

———. 1993. *The Presidential Pulse of Congressional Elections.* Lexington: University Press of Kentucky.

Cann, Damon M. 2008. *Sharing the Wealth: Member Contributions and the Exchange Theory of Party Influence in the U.S. House of Representatives.* Albany, NY: SUNY Press.

Carroll, Royce, and Jason Eichorst. 2013. "The Role of Party: The Legislative Consequences of Partisan Electoral Competition." *Legislative Studies Quarterly* 38 (1): 83–109.

Carson, Jamie L. 2005. "Strategy, Selection, and Candidate Competition in U.S. House and Senate Elections." *Journal of Politics* 67 (1): 1–28.

Chen, Jowei, and Jonathan Rodden. 2013. "Unintentional Gerrymandering: Political Geography and Electoral Bias in Legislatures." *Quarterly Journal of Political Science* 8 (3): 239–69.

Cheney, Richard B. 1989. "An Unruly House: A Republican View." *Public Opinion*, January–February, 41–44.

Cherny, Robert W. 1997. *American Politics in the Gilded Age, 1868–1900.* Wheeling, IL: Harlan Davidson.

Cillizza, Chris. 2015. "It Could Be a Very Long Time before Democrats Are in the House Majority Again." *Washington Post*, January 29, http://www .washingtonpost.com/blogs/the-fix/wp/2015/01/29/it-could-be-a-while-before -democrats-are-in-the-house-majority-again/.

Clark, Jennifer Hayes, Tracy Osborn, Jonathan Winburn, and Gerald C. Wright. 2009. "Representation in U.S. Legislatures: The Acquisition and Analysis of U.S. State Legislative Roll-Call Data." *State Politics and Policy Quarterly* 9 (3): 356–70.

Clubb, Jerome M., William H. Flanigan, and Nancy H. Zingale. 1980. *Partisan Realignment: Voters, Parties, and Government in American History.* Beverly Hills, CA: Sage Publications.

Clymer, Adam. 2008. *Drawing the Line at the Big Ditch: The Panama Canal Treaties and the Rise of the Right.* Lawrence: University Press of Kansas.

Coffey, Daniel J. 2007. "State Party Activists and State Party Polarization." In *The State of the Parties: The Changing Role of Contemporary American Parties*, ed. John C. Green and Daniel J. Coffey, 5th ed. Lanham, MD: Rowman and Littlefield, 75–91.

———. 2011. "More Than a Dime's Worth: Using State Party Platforms to Assess the Degree of American Party Polarization." *PS: Political Science and Politics* 44 (2): 331–37.

Cohen, Richard E. 1977. "House Republicans under Rhodes—Divided They Stand and Fret." *National Journal,* October 29, 1686.

———. 1982a. "His Troops Restless over the Budget, GOP Leader Michel Is on the Spot." *National Journal,* February 20, 316.

———. 1982b. "Nearly Anonymous Insiders Play Key Roles as Aides to Congress's Leaders." *National Journal,* September 11, 1545–49.

———. 1985. "Balanced Budget Plan Forces House Democrats to Get Their Act Together." *National Journal,* November 16, 2586–88.

Cohodas, Nadine. 1987. "Metzenbaum Takes on New Role: Pragmatist." *Congressional Quarterly Weekly Report,* July 18, 1582.

Collins, Susan. 2012. "Yes, the Political Center Can Hold." *Washington Post,* March 9, A15.

Connelly, William F., and John J. Pitney. 1994. *Congress' Permanent Minority?: Republicans in the U.S. House.* Lanham, MD: Rowman and Littlefield.

Cook, Charlie. 2014. "Blocking the Vote." *National Journal,* July 26, http://www .nationaljournal.com/the-cook-report/blocking-the-vote-20140725.

Cook, Timothy E. 1989. *Making Laws and Making News: Media Strategies in the U.S. House of Representatives.* Washington, DC: Brookings Institution.

Cooper, Joseph, and David W. Brady. 1981. "Institutional Context and Leadership-Style: The House from Cannon to Rayburn." *American Political Science Review* 75 (2): 411–25.

Costa, Robert, Paul Kane, and Ed O'Keefe. 2014. "House GOP Leaders Will Bring 'Clean' Debt-Ceiling Bill." *Washington Post,* February 11, A2.

Cottle, Michelle. 2009. "The Retro Man." *New Republic,* November 30, 23.

Cox, Gary W., and Mathew D. McCubbins. 1993. *Legislative Leviathan: Party Government in the House.* Berkeley: University of California Press.

———. 2005. *Setting the Agenda: Responsible Party Government in the U.S. House of Representatives.* New York: Cambridge University Press.

Cox, Ramsey, and Alexander Bolton. 2014. "Senate GOP Blocks Paycheck Bill." *The Hill,* April 9, http://thehill.com/blogs/floor-action/senate/203064-senate -gop-blocks-paycheck-fairness-bill.

Dahl, Robert Alan. 1973. *Polyarchy: Participation and Opposition.* New Haven, CT: Yale University Press.

Davidson, Roger H., and Walter J. Oleszek. 1984. "Changing the Guard in the U.S. Senate." *Legislative Studies Quarterly* 9 (4): 635–63.

DeLay, Tom D., and Stephen Mansfield. 2007. *No Retreat, No Surrender: One American's Fight.* New York: Sentinel.

Delli Carpini, Michael X., and Scott Keeter. 1996. *What Americans Know about Politics and Why It Matters.* New Haven, CT: Yale University Press.

Den Hartog, Chris, and Nathan W. Monroe. 2011. *Agenda Setting in the U.S. Senate: Costly Consideration and Majority Party Advantage.* New York: Cambridge University Press.

Denzin, Norman K. 1970. *The Research Act: A Theoretical Introduction to Sociological Methods.* Chicago: Aldine.

Dewan, Torun, and Arthur Spirling. 2011. "Strategic Opposition and Government Cohesion in Westminster Democracies." *American Political Science Review* 105 (2): 337–58.

Dewar, Helen. 1980. "Party with Reagan: Republicans Gather for a Show of Unity." *Washington Post*, September 16, A3.

———. 1984. "Sen. Byrd Is 'Confident' Facing Today's Election." *Washington Post*, December 12, A2.

Diermeier, Daniel, and Timothy J. Feddersen. 1998. "Cohesion in Legislatures and the Vote of Confidence Procedure." *American Political Science Review* 92 (3): 611–21.

Dovere, Edward-Isaac, and Lauren French. 2015. "White House's Secret Weapon on Trade: Nancy Pelosi." *Politico*, June 3, http://www.politico.com/story/2015/06/white-houses-secret-weapon-on-trade-nancy-pelosi-118565.html.

Downs, Anthony. 1957. *An Economic Theory of Democracy.* New York: Harper and Row.

Draper, Robert. 2012. *Do Not Ask What Good We Do: Inside the U.S. House of Representatives.* New York: Free Press.

Dubin, Michael J. 2007. *Party Affiliations in the State Legislatures: A Year-by-Year Summary, 1796–2006.* Jefferson, NC: McFarland.

Dumain, Emma. 2015. "Pelosi: It's Boehner's Job to Pass Trade Promotion Authority." *Roll Call*, December 10, http://blogs.rollcall.com/218/tpa-pelosi-boehner-job-to-pass-bill/.

Editorial. 2014a. "Congress's Plan to Get Nothing Done." *Washington Post*, September 7, https://www.washingtonpost.com/opinions/congresss-plan-to-get-nothing-done/2014/09/07/2358684e-347c-11e4-a723-fa3895a25d02_story.html.

Editorial. 2014b. "The Governing Trap." *National Review*, November 5, http://www.nationalreview.com/article/392082/governing-trap-editors.

Egan, Patrick J. 2013. *Partisan Priorities: How Issue Ownership Drives and Distorts American Politics.* New York: Cambridge University Press.

Egar, William T. 2015. "Obstruction, Opposition, and Partisan Conflict: Implications of Minority Party Electoral Incentives for the House of Representatives." PhD Dissertation, University of Wisconsin-Madison.

———. Forthcoming. "Tarnishing Opponents, Polarizing Congress: The House Minority Party and the Construction of the Roll Call Record," *Legislative Studies Quarterly.*

Ellis, Christopher, and James A. Stimson. 2012. *Ideology in America.* New York: Cambridge University Press.

Enns, Peter K., and Julianna Koch. 2013. "Public Opinion in the U.S. States: 1956 to 2010." *State Politics and Policy Quarterly* 13 (3): 349–72.

Epstein, Lee, René Lindstädt, Jeffrey A. Segal, and Chad Westerland. 2006. "The Changing Dynamics of Senate Voting on Supreme Court Nominees." *Journal of Politics* 68 (2): 296–307.

Erikson, Robert S., and Gerald C. Wright. 2000. "Representation of Constituency Ideology in Congress." In *Change and Continuity in House Elections,* ed. David W. Brady, John F. Cogan, and Morris P. Fiorina. Stanford, CA: Stanford University Press, 149–77.

Esterberg, Kristin G. 2002. *Qualitative Methods in Social Research.* Boston: McGraw-Hill.

Evans, C. Lawrence. 2001. "Committees, Leaders, and Message Politics." In *Congress Reconsidered,* ed. Lawrence C. Dodd and Bruce I. Oppenheimer, 7th ed. Washington, DC: CQ Press, 217–43.

Evans, C. Lawrence, and Walter J. Oleszek. 2002. "Message Politics and Senate Procedure." In *The Contentious Senate: Partisanship, Ideology, and the Myth of Cool Judgment,* ed. Colton C. Campbell and Nicol C. Rae. New York: Rowman and Littlefield, 107–30.

Everett, Burgess. 2014. "Congress Punts on Issues That Pile Up." *Politico,* July 22, 1.

Farrell, John A. 2001. *Tip O'Neill and the Democratic Century.* Boston: Little, Brown.

Fenno, Richard F., Jr. 1966. *The Power of the Purse: Appropriations Politics in Congress.* Boston: Little, Brown.

———. 1973. *Congressmen in Committees.* Boston: Little, Brown.

———. 1997. *Learning to Govern: An Institutional View of the 104th Congress.* Washington, DC: Brookings Institution.

Fineman, Howard. 1989. "For the Son of C-Span, Exposure = Power." *Newsweek,* April 3, 22.

Fiorina, Morris P., and Samuel J. Abrams. 2009. *Disconnect: The Breakdown of Representation in American Politics.* Norman: University of Oklahoma Press.

Forgette, Richard. 2004. "Party Caucuses and Coordination: Assessing Caucus Activity and Party Effects." *Legislative Studies Quarterly* 29 (3): 407–30.

Frank, Mark W. 2014. "U.S. State-Level Income Inequality Data." Sam Houston State University, http://www.shsu.edu/eco_mwf/inequality.html.

Frates, Chris. 2012. "Health Care Repeal Votes—It's All about Messaging." *National Journal,* July 11, http://www.nationaljournal.com/blogs/influencealley/2012/07/health-care-repeal-vote-it-s-all-about-messaging-11.

Freed, Bruce F. 1976. "House GOP: Its Survival May Be at Stake." *Congressional Quarterly Weekly Report,* June 26, 1634–38.

Fuerbringer, Jonathan. 1988. "The House of Representatives: A House Divided by Partisan Rancor." *New York Times*, March 16, A22.

Gailey, Phil. 1982. "From Majority Leader to Minority Leader." *New York Times*, March 9, A20.

Galbraith, John Kenneth. 1969. *Ambassador's Journal: A Personal Account of the Kennedy Years*. Boston: Houghton Mifflin.

Gallegly, Elton. 2013. "Congress and the Lost Art of Compromise." *Los Angeles Times*, January 14, A23.

Galvin, Daniel. 2010. *Presidential Party Building: Dwight D. Eisenhower to George W. Bush*. Princeton, NJ: Princeton University Press.

Garand, James C. 2010. "Income Inequality, Party Polarization, and Roll-Call Voting in the U.S. Senate." *Journal of Politics* 72 (4): 1109–28.

Garrett, Major. 2005. *The Enduring Revolution: How the Contract with America Continues to Shape the Nation*. New York: Crown Forum.

Gelbart, Marcia. 1996. "House Republicans Launch 'Communications College.'" *The Hill*, July 17, 4.

Gellman, Irwin F. 2015. *The President and the Apprentice: Eisenhower and Nixon, 1952–1961*. New Haven, CT: Yale University Press.

Gimpel, James G., Karen M. Kaufmann, and Shanna Pearson-Merkowitz. 2007. "Battleground States versus Blackout States: The Behavioral Implications of Modern Presidential Campaigns." *Journal of Politics* 69 (3): 786–97.

Gimpel, James G., Frances E. Lee, and Shanna Pearson-Merkowitz. 2008. "The Check Is in the Mail: Interdistrict Funding Flows in Congressional Elections." *American Journal of Political Science* 52 (2): 373–94.

Glass, Andrew. 2007. "Truman Convenes Special Session of Congress July 26, 1948." *Politico*, July 26, http://www.politico.com/story/2007/07/truman-convenes-special-session-of-congress-july-26-1948-005104.

Glassman, Matthew. 2012. "Congressional Leadership: A Resource Perspective." In *Party and Procedure in the United States Congress*, ed. Jacob R. Straus. Lanham. MD: Rowman and Littlefield, 15–34.

Godbout, Jean-François, and Bjørn Høyland. 2011. "Legislative Voting in the Canadian Parliament." *Canadian Journal of Political Science / Revue canadienne de science politique* 44 (2): 367–88.

Gonzales, Nathan L. 2015. "Democrats Might Need to Lose the White House to Win the House Majority." *Roll Call*, February 5, http://blogs.rollcall.com/rothenblog/house-races-2016-white-house-majority/?dcz.

Granat, Diane. 1984. "House Rules Changes Proposed: Democratic and GOP Leaders Named for the 99th Congress." *Congressional Quarterly Weekly Report*, December 8, 3051.

Green, Matthew N. 2010. *The Speaker of the House: A Study of Leadership*. New Haven, CT: Yale University Press.

———. 2015. *Underdog Politics: The Minority Party in the U.S. House of Representatives*. New Haven, CT: Yale University Press.

Griffin, John D. 2006. "Electoral Competition and Democratic Responsiveness: A Defense of the Marginality Hypothesis." *Journal of Politics* 68 (11): 911–21.

Grimmer, Justin. 2013. *Representational Style in Congress: What Legislators Say and Why It Matters*. New York: Cambridge University Press.

Groeling, Tim J. 2010. *When Politicians Attack: Party Cohesion in the Media*. New York: Cambridge University Press.

Groseclose, Tim, and Nolan McCarty. 2001. "The Politics of Blame: Bargaining before an Audience." *American Journal of Political Science* 45 (1): 100–119.

Grossmann, Matthew. 2014. *Artists of the Possible: Governing Networks and American Policy Change Since 1945*. Oxford: Oxford University Press.

Grove, Benjamin. 2005. "In Reid's War Room, the Battle Rages On." *Las Vegas Sun*, November 6, http://lasvegassun.com/news/2005/nov/06/in-reids-war-room-the-battle-rages-on/.

Gutmann, Amy, and Dennis F. Thompson. 2012. *The Spirit of Compromise: Why Governing Demands It and Campaigning Undermines It*. Princeton, NJ: Princeton University Press.

Hallow, Ralph Z. 1991. "Michel Threat: A GOP Surprise." *Washington Times*, September 24, A1.

Hamm, Keith E., and Gary F. Moncrief. 2013. "Legislative Politics in the States." In *Politics in the American States: A Comparative Analysis*, ed. Virginia Gray, Russell L. Hanson, and Thad Kousser, 10th ed. Washington DC: CQ Press, 163–207.

Hanmer, Michael J., and Kerem Ozan Kalkan. 2013. "Behind the Curve: Clarifying the Best Approach to Calculating Predicted Probabilities and Marginal Effects from Limited Dependent Variable Models." *American Journal of Political Science* 57 (1): 263–77.

Hanson, Peter C. 2014a. "Abandoning the Regular Order: Majority Party Influence on Appropriations in the U.S. Senate." *Political Research Quarterly* 67 (3): 519–32.

———. 2014b. *Too Weak to Govern: Majority Party Power and Appropriations in the U.S. Senate*. New York: Cambridge University Press.

Harder, Amy. 2012. "GOP Escalates Messaging Battle on Energy Issues." *National Journal Daily*, July 25.

Harmel, Robert, and Keith E. Hamm. 1986. "Development of a Party Role in a No-Party Legislature." *Western Political Quarterly* 39 (1): 79–92.

Harris, Douglas B. 1998. "The Rise of the Public Speakership." *Political Science Quarterly* 113 (2): 193–212.

———. 2005. "Orchestrating Party Talk: A Party-Based View of One-Minute Speeches in the House of Representatives." *Legislative Studies Quarterly* 30 (1): 127–41.

———. 2006. "Legislative Parties and Leadership Choice: Confrontation or Accommodation in the 1989 Gingrich-Madigan Whip Race." *American Politics Research* 34 (2): 189–222.

———. 2013. "Let's Play Hardball: Congressional Partisanship in a Television Era." In *Politics to the Extreme: American Political Institutions in the Twenty-First Century*, ed. Scott A. Frisch and Sean Q. Kelly. New York: Palgrave Macmillan, 93–115.

Haskins, Ron. 2014. "Congress Kicks the Can Down the Road: Chapter 100." Brookings Institution, December 22, http://www.brookings.edu/research/opinions/2014/12/22-congress-kicks-can-down-road-haskins.

Heberlig, Eric S., and Bruce A. Larson. 2012. *Congressional Parties, Institutional Ambition, and the Financing of Majority Control*. Ann Arbor: University of Michigan Press.

Heclo, Hugh. 2000. "Campaigning and Governing: A Conspectus." In *The Permanent Campaign and Its Future*, ed. Norman J. Ornstein and Thomas E. Mann. Washington, DC: American Enterprise Institute and the Brookings Institution, 1–37.

Helms, Jesse. 2005. *Here's Where I Stand: A Memoir*. New York: Random House.

Herbers, John. 1968. "The Republicans 'Smell Victory.'" *New York Times*, September 15, E3.

Herrnson, Paul S. 1992. "Campaign Professionalism and Fundraising in Congressional Elections." *Journal of Politics* 54 (3): 859–70.

Herszenhorn, David M. 2008. "Word Reaches Congress, as the Market Goes Down, So Goes the Electorate." *New York Times*, October 2, C10.

Hess, Stephen. 1991. *Live from Capitol Hill: Studies of Congress and the Media*. Washington, DC: Brookings Institution.

Hetherington, Marc J. 2001. "Resurgent Mass Partisanship: The Role of Elite Polarization." *American Political Science Review* 95 (3): 619–31.

Hibbing, John, and Elizabeth Theiss-Morse. 1995. *Congress as Public Enemy: Public Attitudes toward American Political Institutions*. Cambridge: Cambridge University Press.

Hix, Simon, and Abdul Noury. Forthcoming. "Government-Opposition or Left-Right? The Institutional Determinants of Voting in Legislatures." *Political Science Research and Methods*.

Holbrook, Thomas M., and Raymond J. La Raja. 2013. "Parties and Elections." In *Politics in the American States*, ed. Virginia Gray, Russell L. Hanson, and Thad Kousser. Washington, DC: CQ Press, 63–104.

Hollander, Catherine. 2014. "Democrats Don't Need Policy Wins to Score Politically." *National Journal: NJ Daily AM*, January 14.

Hook, Janet. 1986. "House Leadership Elections: Wright Era Begins." *Congressional Quarterly Weekly Report*, December 13, 3067.

———. 1987. "House GOP Prepares for Leadership Shuffle." *Congressional Quarterly Weekly Report*, May 16, 959.

———. 1988. "GOP Snipes at How Democrats Run House." *Congressional Quarterly Weekly Report*, May 28, 1437.

———. 1989. "Gingrich's Selection as Whip Reflects GOP Discontent." *Congressional Quarterly Weekly Report*, March 25, 625.

———. 1990. "Republican Contests Reflect Election Woes, Party Rift." *Congressional Quarterly Weekly Report*, December 1, 3997.

"House Refuses to Seat Republican of Indiana." 1985. *New York Times*, February 8, A32.

Howell, William, Scott Adler, Charles Cameron, and Charles Riemann. 2000. "Divided Government and the Legislative Productivity of Congress, 1945–94." *Legislative Studies Quarterly* 25 (2): 285–312.

Howell, William G., and Jon C. Pevehouse. 2007. *While Dangers Gather: Congressional Checks on Presidential War Powers*. Princeton, NJ: Princeton University Press.

Huddy, Leonie, Lilliana Mason, and Lene Aarøe. 2015. "Expressive Partisanship: Campaign Involvement, Political Emotion, and Partisan Identity." *American Political Science Review* 109 (1): 1–17.

Hulse, Carl. 2009a. "As Aisle Gets Wider, Arms Get Shorter." *New York Times*, December 28, A18.

———. 2009b. "Republicans Split on Need to Offer Rival for Budget." *New York Times*, March 14, A9.

———. 2010. "Legislative Hurdles in an Era of Conflict, Not Compromise." *New York Times*, June 20, A20.

Hunt, Albert R. 1981. "Senate Democrats Begin to Regroup." *Wall Street Journal*, December 23, 10.

Iyengar, Shanto, and Sean J. Westwood. 2015. "Fear and Loathing across Party Lines: New Evidence on Group Polarization." *American Journal of Political Science* 59 (3): 690–707.

Jacobson, Gary C. 2013. *The Politics of Congressional Elections*. 8th ed. New York: Pearson Longman.

Jenkins, Shannon. 2006. "The Impact of Party and Ideology on Roll-Call Voting in State Legislatures." *Legislative Studies Quarterly* 31 (2): 235–57.

Jewell, Malcolm E. 1955. "Party Voting in American State Legislatures." *American Political Science Review* 49 (3): 773–91.

———. 1962. *The State Legislature: Politics and Practice*. New York: Random House.

Jewell, Malcolm E., and Sarah McCally Morehouse. 2001. *Political Parties and Elections in American States*. Washington, DC: CQ Press.

Jewell, Malcolm E., and Samuel C. Patterson. 1973. *The Legislative Process in the United States*. New York: Random House.

Jones, Charles O. 1970. *The Minority Party in Congress*. Boston: Little, Brown.

Kahn, Gabriel. 1995. "Bonior Overhauls His Whip Operation," *Roll Call*, January 16.

Kahn, Kim Fridkin, and Patrick J. Kenney. 1999. *The Spectacle of U.S. Senate Campaigns*. Princeton, NJ: Princeton University Press.

Kaiser, Robert G. 2013. *Act of Congress: How America's Essential Institution Works, and How It Doesn't*. New York: Knopf.

Kane, Paul. 2011. "Partisanship Is No Longer Something to Hide on the Hill." *Washington Post*, December 8, A6.

———. 2013. "Congress's Committee Chairmen Push to Reassert Their Power." *Washington Post*, February 16, A4.

———. 2014. "Leadership War Stymies Senate Mission." *Washington Post*, July 21, A3.

Karol, David. 2000. "Divided Government and U.S. Trade Policy: Much Ado about Nothing?" *International Organization* 54 (4): 825–44.

———. 2009. *Party Position Change in American Politics: Coalition Management*. New York: Cambridge University Press.

———. 2012. "How Does Party Position Change Happen? The Case of Gay Rights in the U.S. Congress." Paper presented at the Annual Meeting of the Southern Political Science Association, New Orleans, January.

Keech, William R., and Kyoungsan Pak. 1995. "Partisanship, Institutions, and Change in American Trade Politics." *Journal of Politics* 57 (4): 1130–42.

Kernell, Samuel. 1977. "Presidential Popularity and Negative Voting: An Alternative Explanation of the Midterm Congressional Decline of the President's Party." *American Political Science Review* 71 (1): 44–66.

Kesselman, Mark. 1961. "A Note: Presidential Leadership in Congress on Foreign Policy." *Midwest Journal of Political Science* 5 (3): 284–89.

Key, V. O., Jr. 1949. *Southern Politics in State and Nation*. New York: Knopf.

———. 1955. "A Theory of Critical Elections." *Journal of Politics* 17 (1): 3–18.

———. 1956. *American State Politics: An Introduction*. New York: Knopf.

Klein, Joe. 1995. "The Contemplative Bomb-Thrower." *Newsweek*, January 30, 37.

Klinkner, Philip A. 1994. *The Losing Parties: Out-Party National Committees, 1956–1993*. New Haven, CT: Yale University Press.

Kolodny, Robin. 1998. *Pursuing Majorities: Congressional Campaign Committees in American Politics*. Norman: University of Oklahoma Press.

Koopman, Douglas L. 1996. *Hostile Takeover: The House Republican Party, 1980–1995*. Lanham, MD: Rowman and Littlefield.

Kowalcky, Linda K., and Lance T. LeLoup. 1993. "Congress and the Politics of Statutory Debt Limitation." *Public Administration Review* 53 (1): 14–27.

Krehbiel, Keith. 1998. *Pivotal Politics: A Theory of U.S. Lawmaking*. Chicago: University of Chicago Press.

Krimmell, Katherine. 2013. "Special Interest Partisanship: The Transformation of American Political Parties." PhD Dissertation, Department of Political Science, Columbia University, NY.

Kriner, Douglas L. 2010. *After the Rubicon: Congress, Presidents, and the Politics of Waging War*. Chicago: University of Chicago Press.

Kriner, Douglas, and Liam Schwartz. 2008. "Divided Government and Congressional Investigations." *Legislative Studies Quarterly* 33 (2): 295–321.

Krishnakumar, Anita S. 2005. "In Defense of the Debt Limit Statute." *Harvard Journal on Legislation* 42: 135.

Kucinich, Jackie. 2009. "Boehner Expands GOP Communications Plans." *Roll Call*, April 13, http://www.rollcall.com/issues/54_115/-33933-1.html.

Kucinich, Jackie, and Anna Palmer. 2009. "House GOP Bulks Up Outreach Operation." *Roll Call*, January 7, 3.

Kuntz, Phil. 1992. "GOP Moderates Take a Hit in Caucus Elections." *Congressional Quarterly Weekly Report*, December 12, 3781.

Lamar, Jacob V., and Hayes Gorey. 1989. "An Attack Dog, Not a Lapdog: House Republicans Make Feisty Gingrich Their No. 2 Man." *Time Magazine*, April 3, 22.

Lange, Mark. 2007. "Karl Rove's Wrong Turn." *Christian Science Monitor*, August 17, 9.

Latham, Earl. 1966. *The Communist Controversy in Washington: From the New Deal to McCarthy*. Cambridge, MA: Harvard University Press.

Lawrence, Jill. 2013. "Former House Leaders Say the Current Group Has It Rough." *NJ Daily Extra*, September 23.

Lawrence, John A. 2014. "The Democrats' High-Water Mark." *Politico Magazine*, November 4, http://www.politico.com/magazine/story/2014/11/the-democrats-high-water-mark-came-40-years-ago-112492_full.html#.VFvi7PnF8sY.

Layman, Geoffrey C., and Thomas M. Carsey. 2002. "Party Polarization and 'Conflict Extension' in the American Electorate." *American Journal of Political Science* 46 (4): 786–802.

Layman, Geoffrey C., Thomas M. Carsey, John C. Green, Richard Herrera, and Rosalyn Cooperman. 2010. "Activists and Conflict Extension in American Party Politics." *American Political Science Review* 104 (2): 324–46.

Lee, Frances E. 2009. *Beyond Ideology: Politics, Principles and Partisanship in the U.S. Senate*. Chicago: University of Chicago Press.

———. 2012. "Individual and Partisan Activism on the Senate Floor." In *The U.S. Senate: From Deliberation to Dysfunction*, ed. Burdett A. Loomis. Washington, DC: CQ Press, 110–31.

———. Forthcoming. "Patronage, Logrolls, and 'Polarization': Congressional Parties of the Gilded Age, 1876–1896." *Studies in American Political Development*.

Lenz, Gabriel S. 2013. *Follow the Leader?: How Voters Respond to Politicians' Policies and Performance*. Chicago: University of Chicago Press.

"Lexington: The War of the Words." 2013. *The Economist*, July 13, 32.

Liberatore, Rob. 2008. "Who Knew Lunches Would Lead to Gridlock?" *Politico*, November 20, http://www.politico.com/news/stories/1108/15792.html.

Lijphart, Arend. 1994. *Electoral Systems and Party Systems: A Study of Twenty-Seven Democracies, 1945–1990*. New Haven, CT: Yale University Press.

Link, William A. 2008. *Righteous Warrior: Jesse Helms and the Rise of Modern Conservatism*. New York: St. Martin's Press.

Loomis, Burdett. 1988. *The New American Politician: Ambition, Entrepreneurship, and the Changing Face of Political Life*. New York: Basic Books.

Lott, Trent. 2005. *Herding Cats: A Life in Politics*. New York: ReganBooks.

Lowi, Theodore. 1963. "Toward Functionalism in Political Science: The Case of Innovation in Party Systems." *American Political Science Review* 57 (3): 570–83.

Lubell, Samuel. 1965 [1951]. *The Future of American Politics*. New York: Harper and Row.

MacGillis, Alec. 2014. *The Cynic: The Political Education of Mitch McConnell*. New York: Simon and Schuster.

Mackaman, Frank H., ed. 1981. *Understanding Congressional Leadership*. Washington, DC: Congressional Quarterly Press.

MacNeil, Neil. 1981. "The New Conservative House of Representatives." In *A Tide of Discontent: The 1980 Elections and Their Meaning*, ed. Ellis Sandoz and Cecil V. Crabb Jr. Washington, DC: CQ Press, 65–88.

Madonna, Anthony J., and Kevin Kosar. 2015. "Could the Modern Senate Manage an Open-Amendment Process?" R Street Policy Study No. 42, October 15, http://www.rstreet.org/wp-content/uploads/2015/10/RSTREET42.pdf.

Mahtesian, Charles. 1997. "The Sick Legislature Syndrome." *Governing* 10 (1): 16–20.

Malbin, Michael J. 1977. "The Senate Republican Leaders—Life without a President." *National Journal*, May 21, 76.

Malecha, Gary Lee, and Daniel J. Reagan. 2012. *The Public Congress: Congressional Deliberation in a New Media Age*. New York: Routledge.

Manley, John. 1973. "The Conservative Coalition in Congress." *American Behavioral Scientist* 17: 223–47.

Mann, Thomas E., and Norman J. Ornstein. 2006. *The Broken Branch: How Congress Is Failing America and How to Get It Back on Track*. New York: Oxford University Press.

Mark, David. 2006. *Going Dirty: The Art of Negative Campaigning*. Lanham, MD: Rowman and Littlefield.

Mason, Lilliana. 2015. "I Disrespectfully Agree: The Differential Effects of Partisan Sorting on Social and Issue Polarization." *American Journal of Political Science* 59 (1): 128–45.

Matthews, Donald. 1960. *U.S. Senators and Their World*. Chapel Hill: University of North Carolina Press.

Mayhew, David R. 1974. *Congress: The Electoral Connection*. New Haven, CT: Yale University Press.

———. 1986. *Placing Parties in American Politics: Organization, Electoral Settings, and Government Activity in the Twentieth Century*. Princeton, NJ: Princeton University Press.

———. 2002. *Electoral Realignments: A Critique of an American Genre*. New Haven, CT: Yale University Press.

———. 2005. *Divided We Govern: Party Control, Lawmaking, and Investigations, 1946–2002*. 2nd ed. New Haven, CT: Yale University Press.

McCarty, Nolan. 2015. "Reducing Polarization by Making Parties Stronger." In *Solutions to Political Polarization in America*. New York: Cambridge University Press, 136–45.

McCarty, Nolan, Keith T. Poole, and Howard Rosenthal. 2006. *Polarized America: The Dance of Ideology and Unequal Riches*. Cambridge, MA: MIT Press.

McPike, Erin. 2009. "Bulked Up Machine Pushes GOP Message." *CongressDailyAM*, February 25, 1.

"Medicare Revamp Cuts It Close." 2004. In *CQ Almanac*, 59th ed. Washington, DC: Congressional Quarterly.

Mitchell, Alison. 1999. "Compromise Takes a Holiday." *New York Times*, August 8, E1.

Morehouse, Sarah McCally. 1998. *The Governor as Party Leader: Campaigning and Governing*. Ann Arbor: University of Michigan Press.

Mutz, Diana C. 2015. *In-Your-Face Politics: The Consequences of Uncivil Media*. Princeton, NJ: Princeton University Press.

Nardulli, Peter F. 1995. "The Concept of a Critical Realignment, Electoral Behavior, and Political Change." *American Political Science Review* 89 (1): 10–22.

Nather, David. 2002. "Daschle's Soft Touch Lost in Tough Senate Arena." *CQ Weekly*, July 20, 1920–22.

Newmyer, Tory, and Emily Pierce. 2010. "Bipartisanship Has Few Fans." *Roll Call*, February 1, 1.

Nicks, Denver. 2013. "GOP Hispanic Heritage Month Video Draws Criticism from Activists." *Time Magazine*, September 17, http://swampland.time.com/2013/09/17/gop-hispanic-heritage-month-video-draws-criticism-from-activists/.

Nocera, Joe. 2011. "The Last Moderate." *New York Times*, September 5, A25.

Noel, Hans. 2013. *Political Ideologies and Political Parties in America*. New York: Cambridge University Press.

O'Neill, Tip, and William Novak. 1987. *Man of the House: The Life and Political Memoirs of Speaker Tip O'Neill*. New York: Random House.

Ornstein, Norman J., Thomas E. Mann, and Michael Malbin. 1996. *Vital Statistics on Congress: 1995–1996*. Washington, DC: American Enterprise Institute for Public Policy Research.

———. 2008. *Vital Statistics on Congress, 2008*. Washington, DC: Brookings Institution.

Ornstein, Norman J., Thomas E. Mann, Michael J. Malbin, Andrew Rugg, and Raffaela Wakeman. 2013. "Vital Statistics on Congress: Data on the U.S. Congress—A Joint Effort from Brookings and the American Enterprise Institute." Brookings Institution, July, http://www.brookings.edu/research/reports/2013/07/vital-statistics-congress-mann-ornstein.

Osterlund, Peter. 1988. "House Republicans in Political Purgatory." *Christian Science Monitor*, April 29, 3.

Paddock, Joel. 1998. "Explaining State Variation in Interparty Ideological Differences." *Political Research Quarterly* 51 (3): 765–80.

———. 2005. *State and National Parties and American Democracy*. New York: P. Lang.

Parker, David C. W., and Matthew Dull. 2013. "The Weaponization of Congressional Oversight: The Politics of the Watchful Eye, 1947–2010." In *Politics to the Extreme: American Political Institutions in the Twenty-First Century*, ed. Scott A. Frisch and Sean Q. Kelly. New York: Palgrave Macmillan, 47–70.

Parnes, Amie. 2008. "GOP Senators Using Online System." *Politico*, May 22, http://www.politico.com/news/stories/0508/10537.html.

Patterson, Samuel C. 1962. "Dimensions of Voting Behavior in a One-Party State Legislature." *Public Opinion Quarterly* 26 (2): 185–200.

Patterson, Samuel C., and Gregory A. Caldeira. 1984. "The Etiology of Partisan Competition." *American Political Science Review* 78 (3): 691–707.

Patty, John W. 2008. "Equilibrium Party Government." *American Journal of Political Science* 52 (3): 636–55.

Peabody, Robert L. 1981. "Senate Party Leadership: From the 1950s to the 1980s." In *Understanding Congressional Leadership*, ed. Frank H. Mackaman. Washington, DC: Congressional Quarterly Press, 51–116.

Peters, Ronald M. 1990. *The American Speakership: The Office in Historical Perspective*. Baltimore, MD: Johns Hopkins University Press.

Peterson, R. Eric, Parker H. Reynolds, and Amber Hope Wilhelm. 2010. "House of Representatives and Senate Staff Levels in Member, Committee, Leadership, and Other Offices, 1977–2010." Congressional Research Service, R41366, August 10.

Petrocik, John R. 1996. "Issue Ownership in Presidential Elections, with a 1980 Case Study." *American Journal of Political Science* 40 (3): 825–50.

Pew Research Center. 2009. "The New Washington Press Corps: The Numbers." Project for Excellence in Journalism, July 19, http://www.journalism.org/2009/07/16/numbers/.

———. 2014. "Political Polarization in the American Public: How Increasing Ideological Uniformity and Partisan Antipathy Affect Politics, Compromise, and Everyday Life." June 12, http://www.people-press.org/files/2014/06/6-12 -2014-Political-Polarization-Release.pdf.

———. 2015. "A Deep Dive into Party Affiliation: Sharp Differences by Race, Gender, Generation, Education." April 7, http://www.people-press.org/2015/ 04/07/a-deep-dive-into-party-affiliation/.

Pianin, Eric. 1991. "Michel Enjoys a Political Revival of Sorts." *Washington Post*, November 29, A22.

Pierce, Emily. 2008. "Red Meat on Senate Agenda." *Roll Call*, April 24, 1.

"Politics Goes On." 2002. *The Economist*, September 14, 50.

Poole, Keith T., and Howard Rosenthal. 1997. *Congress: A Political-Economic History of Roll Call Voting.* New York: Oxford University Press.

———. 2011. *Ideology and Congress.* New Brunswick, NJ: Transaction Publishers.

Powell, Larry. 2010. "NCPAC and the Development of Third-Party Expenditures." In *Campaign Finance Reform: The Political Shell Game.* Lanham, MD: Lexington Books, 29–44.

Preston, Mark. 2002. "Carper, Durbin Target Message." *Roll Call*, December 5, 1.

Price, David E. 2004. *The Congressional Experience.* 3rd ed. Boulder, CO: Westview Press.

Raju, Manu. 2008. "Campaign for White House Takes Reins on Capitol Hill." *The Hill*, June 12, 4.

———. 2011. "How Hill Leaders Sow Dysfunction." *Politico*, December 19, http:// www.politico.com/news/stories/1211/70667.html.

Ramirez, Mark D. 2009. "The Dynamics of Partisan Conflict on Congressional Approval." *American Journal of Political Science* 53 (3): 681–94.

Ranney, Austin. 1965. "Parties in State Politics." In *Politics in the American States: A Comparative Analysis*, ed. Jacob Herbert and Kenneth N. Vines. Boston: Little, Brown, 61–99.

———. 1976. "Parties in State Politics." In *Politics in the American States: A Comparative Analysis*, ed. Jacob Herbert and Kenneth N. Vines, 3rd ed. Boston: Little, Brown, 51–92.

Rawls, W. Lee. 2009. *In Praise of Deadlock: How Partisan Struggle Makes Better Laws.* Washington, DC and Baltimore: Woodrow Wilson Center Press with Johns Hopkins University Press.

Rhodes, John J. 1976. *The Futile System: How to Unchain Congress and Make the System Work Again.* McLean, VA: EPM Publications.

Rich, Spencer. 1977. "New Staff, Mission Planned for Senate GOP Policy Unit." *Washington Post*, January 1, A4.

Roberts, Jason M., and Steven S. Smith. 2003. "Procedural Contexts, Party Strategy, and Conditional Party Voting in the U.S. House of Representatives." *American Journal of Political Science* 47 (2): 305–17.

Roberts, Steven V. 1981. "In an Era of Permanent Campaign, Parties Look to 1982." *New York Times*, January 26, A22.

———. 1983. "One Conservative Faults Two Parties." *New York Times*, August 11, A10.

Rogers, David. 2010. "Obey Surveys the House Then and Now." *Politico*, July 23, 8.

Rogers, Steven Michael. 2013. "Accountability in a Federal System." PhD Dissertation, Department of Politics, Princeton University, NJ.

Rohde, David W. 1991. *Parties and Leaders in the Postreform House*. Chicago: University of Chicago Press.

Rosenthal, Alan. 1990. *Governors and Legislatures: Contending Powers*. Washington, DC: CQ Press.

Roshco, Bernard. 1978. "The Polls: Polling on Panama—Si; Don't Know; Hell, No!". *Public Opinion Quarterly* 42 (4): 551–62.

Rossiter, Clinton. 1960. *Parties and Politics in America*. Ithaca, NY: Cornell University Press.

Rothbauer, Paulette M. 2008. "Triangulation." In *The Sage Encyclopedia of Qualitative Research Methods*. Thousand Oaks, CA: SAGE Publications, 893–95.

Rothenberg, Stuart. 2015. "Can Democrats Win the House in 2016?" Rothenberg and Gonzales Political Report, *Roll Call*, http://www.rothenberggonzales.com/news/article/can-democrats-win-the-house-in-2016.

Sandoz, Ellis. 1981. "Introduction: Revolution or Flash in the Pan?" In *A Tide of Discontent: The 1980 Elections and Their Meaning*, ed. Ellis Sandoz and Cecil V. Crabb Jr. Washington, DC: Congressional Quarterly Press, 1–18.

Schaller, Thomas. 2015. "55–45 Politics in a 50–50 Country." *American Prospect*, October 28, http://prospect.org/article/republican-structural-advantage.

Schickler, Eric. 2013. "New Deal Liberalism and Racial Liberalism in the Mass Public, 1937–1968." *Perspectives on Politics* 11 (1): 75–98.

Schickler, Eric, and Kathryn Pearson. 2009. "Agenda Control, Majority Party Power, and the House Committee on Rules, 1937–52." *Legislative Studies Quarterly* 34 (4): 455–91.

Schiller, Wendy J. 2000. *Partners and Rivals: Representation in U.S. Senate Delegations*. Princeton, NJ: Princeton University Press.

———. 2012. "Howard Baker's Leadership in the U.S. Senate." *Baker Center of Applied Public Policy* 4 (2): 28–48.

Schlesinger, Joseph A. 1985. "The New American Political Party." *American Political Science Review* 79:1152–69.

Schram, Martin. 1981. "Minority Boss." *Washington Post*, May 31, A1.

Schwerzler, Nancy J. 1986. "Battle between Byrd, Johnston for Post as Majority Leader Begins to Heat Up." *The Sun*, November 6, 18A.

Sellers, Patrick. 2010. *Cycles of Spin: Strategic Communication in the U.S. Congress.* New York: Cambridge University Press.

Semple, Robert B., Jr. 1972. "Hard to Get a Grip on His Coattails: Nixon." *New York Times,* October 29, E2.

Senior, Jennifer. 2010. "Mr. Woebegone Goes to Washington." *New York,* April 4, http://nymag.com/news/politics/65239/.

Shapiro, Ira. 2012. *The Last Great Senate: Courage and Statesmanship in Times of Crisis.* New York: Public Affairs.

Shaw, Daron R. 2008. *The Race to 270: The Electoral College and the Campaign Strategies of 2000 and 2004.* Chicago: University of Chicago Press.

Shepard, Lyn. 1968. "GOP 'Bullish' on House." *Christian Science Monitor,* October 29, B26.

Shepsle, Kenneth. 1989. "The Changing Textbook Congress." In *Can the Government Govern?,* ed. John Chubb and Paul Peterson. Washington, DC: Brookings Institution, 238–66.

Shor, Boris. 2014. "July 2014 Update: Aggregate Data for Ideological Mapping of American Legislatures." Harvard Dataverse, http://dx.doi.org/10.7910/DVN/26799.

Shor, Boris, Christopher Berry, and Nolan McCarty. 2010. "A Bridge to Somewhere: Mapping State and Congressional Ideology on a Cross-Institutional Common Space." *Legislative Studies Quarterly* 35 (3): 417–48.

Shor, Boris, and Nolan McCarty. 2011. "The Ideological Mapping of American Legislatures." *American Political Science Review* 105 (3): 530–51.

Shufeldt, Gregory, and Patrick Flavin. 2012. "Two Distinct Concepts: Party Competition in Government and Electoral Competition in the American States." *State Politics and Policy Quarterly* 12 (3): 330–42.

Siddon, Arthur. 1980. "GOP Expects Big Gains in Congress." *New York Times,* October 13, 6.

Sigelman, Lee, and Emmett H. Buell. 2004. "Avoidance or Engagement? Issue Convergence in U.S. Presidential Campaigns, 1960–2000." *American Journal of Political Science* 48: 650–61.

Simon, Dennis M., Charles W. Ostrom Jr., and Robin F. Marra. 1991. "The President, Referendum Voting, and Subnational Elections in the United States." *American Political Science Review* 85 (4): 1177–92.

Simon, Richard. 2011. "Congress Turns Bill Titles into Acts of Exaggeration." *Los Angeles Times,* June 19, http://articles.latimes.com/2011/jun/19/nation/la-na-0620-titles-20110620.

Sinclair, Barbara. 1983. *Majority Leadership in the U.S. House.* Baltimore, MD: Johns Hopkins University Press.

———. 1989. *The Transformation of the U.S. Senate.* Baltimore, MD: Johns Hopkins University Press.

——. 1995. *Legislators, Leaders, and Lawmaking*. Baltimore, MD: Johns Hopkins University Press.

——. 2006. *Party Wars: Polarization and the Politics of National Policy Making*. Norman: University of Oklahoma Press.

Slack, Donovan. 2013. "House GOP Tweaks Obama on Budgets and Brackets." Politico44, Blog, *Politico*, http://www.politico.com/blogs/politico44/2013/03/house-gop-tweaks-obama-on-budgets-and-brackets-159749.

Smidt, Corwin D. 2015. "Polarization and the Decline of the American Floating Voter." *American Journal of Political Science*, doi: 10.1111/ajps.12218.

Smith, Hedrick. 1988. *The Power Game: How Washington Works*. New York: Random House.

Smith, Steven. 1989. *Call to Order: Floor Politics in the House and Senate*. Washington, DC: Brookings Institution.

——. 2007. *Party Influence in Congress*. New York: Cambridge University Press.

Smith, Steven S., Ian Ostrander, and Christopher M. Pope. 2013. "Majority Party Power and Procedural Motions in the U.S. Senate." *Legislative Studies Quarterly* 38 (2): 205–36.

Snowe, Olympia J. 2013. "The Effect of Modern Partisanship on Legislative Effectiveness in the 112th Congress." *Harvard Journal on Legislation* 50 (1): 21–40.

Sperling, Godfrey, Jr. 1972. "Nixon Could Win Senate, but Not House." *Christian Science Monitor*, October 31, 1.

Spirling, Arthur, and Iain McLean. 2007. "UK OC OK? Interpreting Optimal Classification Scores for the U.K. House of Commons." *Political Analysis* 15 (1): 85–96.

Squire, Peverill. 1989a. "Challengers in U.S. Senate Elections." *Legislative Studies Quarterly* 14 (4): 531–47.

——. 1989b. "Competition and Uncontested Seats in Us House Elections." *Legislative Studies Quarterly* 14 (2): 281–95.

——. 2007. "Measuring State Legislative Professionalism: The Squire Index Revisited." *State Politics and Policy Quarterly* 7 (2): 211–27.

Stanton, John. 2006. "Frist Launches Message Shop." *Roll Call*, January 19, http://www.rollcall.com/issues/51_69/-11796-1.html.

——. 2008. "Election-Year Rhetoric Trumping Legislation." *Roll Call*, June 12, 3.

——. 2010. "Senate Democrats Building Broad Message Campaign." *Roll Call*, March 18, http://www.rollcall.com/news/-44372-1.html.

——. 2011. "Boehner's Pursuit of Big Deal Irks GOP." *Roll Call*, December 15, http://www.rollcall.com/issues/57_75/Boehner-Pursuit-of-Big-Deal-Irks-GOP-211077-1.html?pos=hftxt.

Steinberger, Paul J. 1980. "Rightism? Wrongism." *New York Times*, November 19, A35.

Steinhauer, Jennifer, and Raymond Hernandez. 2011. "Master of Self-Promotion

Applies Talents to Other Senate Democrats." *New York Times*, March 16, A20.

Stonecash, Jeffrey M., Mark D. Brewer, and Mark D. Mariani. 2003. *Diverging Parties: Social Change, Realignment, and Party Polarization.* Boulder, CO: Westview Press.

Straub, Noelle, and Melanie Fonder. 2001. "GOP Shifts Strategy for New Minority Status." *The Hill*, July 18, 6.

Sundquist, James L. 1983. *Dynamics of the Party System: Alignment and Realignment of Political Parties in the United States.* Washington, DC: Brookings Institution.

Surman, Barry S. 1988. "Cheney Likes Role as Fighter, Peacemaker." *Congressional Quarterly Weekly Report*, December 10, 3476.

Tarrow, Sidney. 1995. "Bridging the Quantitative-Qualitative Divide in Political Science." Review of *Designing Social Inquiry: Scientific Inference in Qualitative Research*, by Gary King, Robert O. Keohane, and Sidney Verba. *American Political Science Review* 89 (2): 471–74.

Theriault, Sean M. 2008. *Party Polarization in Congress.* New York: Cambridge University Press.

———. 2013. *The Gingrich Senators.* New York: Oxford University Press.

Tolchin, Martin. 1981. "Byrd Picks Up the Tune in a Minor Key." *New York Times*, October 25, A4.

———. 1982. "Senate Turns Back Efforts to Modify Tax Cuts for 1983." *New York Times*, May 21, A1.

Toner, Robin. 2005. "Demands of Partisanship Bring Change to the Senate." *New York Times*, May 20, A16.

Tucker, Harvey J., and Ronald E. Weber. 1987. "State Legislative Election Outcomes: Contextual Effects and Legislative Performance." *Legislative Studies Quarterly* 12 (4): 537–53.

US Government Accountability Office. 2006. "Media Contracts: Activities and Financial Obligations for Seven Federal Departments," GAO-06-305, January, http://www.gao.gov/new.items/d06305.pdf.

US House of Representatives. 2004. "The Cannon Centenary Conference: The Changing Nature of the Speakership." Transcript. Washington, DC: Government Printing Office.

Wallner, James I. 2013. *The Death of Deliberation: Partisanship and Polarization in the United States Senate.* Lanham, MD: Lexington Books.

"Washington Update: Congress." 1980. *National Journal*, December 13, 2136–37.

"Washington Update: Policy and Politics in Brief—Scoring Party Points." 1982. *National Journal*, February 20.

Weaver, Warren, Jr. 1972. "Democrats Expected to Retain Control of Both Senate and House in Election." *New York Times*, October 9, 25.

Weber, Vin (interview). 1995. "The Long March of Newt Gingrich." Frontline,

PBS,   http://www.pbs.org/wgbh/pages/frontline/newt/newtintwshtml/weber
.html.

Wehr, Elizabeth. 1987. "GOP Rank-and-File vs. Appropriators: Loyalty Test:
Party First, Committee Second?" *Congressional Quarterly Weekly Report,*
August 1, 1720.

White, Joseph. 1989. "The Functions and Power of the House Appropriations
Committee." PhD Dissertation, Political Science Department, University of
California-Berkeley.

Williamson, Vanessa, Theda Skocpol, and John Coggin. 2011. "The Tea Party
and the Remaking of Republican Conservatism." *Perspectives on Politics* 9
(1): 25–43.

Wilson, George C. 1981. "Democrats Show Fancy Steps." *Washington Post,* December 19, A4.

Wilson, Reid. 2015. "Why the Democratic Path to a House Majority May Run
through a Courtroom." *Washington Post,* May 8, http://www.washingtonpost
.com/blogs/post-politics/wp/2015/05/08/why-the-democratic-path-to-a-house
-majority-may-run-through-a-courtroom/.

Wolfensberger, Don. 2014. "The New Congressional Staff: Politics at the Expense of Policy." FixGov: Making Government Work, Brookings Institution, March 21, http://www.brookings.edu/blogs/fixgov/posts/2014/03/21
-congressional-staff-politics-over-policy-wolfensberger.

Wolfensberger, Donald R. 2001. *Congress and the People: Deliberative Democracy on Trial.* Baltimore, MD: Johns Hopkins University Press.

Wright, Gerald C., and Brian F. Schaffner. 2002. "The Influence of Party: Evidence from the State Legislatures." *American Political Science Review* 96
(2): 367–79.

Zelizer, Julian E. 2004. *On Capitol Hill: The Struggle to Reform Congress and
Its Consequences, 1948–2000.* New York: Cambridge University Press.

———. 2007. "Seizing Power: Conservatives and Congress since the 1970s." In
*The Transformation of American Politics: Activist Government and the Rise
of Conservatism,* ed. Paul Pierson and Theda Skocpol. Princeton, NJ: Princeton University Press, 105–34.

Zucco, Cesar, Jr. 2009. "Ideology or What? Legislative Behavior in Multiparty
Presidential Settings." *Journal of Politics* 71 (3): 1076–92.

Zucco, Cesar, Jr., and Benjamin E. Lauderdale. 2011. "Distinguishing Between
Influences on Brazilian Legislative Behavior." *Legislative Studies Quarterly*
36 (3): 363–96.

Index

Made in the USA
Monee, IL
10 January 2023

24761530R00163